OECD Reviews of School Resources: Austria 2016

Deborah Nusche, Thomas Radinger,
Marius R. Busemeyer and Henno Theisens

OECD
BETTER POLICIES FOR BETTER LIVES

This work is published on the responsibility of the Secretary-General of the OECD. The opinions expressed and arguments employed herein do not necessarily reflect the official views of the OECD or of the governments of its member countries or those of the European Union.

This document and any map included herein are without prejudice to the status of or sovereignty over any territory, to the delimitation of international frontiers and boundaries and to the name of any territory, city or area.

Please cite this publication as:
Nusche, D. et al. (2016), *OECD Reviews of School Resources: Austria 2016*, OECD Reviews of School Resources, OECD Publishing, Paris.
http://dx.doi.org/10.1787/9789264256729-en

ISBN 978-92-64-25670-5 (print)
ISBN 978-92-64-25672-9 (PDF)
ISBN 978-92-64-25771-9 (epub)

Series: OECD Reviews of School Resources
ISSN 2413-4333 (print)
ISSN 2413-3841 (online)

The statistical data for Israel are supplied by and under the responsibility of the relevant Israeli authorities. The use of such data by the OECD is without prejudice to the status of the Golan Heights, East Jerusalem and Israeli settlements in the West Bank under the terms of international law.

Photo credits: Cover © VLADGRIN/Shutterstock.com.

Corrigenda to OECD publications may be found on line at: *www.oecd.org/about/publishing/corrigenda.htm*.

Foreword

This report for Austria forms part of the OECD Review of Policies to Improve the Effectiveness of Resource Use in Schools (also referred to as the School Resources Review, see Annex A for further details). The purpose of the review is to explore how school resources can be governed, distributed, utilised and managed to improve the quality, equity and efficiency of school education. School resources are understood in a broad way, including financial resources (e.g. expenditures on education, school budget), physical resources (e.g. school infrastructure, computers), human resources (e.g. teachers, school leaders) and other resources (e.g. learning time).

Austria was one of the education systems which opted to participate in the country review strand and host a visit by an external review team. Members of the review team were Deborah Nusche (OECD), Thomas Radinger (OECD), Marius R. Busemeyer (University of Konstanz) and Henno Theisens (The Hague University for Applied Sciences). Deborah Nusche co-ordinated the review between January 2015 and January 2016 and Thomas Radinger co-ordinated the review between February and June 2016. The biographies of the members of the review team are provided in Annex B. This publication is the report of the review team. It provides, from an international perspective, an independent analysis of major issues facing the use of school resources in Austria, current policy initiatives, and possible future approaches. The report serves three purposes: i) to provide insights and advice to the Austrian education authorities; ii) to help other countries understand the Austrian approach to the use of school resources; and iii) to provide input for the final comparative analysis of the OECD School Resources Review.

The scope for analysis in this report includes public primary and lower secondary education (including Volksschule, Hauptschule/Neue Mittelschule and AHS Unterstufe). At the request of the Austrian authorities, the focus areas of the Review of School Resources in Austria were: i) funding and governance of school education; ii) organisation of the school offer; and iii) management of the teaching workforce. This report reflects the situation of the Austrian education system at the time of the review visit in June 2015. The review team provided the Austrian Ministry of Education and Women's Affairs (BMBF) with an initial draft report at the beginning of November 2015 to inform the negotiations of the education reform commission comprised of representatives of the federal government and the provinces. The negotiations of the education reform commission resulted in a proposal for education reform that was presented 17 November 2015 and envisaged to be finalised by June 2016 (see Annex 1.1).

The involvement of Austria in the OECD review was co-ordinated by Bernhard Chabera and Andrea Schmölzer of the Department of International Multilateral Affairs at the Austrian Federal Ministry of Education and Women's Affairs. An important part of the involvement of Austria was the preparation of a comprehensive and informative country background report (CBR) on school resources authored by the Federal Institute for Educational Research, Innovation and Development of the Austrian School System (BIFIE) and the Institute for Advanced Studies (IHS). The OECD review team is very grateful to the main authors of the CBR and to all those who assisted them in providing a high-quality informative document. The CBR is an important output from the OECD project in its own right as well as an important source for the review team. Unless indicated otherwise, the data for this report are taken from the CBR. The CBR follows guidelines prepared by the OECD Secretariat and provides extensive information, analysis and discussion in regard to the national context, the organisation of the education system, the use of school resources and the views of key stakeholders. In this sense, the CBR and this report complement each other and should be read in conjunction for a more comprehensive view of the effectiveness of school resource use in Austria.

The OECD and the European Commission (EC) have established a partnership for the project which partly covers participation costs of countries which are part of the European Union's Erasmus+ programme. The participation of Austria was organised with the support of the EC in the context of this partnership. The EC was part of the planning process of the review of Austria (providing comments on the Austrian CBR, participating in the preparatory visit and providing feedback on the planning of the review visit) and offered comments on drafts of this report. The involvement of the EC was co-ordinated by Klaus Körner, Country Desk Officer for Austria as regards education and training, working within the "Country Analysis" Unit of the Directorate for "Lifelong Learning: horizontal policy issues and 2020 strategy", which is part of the Directorate General for Education and Culture (DG EAC) of the European Commission. The review team is grateful to Klaus Körner for his contribution to the planning of the review and for the helpful comments he provided on drafts of this report.*

The review visit to Austria took place between 24 and 30 June 2015. The itinerary is provided in Annex C. The visit was designed by the OECD (with input from the EC) in collaboration with the Austrian authorities. It also involved a preparatory visit by the OECD Secretariat on 9-10 April 2015 with the participation of Klaus Körner from the EC. The review team met with Gabriele Heinisch-Hosek, Federal Minister for Education and Women's Affairs, and other officials of the Federal Ministry of Education and Women's Affairs; the Ministry of Finance; Statistics Austria, the Chamber of Labour (AK), the Chamber of Economy (Wirtschaftskammer Österreich, WKÖ), the Federation of Austrian Industries, the Court of Audit, the Association of Municipalities, national Parents Associations, Teacher Unions and Pupil and Youth Associations, representatives of institutions providing initial teacher education, and researchers with an interest in the effectiveness of school resource use. The team also visited three provinces (Vienna, Salzburg and Burgenland) and six schools, interacting with the federal, provincial and municipal authorities responsible for school education as well school leaders, teachers, parents and students at each school. The intention was to provide the review team with a broad cross-section of information and opinions on school resource use and how its effectiveness can be improved.

The OECD review team is grateful to the many people who gave time from their busy schedules to inform the review team of their views, experiences and knowledge. The meetings were open and provided a wealth of insights. The national co-ordinators Bernhard Chabera and Andrea Schmölzer merit special words of appreciation for sharing their expertise and responding to the many questions of the review team. The courtesy and hospitality we experienced throughout our stay in Austria made our task as a review team as pleasant and enjoyable as it was stimulating and challenging. The OECD review team is also grateful to colleagues at the OECD, especially to Luka Boeskens for analytical support, to Eleonore Morena for key administrative, editorial and layout support and to Yuri Belfali for overall guidance.

This report is organised in four chapters. Chapter 1 provides the national context and background information on the Austrian school system. Chapters 2 to 4 look into three dimensions of

* *This document has been produced with the financial assistance of the European Union. The views expressed herein can in no way be taken to reflect the official opinion of the European Union.*

resource use that were defined as priorities by Austria in collaboration with the OECD: the funding and governance of school education; the organisation of the school offer; and the management of the teaching workforce. Each chapter presents strengths, challenges and policy recommendations.

The policy recommendations attempt to build on and strengthen reforms that are already underway in Austria, and the strong commitment to further improvement that was evident among those the OECD review team met. The suggestions should take into account the difficulties that face any visiting group, no matter how well briefed, in grasping the complexity of the Austrian education system and fully understanding all the issues. This report is the responsibility of the review team. While the team benefited greatly from the Austrian CBR and other documents, as well as the many discussions with a wide range of Austrian personnel, any errors or misinterpretations in this report are the team's responsibility.

Table of contents

Acronyms and abbreviations 11

Executive summary 13

Assessment and recommendations 19
- Context 19
- Strengths and challenges 21
- Policy recommendations 30

Chapter 1. School education in Austria 39
- Context 40
- Structure of the education system 44
- Main features of the school system 47
- Quality and equity of the school system 52
- Notes 58
- References 58
- *Annex* 1.A1. The November 2015 education reform proposal 62
- *Annex* 1.A2. The Austrian education system 67
- *Annex* 1.A3. Distribution of decision-making in public lower secondary education 69

Chapter 2. Funding and governance of school education in Austria 71
- Context and features 72
- Strengths 87
- Challenges 93
- Policy recommendations 101
- Notes 110
- References 111
- *Annex* 2.A1. Data for Chapter 2 115

Chapter 3. Organisation of the school offer in Austria 119
- Context and features 120
- Strengths 129
- Challenges 132
- Policy recommendations 138
- Notes 144
- References 144

Chapter 4. Management of the teaching workforce in Austria 149
- Context and features 150
- Strengths 157

Challenges . . . 165
Policy recommendations . . . 176
Notes . . . 188
References . . . 189

Annex A. The OECD Review of Policies to Improve the Effectiveness of Resource Use in School . . . 193
Annex B. Composition of the OECD Review Team . . . 194
Annex C. Visit programme . . . 196

Tables

1.1. Provinces of Austria . . . 41
1.2. Performance of Austrian students in mathematics, science and reading at the International Benchmarks of Achievement in primary education, TIMSS and PIRLS . . . 52
1.3. Selected indicators of quality and equity in Austrian education, based on PISA 2012 . . . 54
1.4. Adult skills, PIAAC 2012 . . . 57
2.1. Overall public spending on education in different sectors of the Austrian education system (absolute numbers in EUR million and as a percentage of GDP, based on ISCED 97), 2000-11 . . . 73
2.2. Annual per student expenditure on education in equivalent USD converted using PPPs, Austria and neighbouring countries, based on ISCED 2011, 2012 . . . 74
2.3. Variation of per student spending across school types and provinces, 2012 . . . 76
2.A1.1. Comparative data on per student expenditure on education, OECD countries, ISCED 2011, 2012 . . . 115
2.A1.2. Data on expenditure by primary and secondary educational institutions, by resource category, OECD countries with available data, ISCED 2011, 2012 . . . 116
4.1. Annual gross salaries of full-time fully qualified school principals in public schools, 2014/15 . . . 156
4.2. School autonomy over curricula and assessments, PISA 2012 . . . 164

Figures

1.1. Variation in school-age population in Austria compared to the OECD and the EU27 . . . 42
1.2. Percentage of decisions taken at each level of government in public lower secondary education, 2011 . . . 49
1.A2.1. The Austrian Education System . . . 68
1.A3.1. Percentage of decisions taken at each level of government in public lower secondary education, by domain, 2011 . . . 70
2.1. Public and private spending on educational institutions, primary to tertiary education, based on ISCED 2011, 2012 . . . 74
2.2. Per-student expenditure in different types of Austrian schools, 2011-13 . . . 75
2.3. Teachers' salaries relative to earnings for similarly educated workers, 2013 . . . 78

2.4. Lower secondary teachers' salaries at different points in teachers' careers, 2013 79
2.5. Distribution of spending on different school types before and after fiscal transfers, 2012 80
2.6. Funding streams and responsibilities in the Austrian school system 82
2.7. School autonomy in resource allocation in OECD countries, 2012 84
3.1. School density 120
3.2. Average school size 121
3.3. Ratio of students to teaching staff in educational institutions, 2013 122
3.4. Average class size, public and private institutions, by level of education, 2013 122
3.5. School principals' views on adequacy of physical infrastructure 130
3.6. The impact of socio-economic background on education performance 136
3.7. Total number of hours of compulsory instruction time, 2015 136
3.8. Trends in student numbers for HS/NMS and AHS 137
4.1. Ratio of school leader and maximum teacher salaries to the minimum annual statutory salary for teachers, 2014/15 156
4.2. School leader reports on school responsibility for resource management, PISA 2012 166
4.3. Teacher rewards and incentives, TALIS 2008 174

Acronyms and abbreviations

AHS-O	*Allgemein bildende höhere Schule – Oberstufe* – Academic Secondary School, Upper Level
AHS-U	*Allgemein bildende höhere Schule – Unterstufe* – Academic Secondary School, Lower Level
APS	*Allgemeinbildende Pflichtschulen* – General Compulsory School
ASO	*Sonderschule* – Special Needs School
BHS	*Berufsbildene höhere Schule* – Colleges for Higher Vocational Education
BIFIE	*Bundesinstitut für Bildungsforschung, Innovation & Entwicklung des österreichischen Schulwesens* – Federal Institute for Educational Research, Innovation and Development of the Austrian School System
BMBF	*Bundesministerium für Bildung und Frauen* – Austrian Ministry of Education and Women's Affairs
BMS	*Berufsbildene mittlere Schule* – Secondary Technical and Vocational School
BMUKK	*Bundesministerium für Unterricht, Kunst und Kultur* – Federal Ministry for Education, Arts and Culture
BMWFW	*Bundesministerium für Wissenschaft, Forschung und Wirtschaft* – Federal Ministry for Science, Research and Economy (previously BMWF)
BS	*Berufsschule* – Part-time Vocational School
CBR	Country Background Report
EC	European Commission
ESCS	Economic, Social and Cultural Status
EU	European Union
GDP	Gross Domestic Product
HS	*Hauptschule* – General Secondary School
IEA	International Association for the Evaluation of Educational Achievement
ISCED	International Standard Classification of Education
NMS	*Neue Mittelschule* – New Secondary School
OECD	Organisation for Economic Co-operation and Development
PH	*Pädagogische Hochschule* – University College of Teacher Education
PIRLS	Progress in International Reading Literacy Study
PISA	OECD Programme for International Student Assessment
PPP	Purchasing Power Parity
PTS	*Polytechnische Schule* – Pre-vocational School
QIBB	*QualitätInitiative BerufsBildung* – Quality Initiative for Vocational Education and Training
QSR	*Qualitätssicherungsrat für Pädagoginnen- und Pädagogenbildung* – Quality Assurance Council
SCHEP-NEU	*Schulentwicklungsprogramm* – School Development Programme for Federal Schools

SEN	Special Educational Needs
SQA	*Schulqualität Allgemeinbildung* – School Quality in General Education Initiative
TALIS	OECD Teaching and Learning International Survey
TIMSS	Trends in International Mathematics and Science Study
VS	*Volksschule* – Primary School

Executive summary

The Austrian school system benefits from high levels of investment. Although education has also faced some budget cuts and budget pressures seem to be increasing, the recent economic and financial crisis did not yet have a strong impact on the education budget. An international comparison of spending data indicates still relatively high general levels of public investment in education in Austria. The school infrastructure is good and classes are relatively small and student-teacher ratios relatively low. However, there is concern that the country's considerable commitment of resources to education has not sufficiently been translated into educational success as measured through international surveys. In the OECD Programme for International Student Assessment (PISA) 2012, the mean performance of Austrian 15-year-olds was only slightly above the OECD average and below the level of other European countries such as Germany, Switzerland, Belgium and Finland. While Austria had a comparatively small share of low performers, the country also had a small share of top performers. There are also continued concerns about equity. Student's socio-economic background has a key impact on their achievement and educational trajectory through Austria's stratified school system that is characterised by early tracking and selection. Students with an immigrant background are at particular risk of underperformance. Hence, the main challenge does not lie in expanding investments, but in using available resources more effectively and efficiently to improve the quality and equity of schooling.

The governance of school education in Austria is characterised by a complex distribution of responsibilities between the federal and the provincial levels based on a split between federal and provincial schools, a complex distribution of federal funding for teacher salaries of provincial schools, and limited school autonomy for their staff and finances. The present arrangements create structural challenges for the efficient management of school resources. As clear lines of accountability and integrated monitoring systems are lacking, governance arrangements set incentives to over- and misspend, obfuscate the flow of resources, and nourish a culture of mistrust. The distribution of responsibilities leads to the establishment of inefficient parallel structures – including for personnel management – in the form of provincial school boards and school departments of the provinces. And the present distribution of responsibilities prevents a more integrated approach to the governance of the school system. This is evident in the existence of multiple information systems which hampers a comprehensive approach to monitoring the performance of the system; the lack of strategic planning of the school offer as a whole which results in an inefficient organisation of the school network with many small schools; the lack of a comprehensive approach to monitoring and steering the supply and demand for teachers, and the lack of a comprehensive approach to making human resource allocation decisions which, together with negative incentives resulting from funding responsibilities, leads to a lack of administrative and pedagogical support staff.

At the lower secondary level, important steps have been undertaken to harmonise the regulatory regime with the New Secondary School reform, a reform of initial teacher education, and the introduction of a new teacher service code. However, besides needed change in the political willingness of all stakeholders, a full move to comprehensive schooling seems unlikely as long as the split between federal and provincial schools is maintained.

This report analyses the use of school resources in primary and lower secondary education in Austria based on the situation at the time of the visit of the OECD review team in June 2015. The federal government presented a comprehensive reform proposal in November 2015, but at the time of drafting, the political debate was ongoing and it was still unclear which elements would be implemented. This report focuses, in particular, on governance and funding, the organisation of the school offer, and the management of the teaching workforce. It identified the following policy recommendations and suggests prioritising a reform of the current governance arrangements.

Reform the current governance arrangements and improve the transparency of resource flows

Ideally, the governance and funding for all levels of education should be placed under the same regulatory regime ending the formal divide between federal and provincial schools (as well as between federal and provincial teachers). The dual structure of provincial school boards and school departments in the provincial governments should be transformed into a unitary structure. This would eliminate inefficiencies in the current system and create the conditions for integrated and strategic policy making, especially at the lower secondary school level. It would thus also facilitate moving to a more comprehensive school system in the future provided there is sufficient political willingness to delay early tracking and selection among all stakeholders. Given the legacy of Austria's school system and political realities, any future governance and funding arrangement will most likely have to be a political compromise involving both the federal and the provincial levels. The new institutions are thus likely to have a hybrid character with shared responsibilities between the federal and the provincial levels.

The new institutions replacing the provincial school boards and the school departments of the provincial governments should be responsible for recruiting and assigning all teachers to individual schools with funding for all teachers being provided directly by the federal government via the new institutions. This would help align financing and spending responsibilities, render the complex transfer arrangement of teacher funding through the provincial administrations unnecessary, increase the transparency and effectiveness of funding flows and teacher allocation across different schools, and at the same time eliminate some rigidity in the teacher labour market. The employment of other pedagogical support staff, and possibly also of administrative support staff, should also be transferred to the new institutions responsible for teacher recruitment. This would facilitate a broader view of the human resource needs in schools and help to harmonise and equalise levels of support staff in different schools. Schools should gradually receive more autonomy for choosing their personnel, accompanied by effective accountability mechanisms, investments in school leadership capacity, and steps to increase school size. To keep other levels of governance involved in the funding of schools, municipalities and provincial governments could continue to be involved together with the federal level in financing maintenance costs and infrastructure investments.

To facilitate strategic planning, responsibilities should be distributed by levels of education rather than school type. If municipalities remain involved in the funding of schools, it would be important to establish some kind of fiscal equalisation scheme on the provincial level to prevent inequalities between municipalities and schools. It would also be essential to provide incentives and support for a rational organisation of the school offer (e.g. through the creation of municipal school associations (*Schulgemeindeverbände*), school clusters and larger catchment areas). Alternatively, the federal government could devolve all funding responsibilities for infrastructure and maintenance to the provinces and concentrate on the funding of teachers only. If a unified system of teacher funding and allocation that involves the federal and provincial authorities through the new institutions is not feasible and the current system of provincial and federal teachers and the split in responsibilities is maintained, some of the unintended incentives should be addressed. The refunding of teacher costs should be based on actual salary costs rather than nominally low salaries or an equal split between the federal and provincial governments in funding teachers for all general compulsory schools could be introduced, as is the case for vocational schools in dual VET where very little to no overspending occurs.

Austria should explore different ways to introduce more elaborate and needs-based formula funding which takes into account additional factors besides student enrolment to address inequities in a more targeted way and take steps to improve its accountability and controlling instruments. Both these measures would contribute to greater transparency of resource flows and help create greater levels of trust between different levels of government. Formula-based funding has the advantage that the criteria used to distribute funds across schools are made explicit and, therefore, open for informed debate and subject to political scrutiny. Bringing together the different information systems and merging them into an integrated system that links data on students, teachers, schools and resource flows would facilitate more rigorous accountability and monitoring of the use of resources. This is essential in a context in which the federal government is responsible for financing and the provinces are in charge of spending, thus setting problematic incentives and creating a lack of transparency and trust. More integrated data and information systems would allow drawing conclusions about the effective use of resources and thus facilitate more targeted policy interventions. And it would facilitate the monitoring and steering of the teacher labour market.

Provide incentives and support for a rational organisation of the school offer

Austria has a high density of schools and schools are, on average, very small, particularly in primary education and especially in rural and mountainous areas. While it is important to maintain access to schooling for younger children at a reasonable distance from home, and to take broader local and regional development objectives into account, increasing school size up to a certain enrolment level can achieve important economies of scale and free up resources that can be invested in other areas. What is true for school size is true for class size too, and increasing class size could be a further way to increase efficiency. Austria could achieve larger schools and classes through a variety of instruments, including setting and enforcing minimum school and class sizes. Also, one provider could be put in charge of administering several schools. This would imply larger catchment areas that facilitate more rational decisions about the school offer and remove incentives for municipalities to keep their school open in face of required financial transfers to another municipality in case of school closure. The complex process currently required to close down and merge schools should be simplified and other incentives for school consolidation could be introduced, such as additional funding for administrative staff for larger schools or incentives for creating clusters of schools.

Pursue further strategies to increase equity in education through longer common learning time

Austria should consider completing the integration of the New Secondary Schools and the lower level of academic secondary schools as was originally intended with the New Secondary School reform. This would be a logical next step building on previous initiatives to harmonise the education offered in different school types, e.g. with the introduction of a new teacher service code and the reform of initial teacher education. However, if a move towards fully comprehensive schooling at the lower secondary level turns out not to be politically feasible, other options are available. This includes greater collaboration and harmonisation between both school types as well as support for students to move upstream from the New Secondary School to the academic secondary school earlier and more easily. Considering that the New Secondary School has only been introduced recently, the effect of the reform will have to be evaluated in the long run. First evaluations, however, provide mixed results and suggest limited effects on learning outcomes. It will thus be important to evaluate if schools require greater support to implement pedagogical innovations, such as team teaching, effectively. Broader steps to improve the teaching profession and pedagogical leadership would also support the implementation of these pedagogical innovations. Also, Austria should further promote the expansion of integrated all-day schooling. Considering reluctance from parents and schools to introduce integrated models of all-day schooling, Austria could consider introducing a campaign to convince parents and schools of the advantages this brings for children and students.

Develop a vision for teacher professionalism

Building a new conception of the teaching profession that promotes a vision of schools as professional learning communities and teachers that work together as peers to improve teaching and learning for all students would help Austria to make the most efficient use of its teaching workforce. It would help to make teaching a more attractive career and create a more positive discourse around teaching. To support the development of a new vision of teacher professionalism, the OECD review team recommends developing a national teacher profile or standards of practice. This would establish a foundation for teachers to explore their practice and for schools to develop initiatives to improve, and provide orientation for teacher development overall. The views and experiences of teachers should be central for the development of their profession. Teachers in Austria should be given greater responsibility for the self-regulation of their profession and the teacher union should recognise its role in this area beyond the representation of teachers' political interests. In a number of other countries, teacher professional organisations take a leading role in promoting teacher professionalism. The creation of such an organisation is also an option for Austria.

While not a priority at present, working towards a new concept of teacher employment in the medium term could further facilitate the development of a new vision of teacher professionalism. Austria should consider moving to employment under a workload system beyond teaching hours that recognises teachers' wide range of tasks and encourages teachers' involvement in school development. The OECD review team also recommends considering the development of a differentiated career structure that allows for vertical and horizontal progression. A career structure would contribute to promoting a new conception of the teaching profession and increase the attractiveness of the teaching career. Progression in the career structure should be voluntary and be associated with a formal process of evaluation to promote the concept of merit.

Develop the pedagogical leadership of schools

Austria should also take further steps to develop the leadership capacity of its schools. This is essential to promote a new vision of teaching and learning, to ensure the effective management of teachers at a local level, and to provide teachers with opportunities for feedback and professional learning. It is also an important precondition for greater school autonomy. Austria will need to improve the current employment framework of school leaders. This includes steps to further professionalise the recruitment process to reduce the risk for political appointments. The involvement of the school inspectorate and the school forum in the selection process could increase objectivity and help to match candidates to local needs. The development of professional school leadership standards would also help to introduce greater objectivity and, more generally, help to promote a vision of pedagogical leadership. The school leadership profession should play a prominent role in the development of these standards. Considering the apparently low number of applicants, it would be important to analyse the attractiveness of the profession, including the competitiveness of current school leader remuneration compared to teachers and other professions and the possibility to create career development opportunities, such as system leadership roles. To improve pedagogical leadership in schools, the employer of school principals should take more responsibility for the ongoing management of individual school leaders. This could involve the development of personnel management processes such as mandatory individual appraisal. Creating more opportunities for schools to collaborate and facilitating school leadership networks can be a further strategy to foster greater pedagogical leadership and to improve the quality of education across the education system more widely.

Assessment and recommendations

Context

Austria's performance in international student assessments is mixed and there is scope for improvement

In 2011, Austrian primary school students in Year 4 took part in the IEA's TIMSS (Trends in International Mathematics and Science Study) and PIRLS (Progress in International Reading Literacy Study). Austria's results in mathematics and reading in these assessments were considered unsatisfactory compared to 14 participating countries with similar socio-economic characteristics. In both subjects, Austria scored above the international average, but took the last place in its reference group for reading and the third-last for mathematics. In both subjects, the share of Austrian students meeting the Advanced and High International Benchmarks was smaller than the international median. Reading literacy scores have experienced a decline since 2006 and scores for mathematics have decreased since 1995. In science, however, Austria continues to show good results, performing above the international benchmarks across all levels of achievement. In 2012, Austrian 15-year-olds participated in OECD PISA 2012 performing above the OECD average in mathematics (506 vs. 494), at the average in science (506 vs. 501) and below the average in reading (490 vs. 496). In mathematics and reading, Austria fared worse than Germany and Switzerland, but better than or similar to Italy and the Slovak Republic. Since PISA 2003, Austria has slightly narrowed the share of low performing students in all subjects, but at the same time experienced a reduction in its share of top performers. This has resulted in a comparatively small share of students at the bottom, but also at the top of the performance scale in PISA 2012. TIMSS, PIRLS and PISA indicate relatively strong gender gaps in education.

Equity remains a concern in Austria

Students' economic, social and cultural status has an important impact on their performance in PISA 2012. A higher status is associated with better scores in mathematics, reading and science, and more so than in other OECD countries. Students with an immigrant background are at particular risk of underperformance scoring below non-immigrant students in PISA 2012 after controlling for their economic, social and cultural status. This gap has remained unchanged since 2003 and remains well above the OECD average. Students from a socio-economically disadvantaged background and students with an immigrant background are, furthermore, more likely to be low performers than their peers from advantaged and non-immigrant backgrounds. The overall share of resilient students remains below the OECD average. Between-school variance is greater than on average across OECD countries and much of the between-school difference in performance is explained by students' choice of study programmes. Schools are more socio-economically homogenous than in most other OECD countries and school performance is correlated with their students' socio-economic status, although less so than in other OECD countries. However, this still indicates a clustering of students from disadvantaged backgrounds in under-performing schools and related gaps in performance. As data from OECD PIAAC 2012 indicate, parental background remains a strong determinant of children's educational trajectory and access to tertiary education. Austria has the third lowest level of absolute upward mobility among OECD countries.

The governance of school education in Austria is characterised by a complex distribution of responsibilities between the different tiers of government

The Federal Ministry of Education and Women's Affairs (*Bundesministerium für Bildung und Frauen,* BMBF) holds the overall executive authority for school education and the federal government develops and proposes legislation. The nine provinces are responsible for the implementation of all federal legislation through the formulation of implementing legislation. Governing, financing and administrative responsibilities for individual schools are distributed between the federal, the provincial and the municipal levels. There is, thus, a distinction between federal schools (*Bundesschulen*) and provincial schools (*Landesschulen*). Federal schools comprise academic secondary schools (*Allgemein bildende höhere Schule,* AHS) as well as upper secondary vocational schools and colleges (*Berufsbildene mittlere Schule,* BMS, *Berufsbildene höhere Schule,* BHS). Provincial schools include primary schools (*Volksschule,* VS), general lower secondary schools (*Hauptschule,* HS), New Secondary Schools (*Neue Mittelschule,* NMS), special needs schools (*Sonderschule,* ASO), pre-vocational schools (*Polytechnische Schule,* PTS) and part-time upper secondary vocational schools (*Berufsschule,* BS). Federal schools receive their funding directly from the federal government. Provincial schools are financed by the provinces and municipalities using funds which are, however, to a significant extent raised at the federal level and transferred to provinces in accordance with the Fiscal Adjustment Act (*Finanzausgleichsgesetz*). The nine provincial school boards (*Landesschulräte*), which are federal agencies but strongly influenced by the provincial governments, are responsible for administering federal schools. The school departments of the offices of the provincial government (*Schulabteilungen in den Ämtern der Landesregierung*) are responsible for administering provincial schools. In practice, however, this division of responsibilities is less clear-cut. Five out of nine provincial governments have transferred some of their responsibility for provincial schools to the provincial school board. Most tasks associated with the maintenance of provincial schools have in practice been devolved to the municipalities.

Austria has implemented a number of reforms in recent years and in November 2015 the federal government presented a comprehensive reform proposal

In 2013, Austria passed a law to reform some of its school governance structures (*Schulbehörden-Verwaltungsreformgesetz*) abolishing the district education boards which had been in charge of school inspections below the provincial level. Other significant reforms include the introduction of the New Secondary School (NMS) to mitigate the effects of early tracking, a reform of initial teacher education and the introduction of a new teacher service code. Austria has, furthermore, made various changes to its evaluation and assessment framework, introducing, among others, national education standards, standardised national assessments, and a programme for School Quality in General Education (*Schulqualität Allgemeinbildung,* SQA). In November 2015, the federal government presented a proposal for comprehensive education reform. The reform proposal encompasses changes to early childhood education and care; steps to improve the transition from kindergarten to primary education through a school entry phase; greater school autonomy in pedagogical, organisational and financial domains; the creation of model regions in the individual provinces to facilitate the collaboration of different school types and to pilot comprehensive schooling for 6-14 year-olds; a new structure for the joint administration of federal and provincial schools and teachers; and measures to encourage innovation in education. The reform proposal was informed by the work of an expert group on school governance and administration comprising representatives from the federal and provincial governments as well as different federal ministries and the Federation of Austrian Industries (*Industriellenvereinigung*). At the time of drafting, it was unclear how many of the proposals would find their way through the legislative process and the political debate was still ongoing.

Strengths and challenges

Austria has maintained a strong investment in its school system, but may not make the most efficient use of the resources that are available

The Austrian school system benefits from high levels of financial investment. Although some budget cuts were also implemented in the field of education and budget pressures seem to be increasing, the recent economic and financial crisis did not yet have a strong impact on the education budget. Taking both public and private spending on primary, secondary and tertiary education into account, Austria spends a lower share of its gross domestic product (GDP) than the OECD countries on average (4.9% compared to 5.3% in 2012), but still significantly more than the neighbouring Czech Republic, Germany, Italy and the Slovak Republic. When only looking at public expenditure as a share of GDP, however, Austria ranks slightly above the OECD average (4.9% vs. 4.7%). The country also enjoys high levels of public spending per student. In 2012, Austria spent purchasing power equivalent USD 13 189 per student from primary to tertiary education, significantly more than the OECD average of USD 10 220. Austria has, furthermore, recently implemented some reforms in budgeting and outcome-oriented steering that indicate a significant political commitment towards improving efficiency. The general budget process has been reformed to include a set of measurable policy targets and associated indicators that provide guidance and enhance the legitimacy and accountability of policy making. The establishment of the BIFIE (*Bundesinstitut für Bildungsforschung, Innovation & Entwicklung des österreichischen Schulwesens* - Federal Institute for Educational Research, Innovation and Development of the Austrian School System), national education standards (testing) and partially centralised school exams for university entrance qualifications have strengthened the outcome-orientation of the system. However, there is concern that the country's significant resource commitment has not been sufficiently translated into educational success as measured through international assessments. There are also continued concerns about equity in Austria's school system. The main resource challenge for Austria, thus, lies not in expanding investments in education, but in using available resources more effectively and efficiently to improve the quality and equity of education. This also concerns some of the recent reforms, such as the introduction of the NMS and a new teacher service code. These reforms involve quite substantial spending increases. The impact of these investments naturally takes time before they can be fully evaluated, and, depending on the results of these reforms, they may require changes and adaptations.

There is political commitment to allocate additional resources to students from disadvantaged backgrounds and with particular learning needs

The significant investment of public resources in New Secondary Schools (NMS) is one example of this political commitment. The recent transformation of the general secondary schools (HS) into New Secondary Schools (NMS) aims to mitigate the negative effects of early tracking on equity and has been accompanied by a significant increase in public spending to fund more cost-intensive pedagogical approaches, such as team teaching, in this type of school which, on average, has a less advantaged student intake. The political commitment to spend more on students at risk of low performance is also indicated by the joint willingness of the provincial and the federal governments to devote additional teacher resources to students with learning difficulties and language needs. In primary education, students at risk of falling behind can benefit from one remedial teaching hour per week (*Förderunterricht*). Students with difficulties to follow the language of instruction when starting school can receive special support for up to two years as "non-regular students" (*außerordentliche Schüler*). In addition, the federal government provides funding for specialised staff within the general staff plans so schools can offer additional language courses (German as a second language) for students who are not classified as "non-regular students". The provincial school boards have some discretion to allocate additional teaching resources if such needs are identified, often through the school inspection. However, there are some concerns about the effective use of these additional resources from the federal level to improve teaching and learning and about controlling and monitoring how these resources are used.

A high degree of centralisation combined with a strong corporatist tradition can facilitate educational steering and the implementation of education policy

Compared to other federal countries, such as Canada, Germany or Switzerland, legal competencies for education are more centralised at the federal level. For instance, statutory regulations related to teachers' employment conditions and initial teacher education in Austria are passed as federal laws. While the provinces exert considerable influence on the policies of the federal government, this influence is primarily political and to a lesser degree rooted in formal legal competencies, even if the provinces are also responsible for translating central legislation into practice, thus possibly introducing differences in implementation across provinces. The centralisation of policy-making competencies at the federal level limits the number of potential veto players and increases the probability that significant reforms can be passed even against vocal opposition from special interests. But it also carries some risks. Innovation crucially depends on the willingness and political ability of the top of the hierarchy, but the filtering of policy reform proposals at the top depending on the prevailing political interests can prevent the implementation of more encompassing policy innovations. In addition, the many complexities of multi-level governance might contribute to "information overload" on the part of the central government, contributing to bureaucratic bottlenecks and inefficiencies. In Austria, a strong tradition of corporatism – despite its own weaknesses in increasing the number of potential veto players and in prolonging decision-making processes – reduces the risk of these potential disadvantages. It ensures that competing interests of relevant stakeholders balance each other out and precludes one particular set of organised interests from monopolising access to policy making. And it can help prevent problems of "information overload" since intermediary associations such as employers' associations and trade unions supply decision-makers with policy-relevant information. Including different stakeholders in policy formulation can, furthermore, increase the potential for co-operation in the later stages of implementation by building trust and legitimacy and, thus, contribute to lasting change.

The country's complex governance structure provides incentives for overspending, leads to a lack of transparency of resource flows, fuels mistrust, and results in inefficiencies

The governance structure of the Austrian school system is very complex as a result of the split of administrative and fiscal responsibilities for federal and provincial schools. The federal government is the main funder of school education by directly financing the federal schools and by providing funds for the costs of teacher salaries of provincial schools to the provinces through the overall fiscal adjustment arrangements. However, while the federal government holds responsibility for the use and distribution of the teacher resources of federal schools, this is not the case for provincial schools. The federal government has very limited means to steer and control the use and distribution of resources for these schools by the provinces. Clear lines of accountability are lacking and existing monitoring systems are not sufficiently developed. While the federal government and the provinces agree on annual staff plans, the provinces are free to hire more teachers than foreseen in these staff plans and the additional expenditures are partly covered by the federal level. Between 2006 and 2010, the number of teaching positions at general compulsory schools that were not included in the initial budget almost doubled from 1 039 to 2 063. Even though the partial reimbursements of the provinces to the federal government are based on teachers' lower starting salaries whereas the expenditure of the provinces is related to actual salaries, this results in significant additional spending by the federal government. Recent attempts by the federal government to change and confine this practice were met with strong political opposition from the provincial governments and stakeholders and, therefore, failed politically. From the perspective of the provinces, in fact, the resources provided through the general transfer scheme may be insufficient to meet all staffing needs. Besides being unable to prevent the provinces from using more teacher resources than originally agreed upon, the federal government has no direct way of controlling or influencing the distribution of provincial teachers to individual schools. It can be argued that provincial authorities have a better knowledge of local needs and are, therefore, better able to direct resources flexibly to where they are needed. But the lack of transparency about the allocation of resources creates mistrust among stakeholders, particularly so as the federal government is responsible for financing, whereas the provinces are in charge of spending. Systems to monitor the distribution of teachers are in place and they have recently been harmonised, but they remain rather fragmented and decentralised reflecting present governance structures. Also, even though the government has undertaken first steps to improve the efficiency of the administration, the split of responsibilities for federal and provincial schools requires inefficient parallel structures for personnel management in the form of provincial schools boards and school departments of the provincial governments. Present governance arrangements thus result in inefficiencies, fuel mistrust and potential conflicts about the management of resources, and prevent a more integrated approach to governing the school system. The hybrid character of the provincial school boards which are formally federal agencies but also connected to provincial politics in many ways makes the governance structure even more complex.

Schools have a fair degree of pedagogical autonomy, and, in the case of federal schools, some autonomy over their own budget, but overall schools' power to manage their resources is very limited

Austrian schools have a relatively high degree of autonomy in some pedagogical matters. However, Austrian schools have a low degree of autonomy for resource management, except for some areas in the case of federal schools. Federal schools have a certain degree of budgetary autonomy as they are able to rent out their school facilities to generate additional discretionary revenue and they have control over their own accounts, but they have little financial flexibility and cannot transfer funds from one year to the next. Provincial schools, on the other hand, do not have such autonomy in financial matters, thus presenting an inequity in the system. They cannot generate additional income and depend entirely on their municipality for support in maintenance and operating costs. Both federal and provincial schools have very little autonomy in choosing their staff since teacher selection is largely in the hands of the provincial school boards and the school departments of the provincial governments. Individual school leaders can and sometimes do influence decision making at the higher level through personal connections. But this is problematic since it increases the lack of transparency and arbitrariness of decision-making and again creates potential inequities. The limited degree of autonomy has partly been compensated by the establishment of a considerable number of "pilots" by schools (*Schulversuche*), but at a risk of increasing the degree of fragmentation in the whole system. Some teachers and school leaders seem to be wary of greater autonomy as it could change the relationship between school leaders and teachers and increase school leaders' workload. This indicates that greater school autonomy would also require a shift in the culture of school leadership. School leaders need to be better qualified and prepared in order to be able to use the full potential of school autonomy, and require sufficient support to fulfil their role and dedicate themselves to their role as pedagogical leaders.

Austria has made important steps towards the development of an evaluation and assessment framework, but the culture of transparency, evaluation and accountability needs to be further developed

The creation of a Federal Institute for Educational Research, Innovation and Development (BIFIE) has strengthened Austria's capacity for system-level evaluation and evidence-based policy making. The BIFIE collects information about students, teachers and school resources, and thus generates a considerable amount of data for the school system. Austria has also introduced education standards, national standardised assessments and different diagnostic tools. This signifies a shift of attention from teaching to learning and has the potential to improve both quality and equity in education. The recent initiatives to embed a culture of school development planning and self-evaluation through the School Quality in General Education process (SQA) constitute a further important step. However, there is scope to further develop a culture of transparency, evaluation and accountability and to promote the better use of all the information that is already available for decision-making at different levels of the system and by different stakeholders, including schools. The existence of multiple information and quality assurance systems makes a comprehensive approach to monitoring the quality and the performance of the system difficult. There is co-operation between different institutions such as the BIFIE, Statistics Austria, and the statistical section of the Federal Ministry of Education and Women's Affairs (BMBF), but there is room for deepening the collaboration and for better connecting and analysing the different streams of data through one integrated system. The controlling software for the use of teacher resources, for example, is not systematically connected to the other elements of the quality assurance and monitoring system. Similarly, the qualitative information collected through the school inspectorate (e.g. during the SQA process) is not well connected to quantitative data provided by the BIFIE, Statistics Austria, and the federal ministry. More generally, the inspectorate could play a stronger role in improving the quality of education. The inspectorate seems to suffer from a lack of resources – some inspectors are responsible for as many as 100 schools – and mainly provides external advice in case of concrete problems. It does not conduct thematic reviews on specific themes or aggregate the information collected from individual schools as part of system-wide analyses. Also schools seem not to have shifted to an assessment and evaluation culture yet. There is only limited evidence for the systematic and joint analysis and use of assessment results for improvement in schools, for example, and it is not clear to what extent school leaders and teachers are held accountable for results.

Austria has taken first steps to change its school structure towards longer common learning time, but early tracking has remained in place and the introduction of integrated all-day schooling across the country has turned out to be challenging

Early tracking and selection at the age of ten after only four years of primary education is one important explanation for the unequal learning outcomes of students from different demographic and socio-economic backgrounds in Austria. This is similar to other countries for which research provides substantial evidence that early tracking is related to a stronger effect of family background on performance. The New Secondary School reform (NMS) constitutes a significant step to reduce the impact of early tracking and to provide more equitable learning outcomes. Although the NMS has not replaced the lower level of academic secondary schools, it aims to improve the quality of teaching and learning for students in this track and to provide more students with a chance to enter higher education. The NMS and the AHS share a common curriculum and similar educational goals and the NMS benefits from additional resources to develop innovative pedagogical approaches, such as team teaching. The introduction of a new teacher service code and reform of initial teacher education that harmonise the employment conditions and education for different school types promise to raise the quality of teachers at the NMS. However, the NMS reform remained a political compromise and, although the effects of the reform will have to be assessed in the long run, the evidence for the impact of the reform is mixed so far. The systematic management of lower secondary education remains challenging and the full-scale introduction of common schooling seems unlikely as long as there is a lack of political willingness shared by different stakeholders and as long as responsibilities for lower secondary education remain fragmented between the federal level and the provincial level.

The introduction and expansion of all-day schooling constitutes a further initiative to increase common learning time and to make the school system more equitable. Studies on the effects of full-day kindergartens and on the introduction of all-day schooling in Germany show some promising results in terms of quality and equity. All-day schooling in Austria has increased substantially over the past years and in 2014 about 40% of all schools offered one form or another of all-day schooling. This initiative is strongly supported by the federal government and in 2015 available funds amounted to EUR 109 million. However, the expansion of all-day schooling is slower than expected by the federal authorities and the provinces had not requested all available funds until 2015. Schools can opt for fully-integrated all-day schooling or optional afternoon schooling. Even though the evidence suggests that the fully-integrated form promises the greatest returns, schools and parents strongly prefer the optional model.

Small schools are expensive to run, but while individual provinces have been developing some strategies for school consolidation, the rational organisation of the school offer faces a number of obstacles

Austria has a high density of schools and schools are, on average, very small, particularly in primary education and especially in rural and mountainous areas. On average, a primary school in Austria has 107 students, but this differs from 58 students in the Burgenland to 248 students in Vienna. Small rural schools are a pressing, but also sensitive issue in national, regional and local politics, that is likely to become even more important in the years to come given current demographic projections and a downward demographic trend in rural areas. Small average school (and class) sizes in Austria are an important part of the explanation why the Austrian school system is relatively expensive for the quality that it delivers. While it is important to bear broader regional and local development objectives in mind, small schools that have large spaces and high staff numbers for few students are expensive to run and maintain. At the same time, there is little evidence about the impact of small schools on the quality of education and whether small schools improve teaching and learning, also relative to larger schools that are more cost-efficient to operate. In fact, small school size reduces course options within schools, makes it difficult for teachers to learn from peers, and makes it harder for schools to operate with a greater degree of autonomy. Small schools make it difficult to realise other current policy priorities, such as the expansion of all-day schooling. And they drain resources from schools in urban areas as a growing disparity in per student spending between Vienna and the rest of the country illustrate.

Even though the costs of creating large schools in rural areas with low population densities (e.g. for student transportation) need to be taken into account, it thus seems necessary to rationalise the school offer from an education efficiency point of view. Individual provinces, such as Styria and Vorarlberg, have been taking first steps to rationalise the distribution of schools within their province (e.g. through the development of regional education plans and the creation of municipal school associations and associated schools), but Austria as a whole does not have a strategy to consolidate its school offer due to the fragmentation of competences. While decisions about the organisation of the school offer are always also political, there are some structural factors that hinder an efficient organisation. The present governance arrangements result in a fragmented system of school network planning for general compulsory schools. The federal government can plan the organisation of the network of academic secondary schools, but not influence or steer the offer of general compulsory schools which are run by the provinces and the many (sometimes very small) municipalities. The present governance arrangements, in fact, work against an efficient organisation of the school offer. As staff costs are covered by the federal level, the provinces and municipalities have little incentive to plan their networks in rural areas efficiently. Furthermore, the catchment areas of schools tend to coincide with the borders of the municipalities and if a municipality decides to close a school, it needs to compensate a neighbouring municipality for its students attending a school in that other municipality. Other factors, such as insufficient regulations and a lack of strategies to use empty school facilities also play a role. The local responsibility for infrastructure planning of general compulsory schools, furthermore, entails the risk for inequalities in infrastructure investments between poorer and richer municipalities.

Governance arrangements hinder the effective organisation of human resources across the education system and complicate the monitoring and steering of the teacher labour market

The distribution of responsibilities for the organisation and management of human resources between federal, provincial and municipal authorities, and the split in federal and provincial teachers make it difficult to organise the workforce effectively across the school system as a whole based on a broader view of staffing needs. In general compulsory schools, individual provinces are responsible for the distribution of provincial teachers to individual schools with no possibility for the federal government to influence or steer the process. In academic secondary schools, the distribution of federal teachers is the responsibility of the provincial school boards. The distinction into federal and provincial teachers also makes it difficult for teachers to work in different school types, which is particularly problematic in lower secondary education. The New Secondary School Reform has created the first opportunities for teachers from academic secondary schools to work in the NMS as part of a teacher team, but the split in regulatory competencies between the federal and provincial governments makes it difficult to monitor and manage the secondment of academic secondary school teachers. Employment of provincial teachers by individual provinces, furthermore, makes it difficult for teachers to move to another province as statutory rights acquired with increasing seniority may not always be recognised in a different province.

Despite some initiatives to give schools more input into the selection of teachers, schools are still limited in their autonomy to manage their human resources. This may not always ensure that the allocation of teachers matches schools' needs, although input of the school inspections may facilitate some steering. Teachers' age and the age profile of schools seem to be important criteria for the allocation of teachers rather than the schools' profile and needs. It is not clear to what extent the best teachers are allocated to the most disadvantaged schools, also in light of a lack of incentives for teachers to work in specific contexts, such as rural or disadvantaged schools.

There are also concerns about the availability of administrative staff, which can prevent teachers and school leaders from focussing on their core pedagogical responsibilities. The lack of such staff is also partly linked to a lack of school autonomy, and, in the case of general compulsory schools, the complex governance arrangements. Here, municipalities are responsible for the employment of administrative support staff, but they may not have the financial means or willingness to do so as provincial and federal authorities usually compensate for this shortcoming by increasing the number of teachers' working hours. This also creates potential inequities between schools in the absence of a mechanism that would equalise funding levels across municipalities. There is also a need to increase the availability of other professionals who can support schools in their work with young people, i.e. social pedagogues, psychologists and social workers. In line with changing family patterns and increasing diversity and heterogeneity in schools and within classes, these professionals play an important role in supporting the teaching staff and students. The need to integrate a large number of young refugees and asylum seekers into the education system might aggravate these shortcomings further in the near future.

Present governance arrangements also make it challenging to monitor and steer the teacher labour market. The distribution of responsibilities for the employment, monitoring and data management of human resources between federal and provincial authorities for different school types seem to make projections and forecasting overly challenging and require a substantial amount of co-ordination between the different responsible authorities. The monitoring system for federal schools is different and separated from the system used in provincial schools. For example, to gather data on the share of teachers who teach a subject they are not qualified for, it would be necessary to analyse all individual teachers' working contracts filed at the level of the nine provincial school boards or provincial school departments. There do not seem to be major teacher shortages across the country, even though some shortages exist in certain regions or subjects, but considering an expected retirement wave in the near future, sound forward planning and monitoring will be essential to identify existing and emerging shortages.

Austria has introduced a new initial teacher education scheme and a new teacher service code which may raise the status of the profession and improve the teaching workforce

With the introduction of a new teacher service code and a reform of initial teacher education, Austria has undertaken first steps to make teaching more attractive, even though more measures may be needed in the future. This is an urgent issue as Austria faces a considerable retirement wave – according to a parliamentary inquiry about half of all teachers in Austria are expected to retire by 2025. The reform of initial teacher education raises the status of the profession with the requirement that all future teachers will need to acquire a master's qualification. This sends a strong signal that teaching should be a highly-qualified profession and is particularly important for teaching in general compulsory schools which traditionally only required the completion of a three-year bachelor's programme. The introduction of a new teacher service code implies a substantial financial commitment, but it makes teaching more attractive for new teachers. It roughly maintains lifetime earnings, but changes the shape of the salary progression significantly with higher statutory starting salaries and a more compressed slope of the salary scale. Of course, it has to be taken into account that qualification requirements for new teachers have been raised and that new teachers will have to teach slightly more hours. The new teacher education and the new service code also facilitate side entry into teaching for other professionals by recognising experience in other fields to meet qualification requirements and to advance in the salary scale.

The new teacher education and the new service code also promise to improve the quality of the teaching workforce. The new teacher education scheme could help raise the quality of initial teacher education thanks to a number of positive changes. This includes, among others, collaboration between University Colleges of Teacher Education (*Pädagogische Hochschule*, PH), which are strong in pedagogical training, and universities, which have a long tradition in subject-related theory; the lengthening of programmes at PHs; the introduction of obligatory orientation and admissions procedures at universities; and the creation of an independent quality assurance council (*Qualitätssicherungsrat für Pädagoginnen- und Pädagogenbildung*). The new teacher service code is also likely to strengthen the profession by creating some specialist roles for teachers, e.g. in the areas of mentoring, learning and career counselling, and special needs and remedial pedagogy. And it provides stronger in-service development requirements for all teachers and a one-year professional entry phase for all new teachers. Importantly, both the new teacher education and the new service code harmonise the qualifications requirements and working conditions of all new teachers. They, thus, constitute significant milestones to break down barriers between different school types, to create common school form for all children up to age 14, and to create a common teaching profession that feel responsible for raising the achievement of all students in the education system as a whole.

However, the effect of both reforms on the status of the profession and the quality of the workforce remain to be seen. The implementation of the new service code will take about 40 years to apply to all teachers and until then, three different service codes will be in place. The impact of the new initial teacher education similarly will necessarily take time and its implementation faces a number of challenges, including institutional weaknesses of PHs (e.g. limited managerial and organisational autonomy and capacity for research) and universities (e.g. little orientation to practice and weak links to schools).

A stronger professional approach to teaching might be needed and school leaders are not equipped to manage their staff effectively at the local level

The quality of teaching is key for effective learning and considered the single most important factor within schools that impacts student learning. Austria has taken some important steps to increase the quality of teaching, such as the introduction of a new initial teacher education system and the development of quality assurance, school development and self-evaluation practices through the SQA initiative. But there seems to be a need for further reflection in Austria about the nature of teachers' professional work today. The main lever to raise student performance seems to be the provision of additional teaching hours rather than steps to improve teaching practice in schools and classrooms. Recent research on organisational learning has stressed the importance of new ways of working in schools that focus on collaboration, reflective practice, peer observation and continuous professional learning. In Austria, schools do not seem to manage teaching and learning collectively and teachers seem to be rather isolated in their classrooms and to have few opportunities for feedback. Appraisal by the school principal seems to be often concentrated on new teachers, to be less common for more experienced teachers and to have weak links with professional development. Few teachers seem to work as "critical friends" or peer mentors for one another to develop their practice. And teachers have limited sources of external feedback as external teacher appraisal only takes place in case of serious concerns. Strategic approaches to teachers' professional development seem to be rather rare and professional development seems to be mostly the choice of individual teachers.

Teachers' employment framework, that is the career structure and working time arrangements, fail to promote greater teacher professionalism. Even though the new teacher service code provides some opportunities to take on specialist functions, teachers do not benefit from distinct and flexible pathways that would give teachers more development opportunities and recognition, including for those teachers who wish to remain focused on classroom teaching, and help schools meet their needs. And while the new teacher service code provides two hours per week for other tasks, and the service code for provincial teachers stipulates an annual standard of total working hours, the conception of teachers' working time for federal teachers and all new teachers still focuses on teaching hours only. This fails to recognise that effective teaching entails a range of further activities in schools beyond classroom instruction and limits teachers' engagement in broader school development.

Greater teacher professionalism in schools also requires effective management of human resources by school leaders at the local level. Despite some efforts to foster pedagogical leadership in schools in Austria, for instance with the creation of a Leadership Academy, school principals still do not perceive their role as a pedagogical one, but rather as administrative and managerial in nature. And there are a number of issues that make it difficult to strengthen school principals' pedagogical leadership. The profession, which also faces a pending retirement wave, is not very attractive, compensation does not seem to reflect the higher level of responsibility, and appointment processes do not seem to ensure that the best candidates are selected. School leaders, furthermore, lack the autonomy and tools as well as the support from administrative staff and middle leaders to manage their human resources and to incentivise high performance or to respond to underperformance.

Policy recommendations

Align financing and spending responsibilities in one hand

A major challenge in the current governance and funding arrangements is the division of responsibilities between the federal and the provincial governments. Ideally, the governance and funding for all levels of education should be placed under the same regulatory regime ending the formal divide between federal and provincial schools (as well as between federal and provincial teachers). The dual structure of provincial school boards and school departments in the provincial governments should be transformed into a unitary structure. In principle, it is less important whether the newly created institutions are formally provincial or federal agencies, which is ultimately a political decision. The most important point is that a unitary governance structure is created which is able to overcome the formal division between federal and provincial schools and facilitates integrated and strategic policy making, especially at the lower secondary school level. However, out of necessity and given the legacy of Austria's school system, the new institutions are likely to have a hybrid character with shared responsibilities. While the federal government has the formal competencies to pass major legislation in education policy, there is a need for regional flexibility in the implementation of federal laws.

To increase transparency and effectiveness of funding flows, all teachers should be employed by the same employer according to the same standards and all funding for teachers should be provided directly by the federal government via the new institutions. The reforms of initial teacher education and the teacher service code have already set important legal preconditions in this regard. The new institutions should be responsible for teacher recruitment and allocation, while giving schools some autonomy in choosing their personnel. This would align financing and spending responsibilities through involvement of the federal level in the allocation of all teacher resources in the new institutions. Placing the responsibility for the employment of all teachers into one hand would also eliminate some rigidity for teacher mobility stemming from the difficulty to have statutory rights recognised in a different province. Funding all teachers directly by the federal government via the new institutions would render the complex transfer arrangement of teacher funding through the provincial administrations unnecessary. Municipalities and provincial governments could continue to be involved in financing maintenance costs and infrastructure investments, but to facilitate strategic planning for each educational level this involvement should not depend on school type. One option could be to ensure that municipal governments are more strongly involved in the financing of primary schools, the provinces in lower secondary education and the federal government in upper secondary education. However, if municipalities continue to play a strong role in the provision and financing of education, it would be important to establish some kind of transparent fiscal equalisation scheme on the provincial level to prevent inequalities between fiscally weaker and richer municipalities. In the current arrangements, it is not fully transparent how funds provided by the provinces to the municipalities in addition to the funds provided by the federal level via the Fiscal Adjustment Act are distributed between municipalities. Alternatively, the federal government could devolve all funding responsibilities for infrastructure and maintenance to the provinces and concentrate on teacher funding only. In this new division of labour between the provincial and the federal governments, both provincial and the federal governments would continue to be involved in the funding of schools, but the former would be in charge of all infrastructure and maintenance expenditures, whereas the latter would continue to be responsible for financing all teacher resources. While the funding and organisation of the school offer and infrastructure would require co-ordination between the different provinces, the division of labour would be better defined compared to the current situation. Given the history of political struggles between the federal and the provincial governments, any future arrangement will most likely have to be such a political compromise involving both the federal and the provincial levels.

If a unified system of teacher funding and allocation is not feasible and the current system of federal and provincial teachers is maintained, some of the unintended incentives should be addressed. For one, if the system of provincial refunds for overspending on teachers is maintained, the refunding of teacher costs to the federal government should be based on actual salary costs rather than nominally lower salaries. Alternatively, it would be possible to introduce an equal split between the federal and provincial governments in funding teachers for all general compulsory schools as is done in the case of vocational schools, where no or very little overspending occurs. Ideally, however, the responsibility for financing and allocating all teachers should be in one hand, independent of the school type or level of education.

Explore different ways to introduce need-based formula funding

Policy makers should explore different possibilities to introduce more elaborate and needs-based formula funding for the distribution of teaching and other resources. The introduction of needs-based funding formulae can be a highly efficient and transparent method of funding schools. In general, formula-based funding has the advantage that the criteria used to distribute funds across schools are made explicit and, therefore, subject to political scrutiny. This is a significant advantage in terms of transparency compared to a regime with more implicit than explicit criteria for distribution. Transparency is a central precondition for informed debate and priority-setting. In Austria, the introduction of more elaborate and needs-based formula funding would address the lack of transparency and trust resulting from the current relatively rigid system in which the bulk of funding is distributed by student numbers and that stimulates workarounds by the provinces and the municipalities. There are a number of examples from other countries where formula-based funding has been introduced successfully, e.g. in Hamburg, the Netherlands, the Swiss cantons of Berne and Zurich as well as in Toronto (Canada). In the Austrian context, a number of proposals for the design and implementation of formula-based funding that takes different needs of school and socio-economic contexts into account have already been developed and are being discussed. Common to these proposals is the idea that the funding formula according to which resources are distributed between schools should contain elements in addition to simple student numbers that take into account the characteristics of the student population. The choice of variables included in the funding formula is crucial with regard to its impact on equity of funding, but the degree of redistribution and equalisation between different types of schools is fundamentally a political and societal discussion and cannot be decided by scientific criteria. Furthermore, there is a trade-off between "transparency-simplicity and sensitivity to local conditions-complexity". Simple funding formulae, which include only few indicators, are transparent and easy to administer, but do not necessarily pay sufficient attention to the peculiarities of local needs. A shift towards a more elaborate and needs-based formula-based funding system would also require a decision on the share of school funding that comes from needs-based formula funding relative to basic funding. A significant share of the total funding needs to be based on student numbers in order to ensure the stability of basic funding from year to year, topped up by additional funding as determined by needs-based funding formulae. As part of the discussion about the introduction of more elaborate funding formulae, current differences in spending per student across provinces, different geographical areas and school types should be made transparent.

Monitor resource flows and make sure resources are used efficiently

Austria should bring together the different data and information systems and merge them into an integrated system. An integrated system would overcome the present fragmentation by connecting information on students and their performance (currently collected by BIFIE) with data on the use of teacher resources (currently monitored by two different systems in federal and provincial schools) as well as the rich qualitative information available through the quality assurance system. Such an integrated system would facilitate more rigorous accountability and monitoring of the use of resources in a context of decentralised spending powers that sets problematic incentives for the provinces and the municipalities. It would also allow drawing conclusions about the effective use of resources, the relative performance of particular schools and, thus facilitate more targeted policy. Austria could develop a brokerage agency, or equip an existing institution with this function (e.g. BIFIE), to facilitate the sharing of information. Such an agency could also help to promote the use of data, evidence, research and evaluations for decision-making. Streamlining the availability of data on teacher resources and overcoming the current fragmentation that reflects present governance structures would also facilitate the systematic analysis and steering of the teacher labour market. The unification and centralisation of the framework conditions for the school system would also support the transparency of resource flows. Policy makers in Austria have already taken important steps in this regard, e.g. with the introduction of national education standards and the introduction of a new teacher service code. These initiatives have to be sustained and further developed. Efficiency of resource use can, furthermore, be promoted by establishing systematic and high-quality processes of evidence-based policy evaluation, which are still weakly developed in Austria as evidenced by the widespread use of school pilots which are not systematically evaluated.

Rebalance funding across different types of school staff

Policy makers should review the possibilities to create more positions for other types of professionals working in schools, even if it would imply decreasing the number of regular teachers, and strive to harmonise and equalise the funding conditions for administrative staff across school types and levels of education. This should be part of deliberations for a governance reform. The employment of pedagogical support staff could become part of the responsibilities of the new authority responsible for the employment of teachers, while schools could assume responsibility for the recruitment of administrative and maintenance staff, for example. But to limit the administrative burden on schools, the responsibility for the recruitment of administrative staff could also be delegated to the same level as the recruitment for teachers and other pedagogical staff. This would help prevent shortages of staff in schools and avoid inequities in the distribution of personnel resources, which are too dependent on local fiscal and political conditions (in the sector of general compulsory schools). Schools should have some level of influence over staffing decisions and schools with the greatest need for other pedagogical support staff should be given priority.

If the streamlining of overall human resource responsibilities does not prove feasible, the federal authorities could take advantage of their power to set central policies and regulations. Federal authorities could consider the introduction of central standards or guidelines on minimum staff-teacher or staff-student ratios for pedagogical support staff and a minimum number of administrative staff for schools of a certain size. In addition, Austria could further test out innovative and cost-effective ways of organising schools and administrative and pedagogical support. Schools should be encouraged to collaborate more with other social services and non-formal education initiatives to provide support for children and young people in a more open format. Furthermore, there seems to be a need to clarify teachers' roles and responsibilities. Teachers often seem to understand broader tasks, such as subject co-ordination, as administrative tasks, even though they should be seen as part of their involvement in school development.

Enhance school autonomy while creating the conditions for autonomous schools to perform well and while taking steps to prevent inequalities from emerging

A reform of school governance should give schools gradually greater autonomy to select their personnel and teachers while maintaining the equity benefits of a more central teacher recruitment system. Being able to select teachers according to particular criteria (e.g. teaching methods, extracurricular activities, etc.) would allow schools to more effectively shape their profiles. One option would be to allow schools to select part of their teaching force while institutions above the school level remain in charge of recruiting and assigning the remaining part of the teaching force in order to ensure that common standards are applied and that particular schools are not systematically disadvantaged. In Germany, the use of such a mixed system is quite common. Giving schools the full autonomy in hiring teachers carries the risk of amplifying differences between schools, since the more attractive schools will be able to attract the better teachers. Vice versa, not allowing schools any influence on the selection of teaching personnel can lead to misallocations and frustrations and prevent schools from developing a particular profile. Austria could also put further mechanisms into place that work towards equity in teacher allocation. The introduction of salary allowances for schools in disadvantaged areas, for example, could be one option. Such policies have been found to have clear positive effects on teacher recruitment. Schools should also receive more autonomy in financial matters. Allowing the general compulsory schools a degree of financial autonomy similar to the academic secondary schools would be an important first step in mitigating inequalities between different school types. General compulsory schools would, then, be able to tap into own sources of revenue and to maintain their own accounts and operational budgets.

Increased school autonomy needs to be accompanied by effective accountability mechanisms. The SQA process is a good starting point in that respect, but if school autonomy increases, the role of external school evaluation – in a reformed school inspectorate – would also need to be strengthened. Information generated through the quality assurance system needs to be systematically connected with resource management decisions and accompany the process of giving schools greater autonomy. This would allow concentrating additional support to schools that are identified as underperforming in the quality monitoring system or to schools struggling with their new autonomy. Besides accountability, there are other factors that need to go along with school autonomy. Expanding school autonomy requires a redistribution of resources, in particular higher investment in school leadership capacity and administrative personnel. The effect of delegating more autonomy to schools depends on schools' ability to make use of this autonomy in a constructive way and thus requires a strengthening of school leadership and management structures. A critical school size is also necessary in order for schools to be able to effectively use their autonomy. If schools are too small, delegating more responsibilities to the school level may simply overwhelm school leaders with additional work tasks. Considerations about increasing school autonomy should, therefore, go together with discussions about increasing the average school size.

Provide incentives and support for a rational organisation of the school offer

Addressing the issue of a high density of schools and very small average school size is challenging in any school system. For local governments, closing down schools poses difficulties and for parents it is difficult to see "their" school closed. However, in situations with scarce resources, it is important to consider which investments have the highest rate of return and contribute most to the public good. Increasing school size up to a certain enrolment level can achieve important economies of scale, albeit some studies also find that returns to scale diminish and that diseconomies of scale begin to emerge beyond a certain enrolment level. Research shows that, even if consolidation is usually met with opposition, consolidation can end up being positively valued by teachers, parents and students. The broader returns of small schools in rural communities in terms of local and regional development need to be taken into account, but this broader function requires a wider reflection about different strategies and funding solutions beyond education (e.g. from local development funds). In education, increasing average school size would free up resources that could be invested in other areas that can have benefits in terms of equity such as early childhood education and care, the quality of teachers or the further development of all-day schooling. It is, however, important to maintain access to schooling for younger children at a reasonable distance from home and to address other potential negative effects on student well-being, such as weaker links between schools, parents and the local community. What is true for school size is true for class size too, as the small class size in Austria contributes to making education expensive. Increasing class size could be one way to increase efficiency.

Increasing school and class size can be stimulated through a variety of instruments. The most straightforward measure is to set (and enforce) minimum school and class sizes. These can be set at a level that would not require massive school closures and then be increased incrementally towards a desired level over a longer period of time. As an alternative to increasing school size, one provider (such as a regional education centre, a larger municipality or an association of municipalities) could be put in charge of administering several schools. This would also imply larger catchment areas. Once larger catchment areas have been established, a more rational decision can be made about which schools to keep open within the catchment area. Associations of municipalities would also help to simplify the complex system of transfers between municipalities when children from one municipality choose to attend school in a different one. In addition, allowing extra administrative and management budgets for larger schools could help provide incentives for increasing school size. Other obstacles to school consolidation should be removed as well. This includes a simplification of the complex process currently required to close down and merge schools. To address arguments that schools can play a key role for the local community beyond their immediate educational function, alternative institutions could be developed to take over this function of a social hub as part of broader regional and local development initiatives and strategies. These institutions could, in certain cases, also use the vacated former school building. When designing and implementing policies it will be important to learn from the lessons of Austrian provinces and other countries that have successfully increased school size and consolidated their school offer.

Pursue further strategies to increase equity in education by addressing early selection and by further supporting all-day schooling

Austria should consider completing the integration of the NMS and the AHS at the lower secondary level as was originally intended with the NMS reform. This would mean that all Austrian students are in the same type of school until age 14. Although tracking in Poland already took place at a later age, the country provides an example for a successful structural reform that has had a significant success not only in terms of reducing inequities, but also in raising student performance overall. However, if a move towards the full integration of the NMS and the AHS turns out not to be politically feasible, other options are available. One of these would be to reduce the distance between AHS and NMS schools, for example by bringing all lower secondary schools into one hand administratively so that educational planning for the whole age group is more coherent, and common oversight of the curricula, teaching and assessment is strengthened. One step further could be to twin AHS and NMS schools in the same regions, perhaps even to bring them under joint management. This would facilitate transfers across schools and increase the likelihood that the two types of schools grow closer together.

Facilitating better and earlier transitions for students to move upstream from the NMS to the AHS and from one track to another at later moments in their education could help reduce the impact of socio-economic background on student outcomes. The Austrian school system is more flexible than other models of early tracking and selection (e.g. in some German *Länder*) through its diversity of upper secondary vocational tracks which are open to students from the NMS as well. But it would be important to provide better support to students to move up across different school types and to those struggling within a particular track to succeed. Implementing a system of early diagnosis and remedial support for struggling students can be an effective policy tool in this regard. It is also important to facilitate earlier transitions than is currently the case, also bearing in mind the benefits of early intervention for student learning.

Currently, the federal budgets available for all-day schooling are underused, suggesting that the provinces are not moving as quickly as the federal government would like them to. Although all-day schools are increasingly available in Austria, only a small fraction of these offer an integrated form of all-day schooling, which promises the greatest benefits for children from less advantaged socio-economic backgrounds. The introduction of integrated forms is partly hampered by the fact that two-thirds of the parents and the teachers need to agree before schools can opt for the integrated forms of all-day schooling. This is understandable given that integrated all-day schooling affects all students. However, this procedure considerably slows down the further implementation of integrated all-day schooling. To encourage the introduction of integrated all-day schooling, Austria could develop a campaign to bring parents and schools on board. Moreover, Austria needs to address the resulting infrastructure challenges, particularly in urban areas, to make all-day schooling a success.

Develop a vision for teacher professionalism

Building a new conception of the teaching profession that promotes a vision of schools as professional learning communities that work together to improve teaching and learning for all students would help improve the quality of education in Austria. It would also help make teaching a more attractive career and create a more positive discourse around teaching. To support the development of a new vision of teacher professionalism, the OECD review team recommends developing a national teacher profile or standards of practice for the Austrian teaching profession. Such a national teacher profile would establish a foundation for teachers to explore their practice and for school to develop initiatives to improve. It would also provide orientation for the overall teacher development framework, including initial teacher education, professional development and appraisal. Tools and processes like school development planning and self-evaluation through the SQA process, more systematic work in schools with educational standards and assessments, and new opportunities for schools to collaborate could be used to help promote the new vision. The views and experience of teachers and school leaders should be central for the development of their profession. Teachers in Austria should have greater responsibility for the self-regulation of their profession (e.g. in the development of professional standards, the design of teacher education programmes and the definition of entrance criteria) and the teacher union should further recognise its responsibility for the development of the profession beyond the representation of teachers' political interests in terms of employment rights and working conditions. In other countries, such as Australia, Ireland, New Zealand, and Scotland, teacher professional organisations take a lead role in determining processes for the development of teachers, such as the development of professional standards and teacher appraisal. The creation of such an organisation is also an option for Austria.

Working towards a new concept of teacher employment could further facilitate the development of a new vision of teacher professionalism. While this may not be a present priority considering that a new teacher service code is currently being introduced, it should be an objective in the medium term to further develop the conception of employment and working time. Austria should consider moving to employment under a workload system, whereby teachers work a specified number of hours per week. This conception of teacher employment recognises that teachers need time for engaging in a range of other tasks, including the adequate preparation of lessons. It is also likely to improve the opportunities for teachers to formally engage in activities other than teaching at the school level and to work together as peers. School management would be in a better position to foster teacher collaboration, promote whole-school planning and develop professional learning communities. Of course, it is also important that school buildings and facilities provide the conditions for teachers for doing so. In the medium term, Austria should also consider the development of a differentiated career structure that allows for vertical and horizontal progression. A career structure would contribute to promoting a new conception of the teaching profession and increase the attractiveness of the teaching career. The development of a career structure would also provide an opportunity to rethink the administratively complex system of salary allowances for school-level staff which furthermore lacks transparency. The career structure could build on the promising roles that have been established as part of the new teacher service code and the NMS reform and create further roles for school development. The experience of school pilots on middle management could also be institutionalised through the new career structure. Progression in the career structure should be voluntary and be associated with a formal process of evaluation to promote the principle of merit.

Develop pedagogical leadership in schools

Research has highlighted the importance of school leadership for teaching and learning. This provides a strong rationale for implementing policies that ensure the effective management and development of the school leadership profession. Furthermore, as school leaders constitute a relatively small, but central, group of actors in any education system, policies that target school leadership constitute highly cost-effective measures for improving education. Austria has already undertaken steps to foster effective school leadership, but despite long-standing efforts, it has been difficult to foster a cultural change towards greater pedagogical leadership. This is essential in the promotion of a new vision of teaching and learning and to ensure that teachers have sufficient opportunities for regular feedback and professional learning.

The current age profile and the retirement of many school principals provide a window of opportunity to recruit a new generation of school leaders and to instil the necessary cultural change. However, to ensure that promising candidates are selected, the recruitment process will need to be further professionalised to reduce the risk for political appointments. Necessarily, the employer of school principals should take responsibility for the management of school principals, including the recruitment, but the responsibility for recruitment should not be in the hands of a highly politicised body such as the collegiate boards of the provincial school boards. Irrespective of the institution that will take over the employment of school leaders following a reform of the governance structures, the recruitment process should be managed by an administrative body that has the capacity to conduct a high quality recruitment process. To increase objectivity, to match the selection better to the needs of the school, and to increase accountability, further actors, such as the school inspectorate and the school forum, should have greater prominence in the selection process. The development of professional school leadership standards would also help introduce greater objectivity in the selection process by providing a clear reference what kind of skills and competencies school principals should have. More generally, such standards would help promote a vision of pedagogical leadership. In the development of professional school leadership standards, involvement of the school leadership profession should be central. Considering the apparently low number of applicants, it would be important to further analyse the attractiveness of the school leadership profession, including the competitiveness of current school leader remuneration compared to teachers and other professions and the possibility to create career development opportunities for school leaders, such as system leadership roles.

To improve pedagogical leadership in schools, the employer of school principals should take more responsibility for the ongoing management of individual school leaders.

This could involve the development of personnel management processes such as the mandatory individual appraisal. To strengthen school-based teacher appraisal and feedback, school leaders should have opportunities to develop their skills for effective observation, feedback and coaching. Creating more opportunities for schools to collaborate and facilitating school leadership networks can be a further strategy to foster greater pedagogical leadership and to improve the quality of education across the education system more widely. Chile, England (United Kingdom) and New Zealand provide interesting examples in this regard. In Austria, the new Centre for Learning Schools (*Bundeszentrum für Lernende Schulen*) could be expanded to the whole system beyond the NMS, if successful, also to facilitate collaboration between different school types. Also, school leaders in Austria need to benefit from greater support structures through administrative support staff and middle leaders.

Chapter 1

School education in Austria

This chapter presents an overview of the economic and demographic context in Austria, including a description of the present governance arrangements and the distribution of responsibilities for the funding and administration of the system. It also provides a brief description of the Austrian school system for international readers. Finally, it presents evidence on the quality and equity of the Austrian school system.

The statistical data for Israel are supplied by and under the responsibility of the relevant Israeli authorities. The use of such data by the OECD is without prejudice to the status of the Golan Heights, East Jerusalem and Israeli settlements in the West Bank under the terms of international law.

Box 1.1. **Proposal for education reform (November 2015)**

This report reflects the situation of the Austrian education system at the time of the review visit in June 2015. The review team provided the Austrian Ministry of Education and Women's Affairs (BMBF) with an initial draft report at the beginning of November 2015 to inform the negotiations of the education reform commission comprised of representatives of the federal government and the provinces. The negotiations of the education reform commission which were also informed by an Austrian expert group on school administration resulted in an education reform proposal that was presented 17 November 2015. The implementation of the education reform was to be prepared until June 2016. Details of the education reform proposal can be found in Annex 1.1.

This chapter provides the key contextual aspects – political, demographic and economic – for the subsequent analysis. It includes a detailed description of the Austrian education system, including its governance. In addition, it provides an account of recent developments and the main trends and concerns within the Austrian education system in terms of quality and equity.

Context

Situated in the Central European Alps, Austria covers a landlocked, mountainous territory of 83 879 km^2 and has a population of 8.5 million in 2014. It shares a border with Germany and the Czech Republic to the north, Hungary and Slovakia to the east, Slovenia and Italy to the south, and Switzerland and Liechtenstein to the west. Austria's largest cities are the capital Vienna (1.8 million inhabitants), followed by Graz, Linz and Salzburg (all under 300 000 inhabitants) (Statistik Austria, 2015c: 42, 44).

Governance and administration

Austria is a parliamentary republic. The federal constitution governs the separation of powers into the legislative (the National Council [*Nationalrat*] and Federal Council [*Bundesrat*]), the executive (the President as well as the federal government comprising the Chancellor, Vice-Chancellor and federal ministers), and the judiciary (the Constitutional, Administrative, Civil and Criminal Court Systems).

As a federal state based on the principle of local self-administration, Austria is divided into four administrative tiers: the federal, provincial, district and municipal levels. The federal government is divided into departments headed by their respective federal ministers. Below the federal level, Austria consists of nine provinces (*Länder*) (see Table 1.1). The provincial governments (*Landesregierungen*) are headed by governors (*Landeshauptmänner/frauen*) which are elected by the provincial parliaments (*Landtage*). Provinces are represented at the federal level by the members of the National Council. Provinces comprise 95 districts

Table 1.1. **Provinces of Austria**

Province	Capital	Area (km²)	Population (2014)	Population density (people per km², 2014)
Burgenland	Eisenstadt	3 669	287 318	78
Carinthia	Klagenfurt	9 360	555 743	59
Lower Austria	St. Pölten	18 917	1 626 260	86
Upper Austria	Linz	11 717	1 425 980	122
Salzburg	Salzburg	7 050	534 185	76
Styria	Graz	16 251	1 214 930	75
Tyrol	Innsbruck	12 514	721 574	58
Vorarlberg	Bregenz	2 534	375 323	148
Vienna	-	395	1 765 580	4 467
Austria	**Vienna**	**82 409**	**8 506 890**	**103**

Source: OECD (2015a), *Population density* (pop. per km²), *The Regional Database, http://dotstat.oecd.org/?lang=en.*

(*Bezirke*) and the authorities of these districts are organisationally integrated into the provincial administration (Bruneforth et al., forthcoming: 18).

At the lowest level of the administration, Austria is made up of 2 102 municipalities (*Gemeinden*), nearly 80% of which have fewer than 3 000 inhabitants (Bruneforth et al., forthcoming: 18). Each municipality is administered by a municipal office which is managed by a municipal secretary. They are politically represented by an elected municipal council (*Gemeinderat*) headed by a mayor. Municipalities have a constitutional right to self-administration and manage local affairs pertaining to the educational, social, environmental and cultural infrastructure as well as the execution of tasks devolved from the federal or province levels. Due to their limited resources and competences, many smaller municipalities are exempt from duties related to double accounting and controlling procedures (Bruneforth et al., forthcoming: 18).

Demographic characteristics

Population

In 2014, Austria had a population of 8.51 million inhabitants. It exhibits a low level of urbanisation with 45.1% of the population living in predominantly rural regions (well above the OECD average of 25.1%) and only 23.9% living in predominantly urban regions (compared to an average of 48.0% in OECD countries) (OECD, 2013f: 51). In 2014, Austria's average population density of 103 inhabitants/km² was above the OECD average of 37 inhabitants/km², but below the EU28 average of 117 inhabitants/km² and the lowest among all of its neighbours with the exception of Slovenia (OECD, 2015a; Eurostat, 2015). More than half of the Austrian population lives in mountainous regions (European Commission, 2015).

In contrast to most European countries, Austria's population has experienced phases of rapid growth in the early 1990s and 2000s, which exceeded even those of the 1960s. Since 1985, the population has grown by nearly 1 million (13.0%), mainly due to high levels of immigration between 1988 and 1994 and since 2000 (Bruneforth et al., forthcoming: 11). Positive natural growth in five out of nine provinces, mainly due to an increased life expectancy, explains about 6% of the population increase between 2001 and 2011 (Statistik Austria, 2013: 2). The remainder is accounted for by positive net migration into all of Austria's provinces (both from abroad and other parts of the country). Nevertheless, within provinces, population growth has been unevenly distributed with large cities and surrounding districts exhibiting the strongest growth rates. Meanwhile, continued rural-to-urban migration among the young population and a correspondingly lower birth rate have led to negative growth in 35 primarily rural or post-industrial districts between 2001 and 2011 (Statistik Austria, 2013: 5).

Austria's population will continue to grow over the next decades, mainly due to immigration. The population is projected to reach over 9 million inhabitants by 2025 and increase to 9.41 million by 2040 (+10.6% compared to 2014) (Statistik Austria, 2014a). With an average of 1.43 children born to each woman, Austria's total fertility rate lay below the level of replacement and below the OECD average of 1.70 in 2011 (OECD, 2014c: 89). Without further immigration, the population would therefore, after a period of stagnation, decrease to 8.12 million by 2040 (Bruneforth et al., forthcoming: 12). Until 2020, the share of the working age population (20-64 year-olds) is expected to remain stable at around 61.8% before starting to decline to 57.1% in 2030 and 54.3% in 2040 (-12.1%). In the same period, the share of those aged 65 or older is projected to increase steadily from 18.2% in 2013 to 19.5% in 2020 and to reach 26.7% by 2040 (Statistik Austria, 2014a).

The recent decline in the school-age population is expected to reverse in the coming years. As can be seen from Figure 1.1, the 0-4 year-old population has been increasing significantly since 2010 and further growth is expected in the coming years. This increase in the pre-school population is expected to affect the number of children in primary education from 2016 and to eventually reverse the recent downward trend in the secondary school population.

Figure 1.1. **Variation in school-age population in Austria compared to the OECD and the EU27**

1990 = 100

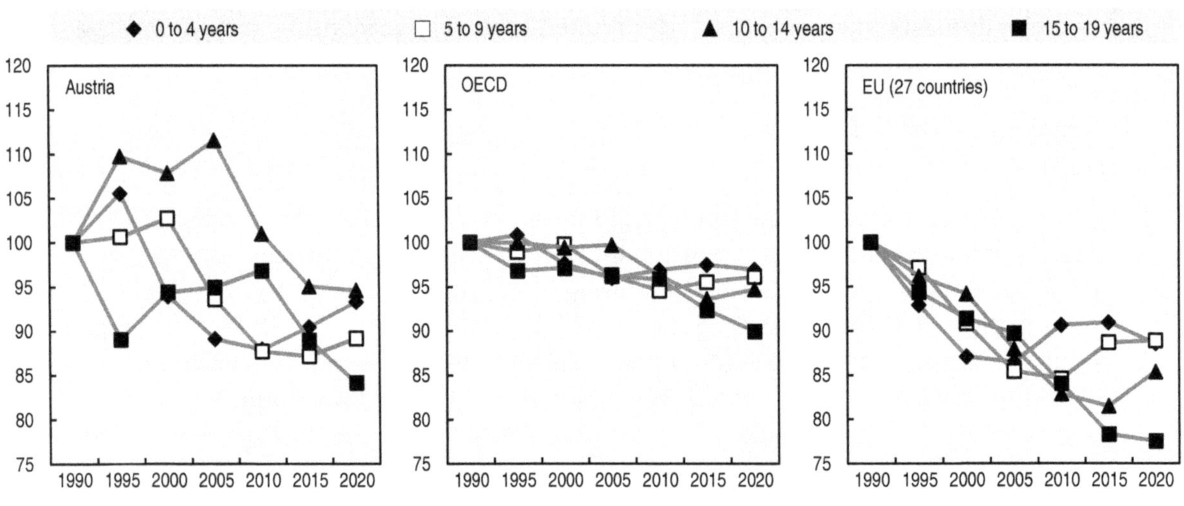

Source: OECD (no date), *Historical population data and projections (1950-2050)*, statistical database, *http://stats.oecd.org/*.

In 2015, 825 500 Austrians (9.62% of the population) were aged between 6 and 15 years and therefore subject to mandatory schooling (Statistik Austria, 2015d). Having declined by about 10% over the last decade, the proportion of 6-15 year-olds is projected to drop further to 9.46% of the population until 2020 (-2.7% compared to 2013) and increase again thereafter until it reaches a share of 9.67% in 2030 (Statistik Austria, 2014a). These trends will vary across the provinces. While Vienna is set to experience a strong increase in the number of students due to its large share of relatively young immigrants, the size of the student population is expected to stagnate in other parts of Austria and to continue to decline until 2030 in provinces such as Ca (Bruneforth et al., forthcoming: 13).

Cultural and language diversity

In 2015, 86.7% of the population had Austrian citizenship. Most of the non-Austrian residents were citizens of Germany (170 000), Turkey (114 000), Serbia (115 000) and Bosnia and Herzegovina (93 000). In recent years, there has also been a marked increase in the number of Bulgarian, Romanian and Hungarian citizens, which – taken together – now amount to 148 000 (a 114% increase since 2010) (Statistik Austria, 2015a).

Language is a central concern related to migration and school education in Austria. The official language of school instruction is German, although members of the Slovenian and Croatian minorities have the right to primary education in their own languages (Bruneforth et al., forthcoming: 13). In 2013, an estimated 19.0% of students in Year 4 and 18.3% of students in Year 8 had parents who were born in countries other than Austria or Germany (Schreiner and Breit, 2014a: 28; Schreiner and Breit, 2014b: 47). In 2010, 22% of all Year 4 students and 68% of those Year 4 students with a non-German background reported to speak German in addition to another language at home. On the other hand, 22% of first-generation immigrant students and 13% of second-generation immigrant students enrolled in the Austrian school system reported not to speak any German with their families (Vogtenhuber et al., 2012: 25). The proportion of children who speak languages other than German at home varies considerably among the Austrian regions. In Vienna, they accounted for more than half of the primary school population, compared to 30% in cities below 50 000 inhabitants and a mere 10% in municipalities and cities below 10 000 inhabitants (ibid.: 36).

Economic growth, unemployment and inequality

With a Gross Domestic Product (GDP) of USD 437.2 billion in 2014, Austria has the 19th biggest economy of the OECD area and a GDP per capita (at Purchasing Power Parity, PPP) of USD 45 800, placing it 16.8% above the OECD average of USD 39 200 (OECD, 2015c: 7). Austria has a very open economy and a large number of successful, export-oriented large and medium sized firms which have helped Austria to attain a high level of material well-being. Despite its resilience throughout the financial crisis, the Austrian economy has stagnated for the past three years with growth rates near the bottom of the EU. With real wages remaining below the pre-crisis level, domestic demand remains weak and falling labour productivity has weakened Austria's international competitiveness. Economic growth is expected to pick up and reach 1.7% by 2017, owing to the depreciation of the Euro, low interest rates and an ongoing income-tax reform which is expected to boost disposable household income and consumption (Bruneforth et al., forthcoming: 11; OECD, 2015c; OECD, 2015e: 65).

Austria's unemployment rate of 5.6% in January 2015 was higher than before or during the crisis and has been on the rise since 2012 while remaining well below that of the OECD area (6.9%) and the Eurozone (11.1%). At 9.5%, unemployment is particularly low among 15-24 year-olds when compared to the OECD and the Eurozone averages (14.3% and 22.6% respectively) (OECD, 2015d).

By international comparison, Austria enjoys low levels of income inequality, as measured by the Gini coefficient, and a high level of redistribution (OECD, 2015c: 26). Nevertheless, income inequality has risen in recent years. Between 2007 and 2011, the real incomes of the richest 10% increased while they fell for the bottom 10% (OECD, 2015f: 24). In addition, low-skilled workers and immigrants have been disproportionately affected by the recent rise in inactivity and unemployment, highlighting the need to improve their labour market integration and educational outcomes (OECD, 2015c: 28). With 61.7% of net private household wealth concentrated among the richest 10% in 2010, Austria had the second highest level of wealth concentration among 18 OECD countries after the United States (76.4%). There is also a persistently large gender pay gap, particularly among Austrian low-income earners. For low-income earners, the gender pay gap is the second largest among all OECD countries (OECD, 2015c: 75).

Structure of the education system

The Austrian education system is organised in five stages: early childhood education and care (kindergarten), primary education, lower secondary education and upper secondary education, and tertiary education (see Annex 1.2 for a diagram of the Austrian education system and Bruneforth et al., forthcoming, for further information).[1] Schooling in Austria is characterised by early selective transitions, a large vocational sector comprising more than half of the students at age 15, and a high degree of differentiation, particularly at the level of upper secondary education (Bruneforth et al., forthcoming: 22). To set the context, this chapter will provide a brief overview of the entire education system, but the remainder of the report will focus on primary and lower secondary education only. A recent OECD study analysed post-secondary vocational education in Austria (see Musset et al., 2013).

Non-compulsory day care (kindergarten) is available for children aged 3 to 5. Attendance at this age is typically subject to a fee which varies among provinces and providers. From the age of 5, half-day kindergarten has been compulsory and provided free of charge since 2010 (Eurypedia, 2015). As envisaged in the federal government's November 2015 reform proposal, a second kindergarten year should become compulsory from the age of 4 onwards, but with an option for parents to opt out (BMBF and BMWFW, 2015, see Annex 1.1). In recent years, participation in early childhood education and care has been increasing for children aged 3 and 4, but remains below the OECD and EU21 average for three-year-olds. In 2013, 71.3% of three-year-olds attended kindergarten (OECD average: 74.0%, EU21 average: 80.4%), compared to 47.5% in 2005; 91.0% of four-year-olds went to kindergarten (OECD average: 87.6%, EU 21 average: 91.2%), up from 82.5% in 2005; and 96.3% of five-year-olds were enrolled in early childhood education and care in 2013 (OECD average: 94.8%, EU21 average: 95.2%) (OECD, 2015b).

Compulsory education lasts for 9 years, from age 6 to age 15, and begins with enrolment in a 4-year primary school (*Volksschule*, VS). Children who are considered "not ready" for primary education but have attained compulsory school age have to attend pre-primary school (*Vorschulstufe*, VSS) for one or two years, depending on the time they need to make the transition to regular primary school. In some schools, pre-primary and primary education is integrated in the same classes.

The completion of primary school (typically at age 10) is followed by four years of lower secondary education. During this first selective transition, students enter different types of lower secondary schools. In theory, the choice of track should depend solely on students' academic ability and interests, but, in practice, students' socio-economic background plays an important role in this transition. Only 29% of the differences in school choice can be explained by differences in student achievement (Bruneforth, Weber and Bacher, 2012: 203).

In the 2013/14 school year, 35% of primary school students transferred to a lower academic secondary school (*Allgemein bildende höhere Schule – Unterstufe*, AHS-U), and 64% to a general secondary school (*Hauptschule*, HS) or New Secondary School (*Neue Mittelschule*, NMS), with the remaining 1% entering international or special needs schools (Eurydice, 2015). The three main types of lower secondary school distinguish themselves as follows:

- **Academic Secondary School, lower level** (*Allgemein bildende höhere Schule – Unterstufe*, AHS-U) constitutes the first stage of the academic secondary school. Its in-depth general curriculum aims to prepare students for progression to higher education. Students are accepted by the AHS-U subject to a strong prior performance in German, reading, and mathematics or by sitting a school entrance exam. From the third year (Year 7) onwards, academic secondary schools are differentiated into three branches emphasising languages, science or economics.
- **General Secondary School** (*Hauptschule*, HS) was traditionally the most frequented type of lower secondary school, attended by 67.9% of Austrian students in Year 5 in 2000/01 (Statistik Austria, 2014c). It provided non-selective access to students and four years of instruction based on differentiated ability groups in the core subjects German, English and mathematics. The successful completion of the HS qualified students to transition to any upper secondary school type including the upper level of academic secondary schools (*Allgemein bildende höhere Schule*, AHS-O). Considering the importance of vocational education in Austria, the vast majority of students went on to attend vocational tracks, some of which also provide the opportunity to attain a general qualification for university entrance (*Matura*) granting access to higher education. In 2013/14, 42.2% of all students achieving such a qualification had attended the HS (Statistik Austria, 2015b). The general secondary school type has been gradually replaced by the New Secondary School since 2008, and since the beginning of the school year 2015/16, all HS have been transformed into NMS.
- **New Secondary School** (*Neue Mittelschule*, NMS) was introduced in 2008 to provide a more inclusive alternative to general secondary schools, avoid early tracking and use innovative pedagogical methods. It has since become the new standard school and has replaced all HS since the school year 2015/16. In 2013/14, 53.1% of students in Year 5 already attended the NMS, compared to 34.1% attending the AHS-U and 8.8% remaining in the HS (Statistik Austria, 2014c). The NMS offers a general curriculum and competence-based approach. Unlike general secondary schools, students are not separated into different ability groups in core subjects, but the NMS apply a differentiated grading scheme depending on student ability in Years 7 and 8. Students are admitted to the NMS after completing their primary education without further pre-requisites except for some specialised schools conducting sports or musical aptitude tests, for example (Eurydice, 2015).

Upper secondary education covers Years 9 to 13 (typical ages 14 to 18) and comprises a range of general and vocational school types. Since compulsory education ends at the age of 15, typically one year after the completion of lower secondary education, students who did not repeat a year or enrol in pre-primary school are obliged to enter upper secondary education for at least one year (e.g. a pre-vocational school). Through this second selective transition, students enter one of the following school types:

- **Academic Secondary School, upper level** (*Allgemein bildende höhere Schule – Oberstufe*, AHS-O) is the continuation of the lower academic secondary school (AHS-U), leading to the general qualification for university entrance (*Matura*) after four years (Years 9 to 12).

Students who attended the AHS-U can enter the AHS-O without further requirements, while the access of former NMS students depends on their prior achievement.

- **Colleges for Higher Vocational Education** (*Berufsbildene höhere Schule,* BHS) last one year longer than the AHS (Years 9 to 13) and offer students a higher-level general and vocational education which, like the AHS-O, grants students a general qualification for university entrance (*Matura*) and qualifies them to enter higher education or higher-level professional occupations. According to the ISCED (International Standard Classification of Education) 2011 classification, Years 12 and 13 at the BHS are classified as a short-cycle tertiary education, and the BHS thus provides a more advanced education than the AHS-O (see Annex 1.3). Admission to the BHS is limited to students who obtained good grades at the end of lower secondary school.
- **Pre-vocational School** (*Polytechnische Schule,* PTS) lasts for one year only and is designed to prepare students for entering part-time vocational schools or an occupation with completion of compulsory education.
- **Part-time Vocational School** (*Berufsschule,* BS) provides part-time specialised education to complement students' company-based apprenticeships for a period of up to four years. Students entering a BS must have completed nine years of prior education and have typically completed Year 9 in a pre-vocational school. After successfully completing the BS, students have the option to gain access to higher education by sitting a series of general higher education entrance examinations (*Berufsreifeprüfungen*) which result in a qualification equivalent to the general qualification for university entrance (*Matura*).
- **Secondary Technical and Vocational School** (*Berufsbildene mittlere Schule,* BMS) provide one to four years (Years 9 to 12) of specialist vocational training providing students with the skills to enter occupations in such fields as engineering, commerce, the arts and crafts. Students can enter the BMS following four years of lower secondary education. As for the BS, students who successfully completed the BMS can gain access to higher education through the general higher education entrance examinations (*Berufsreifeprüfungen*).

Students diagnosed with special educational needs can receive integrated education in regular schools or attend a **Special Needs School** (*Sonderschule,* ASO) which covers nine years, parallel to primary and lower secondary school, followed by an additional pre-vocational year. In the 2013/14 school year, 5.3% of students in primary and lower secondary education (excluding AHS-U) had special educational needs. 61.3% of these students were integrated in regular schools while 38.7% attended one of 307 special needs schools. The proportion of integrated students varies considerably between the provinces, being as high as 80.2% in Styria and as low as 46.0% in Tyrol (Statistik Austria, 2014b).

Austria has a comparatively small private school sector. In 2012, only 7.5% of 15-year-olds attended government-dependent private schools (14.2% in OECD) and 1.1% attended independent private schools (4.1% in OECD), while the vast majority attended public schools (91.4% against an OECD average of 81.7%) (OECD, 2014a, Table C7.2: 417).

Higher Education is provided by public and private universities, universities of applied sciences (*Fachhochschulen*) and university colleges of teacher education (*Pädagogische Hochschulen,* PH). Since the Bologna reform, traditional five-year diploma programmes have largely been replaced by bachelor's degrees lasting 6-8 semesters and master's programmes lasting 2-4 semesters. They are open to students who passed the general higher education entrance examinations (*Berufsreifeprüfungen*) or completed the *Matura* at an AHS-O or BHS. For everyone else, there remains the option to sit a limited higher education entrance examination (*Studienberechtigungsprüfung*) which grants access only to the chosen subject. Graduates from upper secondary programmes are also free to enrol in 1-2 year short-cycle tertiary programmes at technical and vocational institutions (*Kollegs, tertiäre Bildungseinrichtungen*) or schools for mastercraftsmen, foremen, and construction trades (*Werkmeister-, Meister- und Bauhandwerkerschulen*) leading to certificates and diplomas.

Main features of the school system

Policy development and implementation

The governance of school education in Austria is characterised by a complex distribution of responsibilities between the different tiers of government (for a detailed discussion of education governance, see Chapter 2). The federal government's Ministry of Education and Women's Affairs (BMBF) bears the executive authority for all aspects pertaining to school education, including compulsory, technical and vocational, as well as higher-level secondary education. It develops and proposes legislation on education standards, curricula and teaching, including teachers' remuneration, training and retirement as well as private schools and educational authorities. The nine provinces are responsible for the implementation of all federal legislation pertaining to school education through the formulation of implementing legislation (Eurypedia, 2015).

Unlike in the federal systems of Germany and Switzerland, the vast majority of Austrian tax revenue is generated at the federal level (87% in 2014) rather than by the provinces themselves. Through the Fiscal Adjustment Act (*Finanzausgleichsgesetz*), these funds are then partially redistributed among the provinces and municipalities based on quotas which are renegotiated among the different tiers of government every four years. This system creates a split of financing and spending responsibilities, typical for Austrian federalism (Bruneforth et al., forthcoming: 15).

The distribution of governing and financing responsibilities differs between so-called federal schools and provincial schools:

- **Federal schools** (*Bundesschulen*) comprise academic secondary schools (AHS) as well as upper secondary vocational schools and colleges (BMS, BHS).
- **Provincial schools** (*Landesschulen*) include primary schools (VS), general lower secondary schools (HS), New Secondary Schools (NMS), special needs schools (ASO), the pre-vocational schools (PTS) and part-time upper secondary vocational schools (BS).

Federal schools receive their funding directly from the federal government while provincial schools are financed by provinces and municipalities using funds which are, however, to a significant extent raised at the federal level and transferred to provinces in accordance with the Fiscal Adjustment Act (for a detailed discussion of school funding, see Chapter 2).

The administrative responsibility for schools is formally divided between the nine provincial school boards (*Landesschulräte*) and the school departments of the offices of the provincial government (*Schulabteilungen in den Ämtern der Landesregierung*). The provincial school boards are responsible for administering federal schools which encompasses all aspects of their establishment, maintenance and closure, as well class sizes, staffing and teaching time. As federal agencies, the provincial school boards are under the constitutional authority of the federal minister. However, the provincial school boards' decision making bodies, the collegiate boards (*Kollegien*), are presided over by the provincial governor and composed of members nominated by political parties in proportion to their share of seats in the provincial parliament. The school departments of the offices of the provincial government are responsible for administering provincial schools. In practice, however, this division of responsibilities is less clear-cut: five out of nine provincial governments have transferred some of their responsibility for provincial schools to the provincial school board. Furthermore, most tasks associated with the provision and maintenance of provincial schools, apart from teaching staff decisions, have in practice been devolved to the municipal level, including the provision of school buildings, infrastructure and non-teaching staff such as janitors. Provinces support municipalities in carrying out these duties by administering allocated funds and have retained their responsibility for vocational, agriculture and forestry schools (Eurypedia, 2015).

Austria's 95 districts (*Bezirke*) no longer have any administrative involvement in the school system since a reform (*Schulbehörden-Verwaltungsreformgesetz*) transferred their responsibilities to the provincial level in 2013 (Bruneforth et al., forthcoming: 33).

As envisaged in the federal government's November 2015 reform proposal, the responsibility for the administration of both federal and provincial schools should pass to a new federal-provincial authority, the education directorates (*Bildungsdirektionen*). These new directorates should hold all powers presently held by the provincial school boards and the school departments of the offices of the provincial government, including the organisation of the federal and the provincial teachers, the external school organisation, administrative staff and the school inspection (BMBF and BMWFW, 2015; see Annex 1.1).

School autonomy and school leadership

Austrian schools enjoy a relatively limited degree of autonomy, particularly in resource use and management (see also Chapter 2). As shown in Figure 1.2, lower secondary schools take 31% of key decisions (compared to an OECD average of 41%) while the central or provincial governments – the latter are referred to as the "state" level in Figure 1.2 – take 55% of decisions (compared to 36% across the OECD) in 2011. Another 14% of decisions are taken at the local level, compared to 17% across the OECD (OECD, 2012, Table D6.1: 512).

A closer look at the different domains of decision-making[2] reveals differences in decision-making power depending on the types of decisions considered (see Annex 1.3 for figures showing the distribution of decision-making responsibilities by domain). Decisions in the domain of personnel management are shared between the federal, provincial, municipal and school levels, although lower secondary schools only take 4% of decisions (compared to 31% across the OECD). Schools also have comparatively little say in the domain of planning and structures, taking 10% of decisions (compared to 24% across the OECD), while 70% of decisions are taken at the federal and 20% at the provincial level. Decisions on resource management – including the allocation of resources for teaching-staff, non-teaching staff, capital and operating expenditure and professional development of principals and teachers – are relatively evenly distributed among the federal, provincial, municipal and school levels, with schools taking 21% of decisions (compared to 32% in the OECD). However, schools have little control over the staff plans which govern the financing of teaching personnel and are not normally permitted to select teachers themselves as they are allocated by the school departments of the offices of the provincial governments and provincial school boards. In contrast, schools have a high degree of autonomy when it comes to the organisation of instruction, taking 89% of relevant decisions in this domain

Figure 1.2. **Percentage of decisions taken at each level of government in public lower secondary education, 2011**

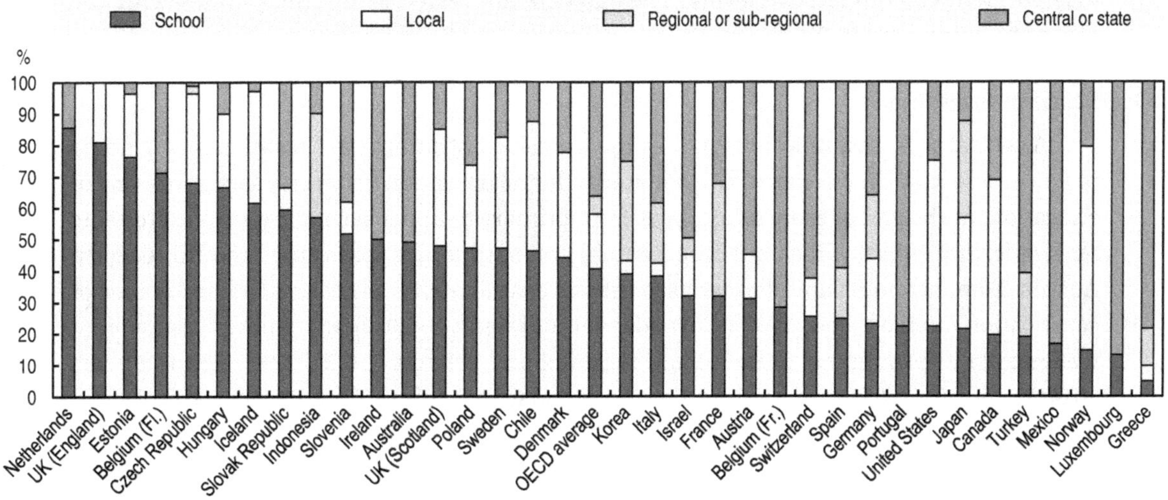

Note: Countries are ranked in descending order of the percentage of decisions taken at the school level.
Source: OECD (2012), *Education at a Glance 2012: OECD Indicators, http://dx.doi.org/10.1787/eag-2012-en*, Table D6.1, See Annex 3 for notes.

(above the OECD average of 75%), while the remaining 11% are taken at the federal level (OECD, 2012, Table D6.2a/: 513f.).

Since the 1990s, schools have been granted increased discretion over the implementation of curricula and have been encouraged to develop pedagogical priorities and subject-related profiles. However, the still rather limited autonomy of schools overall has led schools to initiate numerous pilot projects which allow them to deviate from some standard regulations (Bruneforth et al., forthcoming: 27, 50). The federal government's November 2015 proposal for education reform foresees giving schools further autonomy in pedagogical, organisational and financial domains as well as a reduction in school pilots (see Annex 1.1).

Education goals, assessment and evaluation

Education goals

The Austrian national constitution defines the objectives of the education system, among others, to ensure a maximum level of educational attainment independent of an individual's family background, origin or social situation and to prepare students to contribute to society's economic and cultural life. Austria's constitution distinguishes between the goals of different school types, thus enshrining the diversified nature of its school offer.

The educational mandate of Austrian schools is regulated by the federal School Organisation Act (*Schulorganisationsgesetz*, SchOG) based on subject curricula, broad educational objectives and a list of goals pertaining to cross curricular competences formulated by the Ministry of Education and Women's Affairs (BMBF). In 2008, Austria introduced measurable national education standards to guide teaching, learning and assessment practices. They include attainment targets which define students' expected learning outcomes at the end of primary education (Year 4) for mathematics and German as well as the end of lower secondary education (Year 8) for mathematics, German, and

English. Following a baseline test in 2009/10, standardised national assessments with no stakes for students were implemented in 2011/12 to assess student performance relative to four pre-defined competence levels. The subjects are tested in five-year cycles with the first to be completed in 2016.

Student assessment

A central policy framework regulates the frequency of summative assessments, grading practices and how they are used to evaluate students' transition between years and levels of education. At the end of every school year from primary to upper secondary school, students receive formal reports which are based entirely on summative assessments. Until recently, Austria did not conduct any standardised central examinations affecting students' grades or certification (unlike 26 out of 37 OECD education systems in 2012) and student assessment was mostly implemented by individual teachers and schools (OECD, 2013d). In the years 2014/15 and 2015/16 respectively, academic secondary schools (AHS) and colleges for higher vocational education (BHS) introduced compulsory standardised leaving examinations. These exams comprise a written pre-academic paper (AHS) or diploma work (BHS), standardised written tests in core subjects as well as oral exams and are intended to increase objectivity, transparency and students ability to move on to higher education. Formative assessment is expected to take place, but not regulated by a central policy framework (Eurypedia, 2015; OECD, 2015b; OECD, 2013d).

School evaluation

Up until 2012, Austria did not have a nationwide legal framework governing the evaluation of schools. External inspections were carried out by the school inspectorate at the province or district level, based on the schools' self-evaluation and the credibility of their internal quality development system. Due to a lack of common regulations regarding evaluation criteria and their frequency, however, the form and intensity of evaluations varied considerably among schools. It has also not been mandatory for schools to conduct self-evaluations. As a result, most schools did not benefit from regular feedback (Specht and Sobanski, 2012; OECD, 2013d). In the OECD 2008 Teaching and Learning International Survey (TALIS), 35.2% of Austrian lower secondary teachers reported that their school had received neither an external evaluation nor self-administered an evaluation over the past five years – the highest figure across participating countries (OECD, 2009, Table 5.1: 174). And for the OECD Programme for International Student Assessment (PISA) 2012, only 20.3% of 15-year-olds were in a school whose principal reported the existence of external evaluations as a quality assurance and improvement mechanism, also the lowest value among OECD countries (OECD average: 63.2%) (OECD, 2013b, Table IV.4.32).

In 2012, the Federal Ministry for Education, Arts and Culture (BMUKK) introduced a coherent framework for external school evaluations and made self-evaluation compulsory (see Chapter 2). Furthermore, a 2013 initiative to enhance school quality (*Schulqualität Allgemeinbildung*, SQA) now requires schools to create development plans and implement periodic performance reviews. A corresponding initiative (*QualitätsIniative BerufsBildung*, QIBB) exists for vocational schools. The 2011/12 introduction of national standardised assessments without stakes for students of Years 4 and 8 has also added a new source of quantitative feedback at the school and system level. Schools now receive standardised feedback on their students' performance and teachers obtain the aggregate results of the students they teach.

Education system evaluation

Austria has strengthened its capacity for system-level evaluation and evidence-based policy making over the past years. Responsibilities for education system evaluation are now shared between the Federal Ministry of Education and Women's Affairs (BMBF) and the Federal Institute for Education Research, Innovation and Development of the Austrian School System (BIFIE). The BIFIE was created in 2008 and carries out the majority of evaluation activities by implementing educational standards, developing the centralised school leaving exam and establishing the ongoing system of educational monitoring.[3] Since 2009, the BIFIE also produces a triennial national education report (*Nationaler Bildungsbericht Österreich*) providing data on the context, inputs, processes and outcomes of education in order to increase accountability and provide advice for future policy development (OECD, 2013d: 108).

Austria is a regular participant in most major international comparative studies of student performance, including TIMSS, PIRLS and PISA.[4] Aggregate results from the national standardised assessments provide additional data to analyse the quality of the education system and factors associated with student performance.

Work programme of the Austrian Federal Government 2013-18 and November 2015 education reform proposal

The 2013-18 federal government has defined its education reform priorities in its coalition contract (Austrian Federal Chancellery, 2013) as well as a six-point programme (Austrian Federal Chancellery, 2014). According to these programmes, by 2016/17, the last year of kindergarten (Early Childhood Education and Care, ECEC) should be connected with Years 1 and 2 of primary education to form a joint school-entry phase (*Schuleingangsphase*), following an initial trial and evaluation in 35 selected schools in 2014/15. This measure is designed to facilitate the transition from early childhood education and care to primary education and offer targeted support to students in need of German-language learning. In addition, the government has proposed to increase school autonomy with regard to the timing of instruction and break times, the creation of individualised academic profiles and the role of school leaders in selecting teaching personnel. In order to respond to parents' increased demand for day care and to promote equity, the government also aims to expand the offer of all-day schooling and establish criteria for the organisation of both instruction and leisure time (Bruneforth et al., forthcoming: 29). Furthermore, the government announced that it plans to increase the frequency of physical exercise during the school day, introduce compulsory career guidance for students of lower secondary schools and alleviate teachers' burden of administrative work. The work programme further sets out to reduce the number of low-skilled adults by means of offering free educational programmes and the opportunity to catch up on compulsory school-leaving qualifications.

In November 2015, the federal government presented a proposal for comprehensive education reform which encompasses changes to early childhood education and care, steps to improve the transition from kindergarten to primary education through a school entry phase, greater school autonomy in pedagogical, organisational and financial domains, the creation of model regions in the individual provinces to facilitate the collaboration of different school types and to pilot comprehensive schooling for 6-14 year-olds, a new structure for the joint administration of federal and provincial schools and teachers, and measures to encourage innovation in education (BMBF and BMWFW, 2015, see Annex 1.1). This reform proposal was informed by the work of an expert group on school governance and administration (BMBF, 2015). The implementation of the reform proposed in November 2015 was still in development at the time of drafting this report.

Quality and equity of the school system

Access, participation and performance

Austria's performance in international student assessments is mixed and varies between the examined subjects and years. In Year 4 (age 10-11) of primary school, Austrian students take part in the IEA's (International Association for the Evaluation of Educational Achievement) Trends in Mathematics and Science Study (TIMSS) and the Progress in International Reading Literacy Study (PIRLS). In 2011, Austria's results in mathematics and reading were considered unsatisfactory when compared to 14 countries with similar socio-economic and political characteristics. In both subjects, Austria scored above the international average, but took the last place in its reference group for reading and the third-last for mathematics (BIFIE, 2012). In mathematics, 2% of students met the TIMSS Advanced and 26% the High International Benchmark respectively, compared to the international medians of 4% and 28%. In reading, 5% of students met the PIRLS Advanced and 39% the High International Benchmark. This placed Austria below the international medians of 8% and 44%. In science, Austrian primary school students continue to show good results, performing above the international benchmarks across all levels of achievement (see Table 1.2). Girls performed consistently worse than boys in mathematics and science, while the opposite was true for reading. There has been a worrying decline in both reading literacy scores since 2006 and mathematics since 1995 (Mullis et al., 2012a; Mullis et al., 2012b; Martin et al., 2012).

Table 1.2. **Performance of Austrian students in mathematics, science and reading at the International Benchmarks of Achievement in primary education, TIMSS and PIRLS**

Percentages of students reaching international benchmarks in TIMSS and PIRLS

	Austria	International median
Low international benchmark (400)		
Mathematics (TIMSS)	95	90
Science (TIMSS)	96	92
Reading (PIRLS)	97	95
Intermediate international benchmark (475)		
Mathematics (TIMSS)	70	69
Science (TIMSS)	79	72
Reading (PIRLS)	80	80
High international benchmark (550)		
Mathematics (TIMSS)	26	28
Science (TIMSS)	42	32
Reading (PIRLS)	39	44
Advanced international benchmark (625)		
Mathematics (TIMSS)	2	4
Science (TIMSS)	8	5
Reading (PIRLS)	5	8

Source: Mullis, I.V.S. et al. (2012a), *PIRLS 2011 International Results in Reading, http://timssandpirls.bc.edu/pirls2011/downloads/P11_IR_FullBook.pdf*, p. 68; Mullis, I.V.S. et al. (2012b), *TIMSS 2011 International Results in Mathematics, http://timssandpirls.bc.edu/timss2011/downloads/T11_IR_Mathematics_FullBook.pdf*, p. 90; Martin, M.O. et al. (2012), *TIMSS 2011 International Results in Science, http://timssandpirls.bc.edu/timss2011/downloads/T11_IR_Science_FullBook.pdf*, p. 86.

In the OECD Programme for International Student Assessment (PISA) 2012, Austrian 15-year-olds performed above the OECD average in mathematics (506 vs. 494), at the average in science (506 vs. 501) and below the average in reading (490 vs. 496). In mathematics, the performance of Austrian students returned to the level of 2003 and 2006, performing better than Italy or the Slovak Republic, but below Switzerland and Germany, and comparable with Australia and Vietnam. In science, Austrian 15-year-olds performed around the OECD average, following stronger results in 2006. In reading, the performance of Austrian students has fallen below the OECD mean after having achieved average results in 2003 and 2006. Austria fares considerably worse than neighbouring Switzerland and Germany (almost 20 points behind), comparable to Italy, the Czech Republic or Hungary, and better than the Slovak Republic (OECD, 2014b, Table I.A: 19). Although many students assessed in PISA have already entered institutions of upper secondary education (which are not the main focus of this report), their performance at age 15 reflects, at least to some extent, the quality of education they have received throughout compulsory schooling until the age of 14.

Austria has comparatively small shares of students both at the bottom and top of the performance scale (see Table 1.3). In mathematics, Austria's share of low achievers is significantly smaller than that across the OECD (18.7% compared to 23.0%) and the picture is similar for science (15.8% compared to 17.8%). In reading, Austria has a higher share of low achievers than the OECD countries on average (19.5% compared to 18.0%). Between 2003 and 2012, Austria slightly narrowed the share of low performing students in all subjects. However, Austria has at the same time experienced a reduction in its share of top performers. In reading, the share of top performers significantly decreased by 2.8 percentage points since 2003 and is now below the OECD average. While Austria has maintained its share of top performers in mathematics around the OECD average, the share of top performers in science also decreased. The fact that 11% of Austrian 15-year-olds were considered "at risk" (below Proficiency Level 2) in reading, mathematics *and* science suggests that performance deficits are concentrated in a group of students which might leave school without the skills necessary to succeed on the labour market (OECD, 2014b; OECD, 2016).

Together with Hungary, Austria has the largest gender gap in mathematics performance with boys scoring 29 points higher than girls, taking programme level and designation into account. This constitutes a difference nearly twice as large as the OECD average of 17 points in 2012 and a dramatic increase since 2003 (OECD, 2014b, Table I.2.26).

Equity in education remains an important concern in Austria, given its steep socio-economic performance gradient, a high level of intergenerational reproduction and performance differences between immigrant and non-immigrant migrant students (see Table 1.3). 15.8% of the variation in mathematics performance in PISA 2012 is explained by students' socio-economic status (compared to an OECD average of 14.8%), and a one-unit increase in a student's economic, social and cultural status (ESCS) is associated with scoring 43 points higher in mathematics (compared to 39 points across the OECD, which is nearly the equivalent of an entire year of education). In reading, it is associated with scoring 42 points higher (compared to the OECD average of 38 points), and in science with a 46 point increase (compared to the OECD average of 38 points) (OECD, 2013a, Table II.2.1: 174f.). The share of resilient students remains below the OECD average. Students with an immigrant background are at particular risk of underperformance. In PISA 2012, students with an immigrant background scored an average of 33 score points lower in mathematics than non-immigrant students, controlling for their ESCS. This gap has remained unchanged since 2003 and remains well above the OECD average of 23 points (OECD, 2013a, Table II.3.4b: 229). Students from a socio-economically disadvantaged background and students with an immigrant background are, furthermore, more likely to be low performers than their peers from advantaged and non-immigrant backgrounds. The difference between socio-economically advantaged and disadvantaged students in the share of low performers in mathematics amounted to 27.5% (OECD average: 27.7%). For immigrant students and students without an immigrant background, the difference in the share of low performers in mathematics was 22.1%, significantly higher than on average across OECD countries (14.2%) (OECD, 2016). Parental background remains a strong determinant of children's educational trajectory and access to tertiary education. Based on analysis for the OECD 2012 Programme for the International Assessment of Adult Competencies (PIAAC), children of parents with tertiary educational qualifications (ISCED-97 levels 5A, 5B and 6) have 5.1 times higher odds of attaining such a qualifications than those of parents with lower secondary qualifications or less, compared to 4.5 across the OECD (OECD, 2014a, Table A4.1b: 93). Only 29% of Austrian 35-64 year-olds have a higher educational attainment than their parents, which is the third lowest level of absolute upward mobility in the OECD. Mobility is particularly low for women (25%, compared to 33% for men) (OECD, 2014a, Table A4.4: 100).

Table 1.3. **Selected indicators of quality and equity in Austrian education, based on PISA 2012**

	OECD average (2012)	Austria (2012)	Austria (2003; for science, 2006)
Percentage of top performers			
Mathematics	12.6	14.3	14.3
Reading	8.4	5.5	8.3
Science	8.4	7.9	10.0
Percentage of low achievers			
Mathematics	23.0	18.7	18.8
Reading	18.0	19.5	20.7
Science	17.8	15.8	16.3
Difference in performance between the 90th and 10th percentiles (in score points)			
Mathematics	239	240	242
Reading	242	238	263
Science	239	240	255
Percentage of overall variation in student performance explained by students' socio-economic status			
Mathematics	14.8	15.8	15.1
Reading	13.1	15.3	n/a
Science	14.0	18.3	15.4
Percentage of resilient students	6.1	5.6	6.2
Difference in mathematics performance between immigrant and non-immigrant students after accounting for ESCS (in score points)	23	33	37
Between school variance in mathematics performance (as percentage of total)	36.8	47.7	48.9
Within school variance in mathematics performance (as percentage of total)	63.3	50.8	49.5

Note: Top performers = students performing at PISA level 5 and above; Low performers = students performing below PISA level 2; Resilient students = students in bottom quarter of ESCS who perform among the top 25% of students after accounting for ESCS.
Source: OECD (2013a), *PISA 2012 Results: Excellence through Equity (Volume II): Giving Every Student the Chance to Succeed, http://dx.doi.org/10.1787/9789264201132-en*, Tables II.2.1, II.A, II.2.7b, II.3.4b, II.3.7, II.2.8b; OECD (2014b), *PISA 2012 Results: What Students Know and Can Do (Volume I, Revised edition, February 2014): Student Performance in Mathematics, Reading and Science, http://dx.doi.org/10.1787/9789264208780-en*, Tables I.A, I.2.1b, I.4.1b, I.4.3d, I.5.3a/d.

As can be expected in a highly differentiated and hierarchical school system, there are considerable performance differences between schools in Austria. The academic selectivity of schools is associated with a 36 point increase in mathematics scores among 15-year-olds, compared to just 5.9 points across the OECD (OECD, 2013b, Table IV.1.12b: 240). These results are confirmed by national standardised assessments: among Year 8 students enrolled in the NMS or HS, 24% failed to reach the standards for mathematics and another 33% did not score above level 1 while only 1% of students enrolled in the AHS failed to meet the standard and only 12% failed to reach level 2 (Schreiner and Breit, 2013: 21). As a result, in PISA 2012, between school variance in mathematics performance stood at 48.1% of the OECD average total variation. In contrast, only 36.9% of performance differences are observed between schools across OECD countries. Accordingly, Austria has a low index of academic inclusion[5] of 51.6, compared to the OECD average of 64.1 (OECD, 2013a, Table II.2.8a/b: 196ff).

Much of the between-school difference in performance is explained by students' choice of study programmes (65%, compared to 40% across the OECD), i.e. whether students were enrolled in programmes designed to give direct access to the labour market, further vocational studies or the next programme level, which highlights the stratification among Austria's different school types (OECD, 2013a, Table II.2.9a: 201). However, schools are also more socio-economically homogenous than in most other OECD countries (OECD, 2015c: 28) and school performance is correlated with their students' ESCS, giving rise to equity concerns. In particular, 17.4% of the between school variation is explained by schools' different socio-economic composition. Although this figure is lower than the OECD average of 27.8%, it indicates a clustering of students from disadvantaged backgrounds in under-performing schools or school types and corresponding educational gaps (OECD, 2013a, Table II.2.9a: 200).

Unlike in various other OECD countries in which students in schools located in towns (3 000 to about 100 000 inhabitants) outperform students in rural schools (fewer than 3 000 inhabitants), and students in city schools (more than 100 000 inhabitants) outperform students in town schools after taking socio-economic status into account, performance differences between students in rural, town and city schools in Austria are not statistically significant (OECD, 2013a, Table II.3.3a).

National data indicate that year repetition occurs at all levels of the Austrian school system, but that repetition is highest in upper secondary education, particularly in upper academic secondary schools (AHS-O) (Statistik Austria, 2015b: 55). For OECD PISA 2012, 11.9% of 15-year-old students in Austria reported having ever repeated a year, compared to 12.4% across the OECD. Year repetition in primary and lower secondary education in Austria as reported by 15-year-olds (5.1% and 4.9% respectively) is significantly lower than in Germany (10.3% and 12.8% respectively) and Switzerland (13.2% and 8.1% respectively), and also lower than on average across OECD countries (7.1% and 5.7% respectively). At the upper secondary level (3.6%), however, year repetition is higher than in Germany (0%) and Switzerland (0.5%) and on average across OECD countries (2.1%) (OECD, 2013b, Table IV.2.2). Year repetition is more frequent for boys than for girls and considerably more common among students with a non-German mother tongue. In 2012/13, 5.7% of students with a non-German mother tongue repeated a year in the NMS and 15.0% in the AHS-U, compared to overall rates of 3.2% and 8.1% respectively (BILDOK, cited in Bruneforth et al., forthcoming: 40).

In 2012, Austrian students reported the highest level of overall well-being as measured by an index of sense of belonging at school across all OECD countries participating in PISA 2012 (OECD, 2013e, Table III.2.3d: 252). However, there are relatively strong discrepancies between the experience of socio-economically advantaged and disadvantaged students. For example, 85.9% of socio-economically advantaged students reported to be satisfied with their school, compared to 79.1% of disadvantaged ones (OECD, 2013e, Table III.2.3c). Also, bullying, which can contribute to emotional and behavioural problems, including anxiety and depression, weak performance in school, and increased absenteeism and truancy, constitutes a significant problem in Austrian schools. According to data from the World Health Organization's (WHO) Health Behaviour in School-aged Children survey for 2009/10, 40% of children aged 11, 13 and 15 reported having been bullied at school at least once in the past couple of months (UNICEF Office of Research, 2013).[6] In 2008, the Federal Ministry for Education, Arts and Culture (BMUKK) implemented a national strategy for preventing violence and bullying at school (*Nationale Strategie zur Gewaltprävention*), the effects of which are not yet reflected in the WHO data.[7]

Attainment, adult skills and labour market outcomes

The level of educational attainment in Austria has steadily increased over the past decades and is among the higher ones within the OECD area. Only 16% of adults have attained less than upper secondary education (ISCED 2011 levels 0, 1 and 2), compared to 24% across the OECD. The proportion of adults who have attained at least upper secondary education (ISCED 2011 levels 3 and higher) has steadily increased across cohorts and remains above the OECD average for all age groups, including 90% of 25-34 year-olds, 86% of 35-44 year-olds, 83% of 45-54 year-olds and 75% of 55-64 year-olds (compared to 83%, 80%, 74% and 66% across the OECD) (OECD, 2015b, Tables A1.1a, A1.2a: 39f.). A notable 48% of adults whose highest level of education is upper secondary or post-secondary non-tertiary education (ISCED 2011 levels 3 and 4) have completed a vocational programme, compared with 26% across the OECD (OECD, 2015b, Table A1.5a: 45). 30% of the adult population aged 25-64 held a tertiary qualification (ISCED 2011 levels 5, 6, 7 or 8) in 2014, compared with an OECD average of 33%. A comparatively large share of adults with a tertiary education in Austria has completed a short cycle tertiary programme (ISCED 2011 level 5): 15% of 25-64 year-olds have completed such a programme, almost double the OECD average of 8%. Only 13% of 25-64 year-olds have attained a bachelor's or master's degree or equivalent qualification (ISCED 2011 levels 6 and 7), significantly less than the OECD average of 27% (OECD, 2015b, Tables A1.3a and A1.1a: 39, 41).

In 2012, the proportion of women who only achieved basic education was 23.2% compared to 14.9% for men (Statistik Austria, 2015b: 91). This attainment gap has significantly narrowed compared to previous decades. In 2014, 89% of women aged 25-34 had completed at least upper secondary education (ISCED 2011 level 3 and higher) and 23% had attained a bachelor's or master's degree or equivalent (ISCED 2011 qualifications 6 and 7), compared to 91% and 18% of men (OECD, 2015b, Table A1.3b and A1.2b).

The OECD 2012 PIAAC indicates that the skills of Austrian 16-65 year-olds are lower than average in literacy (see Table 1.4), above average in numeracy and at the average of participating OECD countries for problem solving with fewer adults at the top, but also at the bottom of the distribution. Younger adults aged 16-24 years showed average problem solving and literacy skills and above average numeracy skills (OECD, 2013c). Compared to the skills of 15-year-olds assessed in the PISA 2012 test, literacy skills are better among the slightly older cohorts. This might indicate a good capacity of the Austrian labour market and adult education system to foster skills beyond compulsory education.

Like in other countries, educational attainment in Austria has a significant impact on success in the labour market. In 2014, the employment rates among adults with tertiary education (ISCED 2011 Levels 5, 6, 7 and 8) were 32 percentage points higher than those of

Table 1.4. **Adult skills, PIAAC 2012**

	Austria	OECD average
Mean proficiency score (16-65 year-olds)		
Literacy	269.5	272.8
Numeracy	275.0	268.7
Percentage scoring at Level 2 or 3 in problem-solving in technology-rich environments (16-65 year-olds)	32.4	34.0
Mean proficiency score (16-24 year-olds)		
Literacy	277.7	279.6
Numeracy	279.3	271.3
Percentage scoring at Level 2 or 3 in problem-solving in technology-rich environments (16-24 year-olds)	50.7	50.7
Proportion of low-skilled adults (16-65 year-olds) with skills at or below Proficiency level 1 (%)		
Literacy	15.3	15.5
Numeracy	14.3	19.0
Proportion of adults opting out of the computer-based assessment, failing the ICT core, or without computer experience (%)	24.9	24.4

Source: OECD (2013c), *OECD Skills Outlook 2013: First Results from the Survey of Adult Skills, http://dx.doi.org/10.1787/9789264204256-en*, Tables A2.1, A2.4, A2.5, A2.6a, A3.2, A2.10a/b.

adults with only below upper secondary education (ISCED 2011 Levels 0, 1 and 2), compared to a 28 percentage point difference across the OECD (OECD, 2015b, Table A5.3a: 107f.). Adults with tertiary education were also the least vulnerable in terms of unemployment (3.7% compared to 10.8% of those with below upper secondary qualification). This unemployment gap of 7.1 percentage points (compared to 7.7 in the OECD) was even more pronounced among young adults (25-34 years) whose unemployment rates differed by 13.3 percentage points among the two groups (compared to 11.6 in the OECD) (OECD, 2015b, Table A5.4a: 110f.). However, Austria has one of the largest gaps in labour market outcomes among different age groups. While 83% of younger adults (25-34 years) with upper secondary or post-secondary non-tertiary education were employed in 2014, only 44% of older adults (55-64 years) with the same educational level were (OECD, 2015b, Table A5.3a: 108f). Like in other countries with a strong vocational education and training system, graduates from vocational programmes in Austria fare well on the labour market and often better than their peers from general programmes. In 2014, students who had attained a vocational upper secondary qualification had a lower risk of unemployment as opposed to graduates with a general qualification (4.3% vs. 6.0%) (OECD, 2015b, Table A5.5a: 113). Students completing a vocational course also had a higher employment rate than those who completed a general upper secondary education (ibid). The Austrian labour market is not only sensitive to qualifications, but also to skills. Employment rates are more than 10 percentage points higher among adults with literacy proficiency Levels 4 or 5 in PIAAC, compared to those who scored at Level 2, regardless of their educational attainment – one of the largest effects in the OECD (OECD, 2014a, Table A5.7a [L]: 127).

Regardless of educational attainment, there is a persistent gender pay gap. In 2013, 25-64 year-old women in full-time employment could expect to earn only around 80% of their male equivalents' salary, whether they have an upper secondary or post-secondary non-tertiary education (ISCED 2011 level 3 and 4) or a lower qualification (ISCED 2011 levels 0, 1 and 2) (OECD average: around 75%). Women with tertiary education (ISCED 2011 levels 5, 6, 7 and 8) in full-time employment, earned only 69% of what a man with the same qualification could expect, less than the OECD average of 73% and the EU21 average of 74% (OECD, 2015b,

Table A6.2a: 126). The gender disparity is even more pronounced when earnings from all types of employment are taken into account. In 2013, working age women (24-64 year-olds) with tertiary education (ISCED 2011 levels 5, 6, 7 and 8) reported incomes at 57% of men's earnings (69% in the OECD and in EU21 countries), women with upper secondary or post-secondary non-tertiary education (ISCED 2011 levels 3 and 4) received 61% (70% in the OECD, 72% in EU21 countries) and those with lower secondary qualifications or less (ISCED 2011 levels 0, 1 and 2) earned 66% (69% in the OECD, 72% in EU21 countries). These disparities have shown little to no sign of narrowing over the past decade (OECD, 2015b, Table A6.2b).

Notes

1. The following websites also provide further details: Austrian Federal Ministry of Education and Women's Affairs (*www.bmbf.gv.at/enfr/school/schools.html*) and Eurydice (*https://webgate.ec.europa.eu/fpfis/mwikis/eurydice/index.php/Austria:Overview*).
2. The four domains of decision-making defined by the OECD (2012) comprise the following areas: **Organisation of instruction:** student admissions; student careers; instruction time; choice of textbooks; choice of software/learningware; grouping of students; additional support for students; teaching methods; day-to-day student assessment. **Personnel management:** hiring and dismissal of principals, teaching and non-teaching staff; duties and conditions of service of staff; salary scales of staff; influence over the careers of staff. **Planning and structures:** opening or closure of schools; creation or abolition of a grade level; design of programmes of study; selection of programmes of study taught in a particular school; choice of subjects taught in a particular school; definition of course content; setting of qualifying examinations for a certificate or diploma; accreditation (examination content, marking and administration). **Resource management:** allocation and use of resources for teaching staff, non-teaching staff, capital and operating expenditure, professional development of principals and teachers.
3. According to a bill of the federal government submitted to parliament in November 2015, responsibility for the central school leaving exam at the end of upper secondary education is going to be transferred to the Ministry of Education and Women's Affairs (BMBF) by the end of 2016.
4. Austria decided not to participate in the 2015 round of assessment for TIMSS.
5. Calculated as 100*(1-rho), where rho stands for the intra-class correlation of performance, i.e. the variation in student performance between schools, divided by the sum of the variation in student performance between schools and the variation in student performance within schools.
6. The 2009/10 Health Behaviour in School-aged Children survey asked young people aged 11, 13 and 15 how often they had been bullying others and how often they had been bullied by others at school in the past couple of weeks. The children who took part in the survey were given the following definition of bullying: "We say a student is being bullied when another student, or a group of students, say or do nasty and unpleasant things to him or her. It is also bullying when a student is teased repeatedly in a way he or she does not like or when he or she is deliberately left out of things. But it is not bullying when two students of about the same strength or power argue or fight. It is also not bullying when a student is teased in a friendly and playful way."
7. For further information in German, see *www.schulpsychologie.at/gewaltpraevention/nationale-strategie*.

References

Austrian Federal Chancellery (2014), "Der Weg zur besten Bildung: 6-Punkte-Programm" [The Way Towards the best Education: 6 Step Programme], *Regierungsklausur26./27*, Schladming, Federal Press Service, Vienna, *www.bka.gv.at/DocView.axd?CobId=57183*.

Austrian Federal Chancellery (2013), *Work programme of the Austrian Federal Government 2013-2018*, Federal Press Service, Vienna, *www.bka.gv.at/DocView.axd?CobId=53588*.

BIFIE (2012), *PIRLS & TIMSS 2011, Schülerleistungen in Lesen, Mathematik und Naturwissenschaft in der Grundschule. Erste Ergebnisse [PIRLS & TIMSS 2011, Student Performance in Reading, Mathematics and Science in Primary School. First Results]*, *www.bifie.at/system/files/buch/pdf/ErsteErgebnisse_PIRLSTIMSS2011_web.pdf*.

BMBF (2015), *Freiraum für Österreichs Schulen: Empfehlungen zur neuen Steuerung, Expert/innenarbeitsgruppe Schulverwaltung [Freedom for Austria's Schools: Recommendations for New Steering, Expert Working Group on School Administration]*, Bundesministerium für Bildung und Frauen, Vienna.

BMBF and BMWFW (2015), *Bildungsreformkommission Vortrag an den Ministerrat [Education Reform Commission Presentation to the Council of Ministers]*, Bundesministerium für Bildung und Frauen, Vienna, *www.bmbf.gv.at/ministerium/vp/2015/20151117.pdf?55kaz6*.

Bruneforth, M. et al. (forthcoming), *OECD Review of Policies to Improve the Effectiveness of Resource Use in Schools, Country Background Report for Austria*, Bundesministerium für Bildung und Frauen, Vienna.

Bruneforth M., C. Weber and J. Bacher (2012), "Chancengleichheit und garantiertes Bildungsminimum in Österreich" [Equality of opportunities and guaranteed minimum education standards in Austria], in B. Herzog-Punzenberger (ed.), *Nationaler Bildungsbericht Österreich 2012, Band 2: Fokussierte Analysen bildungspolitischer Schwerpunktthemen [National Education Monitoring Report for Austria 2012. Volume 2: Focussed Analysis of Key Areas of Education Policy]*, Leykam, Graz, pp. 189-229.

European Commission (2015), *Country Profiles. Key Indicators: Österreich*, Directorate-General Regional and Urban Policy Analysis Unit B1, *www.ec.europa.eu/regional_policy/sources/docgener/informat/country2020/country_at_en.pdf*.

Eurostat (2015), Population density - Persons per km^2 (indicator tps00003), *www.ec.europa.eu/eurostat/tgm/table.do?tab=table&init=1&language=en&pcode=tps00003&plugin=1*.

Eurypedia (2015), European Encyclopedia on National Education Systems: Austria, *https://webgate.ec.europa.eu/fpfis/mwikis/eurydice/index.php/Austria:Overview*.

Martin, M.O. et al. (2012), *TIMSS 2011 International Results in Science*, International Association for the Evaluation of Educational Achievement (IEA), Amsterdam and TIMSS and PIRLS International Study Center, Boston, *http://timssandpirls.bc.edu/timss2011/downloads/T11_IR_Science_FullBook.pdf*.

Mullis, I.V.S. et al. (2012a), *PIRLS 2011 International Results in Reading*, International Association for the Evaluation of Educational Achievement (IEA), Amsterdam and TIMSS and PIRLS International Study Center, Boston, *http://timssandpirls.bc.edu/pirls2011/downloads/P11_IR_FullBook.pdf*.

Mullis, I.V.S. et al. (2012b), *TIMSS 2011 International Results in Mathematics*, International Association for the Evaluation of Educational Achievement (IEA), Amsterdam and TIMSS and PIRLS International Study Center, *Boston, http://timssandpirls.bc.edu/timss2011/downloads/T11_IR_Mathematics_FullBook.pdf*.

Musset, P. et al. (2013), *A Skills beyond School Review of Austria*, OECD Reviews of Vocational Education and Training, OECD Publishing, Paris, *http://dx.doi.org/10.1787/9789264200418-en*.

OECD (2016), *Low-Performing Students: Why They Fall Behind and How to Help Them Succeed*, PISA, OECD Publishing, Paris, *http://dx.doi.org/10.1787/9789264250246-en*.

OECD (2015a), Population density (pop. per km^2), *The Regional Database* (database), OECD.Stat, *http://dotstat.oecd.org/?lang=en*.

OECD (2015b), *Education at a Glance 2015: OECD Indicators*, OECD Publishing, Paris, *http://dx.doi.org/10.1787/eag-2015-en*.

OECD (2015c), *OECD Economic Surveys: Austria 2015*, OECD Publishing, Paris, *http://dx.doi.org/10.1787/eco_surveys-aut-2015-en*.

OECD (2015d), "Labour: Labour market statistics", *Main Economic Indicators* (database), *http://dx.doi.org/10.1787/data-00046-en*.

OECD (2015e), *OECD Economic Outlook*, OECD Publishing, Paris, http://dx.doi.org/10.1787/eco_outlook-v2015-2-en.

OECD (2015f), *In It Together: Why Less Inequality Benefits All*, OECD Publishing, Paris, *http://dx.doi.org/10.1787/9789264235120-en*.

OECD (2014a), *Education at a Glance 2014: OECD Indicators*, OECD Publishing, Paris, *http://dx.doi.org/10.1787/eag-2014-en*.

OECD (2014b), *PISA 2012 Results: What Students Know and Can Do (Volume I, Revised edition, February 2014): Student Performance in Mathematics, Reading and Science*, PISA, OECD Publishing, Paris, *http://dx.doi.org/10.1787/9789264208780-en*.

OECD (2014c), *Society at a Glance 2014: OECD Social Indicators*, OECD Publishing, Paris, *http://dx.doi.org/10.1787/soc_glance-2014-en*.

OECD (2013a), *PISA 2012 Results: Excellence through Equity (Volume II): Giving Every Student the Chance to Succeed*, PISA, OECD Publishing, Paris, *http://dx.doi.org/10.1787/9789264201132-en*.

OECD (2013b), *PISA 2012 Results: What Makes a School Successful (Volume IV): Resources, Policies and Practices*, PISA, OECD Publishing, Paris, *http://dx.doi.org/10.1787/9789264201156-en*.

OECD (2013c), *OECD Skills Outlook 2013: First Results from the Survey of Adult Skills*, OECD Publishing, Paris, *http://dx.doi.org/10.1787/9789264204256-en*.

OECD (2013d), *OECD Synergies for Better Learning: An International Perspective on Evaluation and Assessment*, OECD Publishing, Paris, *http://dx.doi.org/10.1787/9789264190658-en*.

OECD (2013e), *PISA 2012 Results: Ready to Learn: Students' Engagement, Drive and Self-Beliefs*, PISA, OECD Publishing, Paris, *http://dx.doi.org/10.1787/9789264201170-en*.

OECD (2013f), *OECD Regions at a Glance 2013*, OECD Publishing, Paris, *http://dx.doi.org/10.1787/reg_glance-2013-en*.

OECD (2012), *Education at a Glance 2012: OECD Indicators*, OECD Publishing, Paris, *http://dx.doi.org/10.1787/eag-2012-en*.

OECD (2009), *Creating Effective Teaching and Learning Environments: First Results from TALIS*, OECD Publishing, Paris, *http://dx.doi.org/10.1787/9789264068780-en*.

OECD (no date), *Education GPS*, *http://gpseducation.oecd.org*.

OECD (no date), *Historical population data and projections (1950-2050)*, statistical database, *http://stats.oecd.org/*.

Schreiner, C. and S. Breit (eds.) (2014a), *Standardüberprüfung 2013, Mathematik, 4. Schulstufe, Bundesergebnisbericht [Report on the Federal Results in the Standardised Assessment in Mathematics, Year 4, for 2013]*, *www.bifie.at/system/files/dl/01_BiSt-UE_M4_2013_Bundesergebnisbericht.pdf*.

Schreiner, C. and S. Breit (eds.) (2014b), *Standardüberprüfung 2013, Englisch, 8. Schulstufe, Bundesergebnisbericht [Report on the Federal Results in the Standardised Assessment in English, Year 8, for 2013]*, *www.bifie.at/system/files/dl/01_BiSt-UE_E8_2013_Bundesergebnisbericht_gesamt.pdf*.

Schreiner, C. and S. Breit (eds.) (2013), *BIFIE Standardüberprüfung 2012, Mathematik, 8. Schulstufe, Bundesergebnisbericht [Report on the federal results in the standardised assessment in Mathematics, Year 8, for 2012]*, *www.bifie.at/system/files/dl/01_BiSt-UE_M8_2012_Bundesergebnisbericht.pdf*.

Specht, W. and F. Sobanski (2012), *OECD Review on Evaluation and Assessment Frameworks for Improving School Outcomes: Country Background Report for Austria*, Bundesminiterium für Unterricht, Kunst und Kultur (BMUKK), Vienna, *www.oecd.org/edu/evaluationpolicy*.

Statistik Austria (2015a), *Statistik des Bevölkerungsstandes. Bevölkerung zu Jahresbeginn seit 2002 nach detaillierter Staatsangehörigkeit* [Population statistics. Population at the beginning of the year since 2002 disaggregated by nationality], Bundesanstalt Statistik Österreich, Vienna, *www.statistik.at/web_de/statistiken/menschen_und_gesellschaft/bevoelkerung/bevoelkerungsstruktur/bevoelkerung_nach_staatsangehoerigkeit_geburtsland/index.html*.

Statistik Austria (2015b), *Bildung in Zahlen 2013/14, Schlüsselindikatoren und Analysen [Education in Figures 2013/14, Key Indicators and Analyses]*, Bundesanstalt Statistik Österreich, Vienna, *www.statistik.at/web_de/services/publikationen/5/index.html?includePage=detailedView&pubId=508&sectionName=Bildung,+Kultur*.

Statistik Austria (2015c), *Statistisches Jahrbuch 2015 [Statistical yearbook 2015]*, Bundesanstalt Statistik Österreich, Vienna, *www.statistik.at/web_de/services/stat_jahrbuch*.

Statistik Austria (2015d), *Bevölkerung am 1.1.2015 nach Alter und Bundesland – Insgesamt* [Population 1.1.2015 by Age and Province – Total], Bundesanstalt Statistik Österreich, Vienna, *www.statistik.at/web_de/statistiken/menschen_und_gesellschaft/bevoelkerung/bevoelkerungsstruktur/bevoelkerung_nach_alter_geschlecht/023470.html*.

Statistik Austria (2014a), *Bevölkerungsprognose 2014. Vorausberechnete Bevölkerungsstruktur für Österreich 2013-2075 laut Hauptszenario (ausführliche Tabellen)* [Population Forecast 2014. Calculated Population Structure for Austria 2013-2075 According to the Main Scenario (Detailed Tables)], Bundesanstalt Statistik Österreich, Vienna, *www.statistik.at/web_de/statistiken/menschen_und_gesellschaft/bevoelkerung/demographische_prognosen/bevoelkerungsprognosen/index.html*.

Statistik Austria (2014b), *Schülerinnen und Schüler mit sonderpädagogischem Förderbedarf 2013/14* [Students with Special Educational Needs 2013/14], Bundesanstalt Statistik Österreich, Vienna, *www.statistik.at/web_de/statistiken/menschen_und_gesellschaft/bildung_und_kultur/formales_bildungswesen/schulen_schulbesuch/index.html*.

Statistik Austria (2014c), *Verteilung der Schülerinnen und Schüler in der 5. Schulstufe 2013/14 Vergleich mit den Jahren 1980/81, 1990/91, 2000/01, 2010/11, 2011/12 und 2012/13* [Distribution of Students in Year 5 2013/14 Comparison with the Years 1980/81, 1990/91, 2000/01, 2011/12 and 2012/13], Bundesanstalt Statistik Österreich, Vienna, *www.statistik.at/wcm/idc/idcplg?IdcService=GET_PDF_FILE&RevisionSelectionMethod=LatestReleased&dDocName=029659.*

Statistik Austria (2013), *Registerbasierte Statistiken Demographie (RS) Kalenderjahr 2013 [Register-based Demography Statistics Calendar Year 2013]*, Bundesanstalt Statistik Österreich, Vienna, *www.statistik.at/web_de/statistiken/menschen_und_gesellschaft/bevoelkerung/index.html.*

UNICEF Office of Research (2013), *Child Well-being in Rich Countries: A Comparative Overview*, Innocenti Report Card 11, UNICEF Office of Research, Florence, *www.unicef-irc.org/publications/683.*

Vogtenhuber, S., L. Lassnigg and M. Bruneforth (2012), "Kontext des Schul- und Bildungswesens" [Context of the School and Education System], in BIFIE, *Nationaler Bildungsbericht Österreich 2012 [National Education Monitoring Report for Austria 2012]*, *www.bifie.at/system/files/buch/pdf/NBB2012_Band1_gesamt_0.pdf.*

ANNEX 1.A1

The November 2015 education reform proposal

In November 2015, an education reform commission comprising representatives of the federal government and the provinces presented a proposal for education reform in Austria. The education reform proposal was informed by the work of an expert commission in Austria that resulted in the paper *Freiraum für Österreichs Schulen: Empfehlungen zur neuen Steuerung* [Freedom for Austria's schools: Recommendations for new steering] (BMBF, 2015) and a draft report of the OECD school resources review of Austria. The November 2015 proposal suggested the following reforms.

1) Early childhood education and care: Strengthening kindergarten as an educational institution

- Introduction of a standardised national "education compass" for all children aged 3.5 and above (in analogy to the best practice "mother-child passport").
- Second compulsory kindergarten year for everyone, with the possibility for parents to opt out.
- Development of a compulsory standardised national quality framework by the end of 2016 in consultation with the provinces.
- Continuing documentation of language levels and development using a portfolio system ("education compass").
- Further development of educational institutions for kindergarten teachers (*Bildungsanstalten für Kindergartenpädagogik*, BAKIP).
- Recognition of (tertiary) qualifications for professional qualifications from the new BHS for Elementary Pedagogy (formerly BAKIP) with the appropriate proof of practical experience to facilitate side entry.
- Development of integrated further education opportunities at associate institutions (university colleges of teacher education, universities) and provincial academies for elementary pedagogues and primary teachers.
- Stronger research in the field of early childhood education and care and participation in international projects (e.g. OECD) on elementary pedagogy and supporting early childhood development.

2) Transition to school, primary education, and support for language development

- NEW Admission of students.

- Data exchange with the creation of a national basis for disclosure and use of formative student information and data between kindergarten and primary school.
- Further development and comprehensive expansion of co-operation between kindergarten and primary school teachers (network schools).
- Joint staff meetings with the school supervisors from the school inspection of early childhood education and care and primary education.
- Orientation and participation in the latest international research and development projects (OECD and EU), transfer of international expertise.
- Updating and further development of primary school curricula.
- Autonomous opportunity for teaching across school years with flexible internal differentiation.
- Autonomy for schools to implement alternative student assessments for primary school Years 1 to 3.
- Introductory language courses in schools.

3) School autonomy

a) More pedagogical, organisational, staff and financial autonomy

- Greater flexibility to devise learning groups according to pedagogical targets and more opportunities for the flexible formation of classes and groups.
- Greater autonomy for schools to determine their focus and curriculum timetables where this will enhance the quality of learning.
- A massive reduction in the number of school pilots from 2017/18.
- Benchmark of 200 to 2 500 students, with a range of 10% of fluctuation for autonomous schools or administrative bodies.
- Ongoing partnerships between schools and boards like the school forum or the school community committee.
- Development of a comprehensive long-term school concept that entails the school profile, mission statement, etc. by the NEW administrative bodies (school cluster), and production of annual pedagogical quality reports by individual schools.
- Responsibility for the organisation of the work schedule for the school leadership.
- Greater flexibility for the adaptation of school hours to meet the demands of the work schedules of parents and guardians.
- Autonomy for school leadership to set aside time for quality development projects and annual planning with all staff outside of teaching hours.

b) Greater autonomy for human resource management to increase the organisational potential and responsibility of school leadership

- Organisation of school leadership (principals, deputy principals and middle management) as a separate professional group (5-year contracts and a standardised job profile and recruitment process).
- Selection of staff through school leadership in consultation with the education authority, with a veto right against new staff appointment for school leadership.
- Responsibility for school leadership for staff development and performance evaluations (with support of middle leaders).

- Responsibility for further training arrangements and their approval, including exemptions, in the hands of the school leadership within the available resources (travel expenses). Availability of further training courses through university colleges of teacher education (PH).
- Involvement of school leadership in decisions pertaining to the employment of staff, such as contract renewal.

c) Greater financial autonomy to facilitate the efficient and needs-based use of resources

- Possibility to convert teaching staff positions into support staff positions, e.g. for pedagogical assistance (up to 5% of staff).
- Autonomy for schools to deploy external teaching staff for special areas of focus within the scope of the resources provided.
- Flexibility in assigning and planning the current regulations on administrative tasks in schools (e.g. updating of teaching materials and other ancillary services) in accordance with the needs of the individual school.
- Depending on the school authority model, direct availability of certain financial resources to autonomous schools or school clusters (NEW administrative body) as part of a global budget for material expenditure (e.g. material expenditure for students, text books, missions, transportation, overheads, equipment, etc.).
- Permission for third-party funding for schools within the legal framework.

d) Evidence-based quality control and (pedagogical) monitoring of results to help schools develop

- Responsibility of the federal government for the central specifications of education targets, curricula, education standards, and for auditing resources and monitoring results.
- Responsibility of the federal government for the entire strategic planning and result-oriented management of these areas.
- Responsibility for autonomous schools for their operative implementation and pedagogical organisation.
- Production of annual school-specific quality reports by autonomous schools (with the support of the NEW school inspections) in order to ensure ongoing quality control and transparent documentation (for the school partners and the central authorities).
- Regular collection of data (indicators, figures and measurements) on learning progress, school climate, educational pathways and transitions, social composition, the result-oriented use of resources etc. through the federal authorities. Availability of these data to schools as well as the quality control body (NEW school inspection) in order to inform further development measures.
- Self-evaluation and peer evaluation by schools to complement central quality control mechanisms.
- Quality development within schools with clear written development plans and target agreements with the support of NEW school inspection.
- Presentation of a national school quality report collecting the results of the school quality control areas to the parliament on a three-year basis.

4) Model regions: schools for 6-14 year-olds

The aim is to create a school in which students can enjoy optimal development of their individual abilities and to pilot comprehensive schooling for this age group. This requires a supporting pedagogic, staff-related and organisational framework, which is provided by internal differentiation and individualisation, as well as a good mixt of all children within one peer group. New Secondary Schools, academic secondary schools (lower level) and special needs schools are part of the region; primary schools and kindergartens or day nurseries can also participate. In a model region all schools within the region are integrated.

- Schools may be combined in a school association ("region"). The model region will be established on the basis of concepts developed by the provinces, subject to approval by the Federal Ministry of Education and Women's Affairs (BMBF).
- A model region may only extend across one province.
- The total number of individual schools in the model regions must not amount to more than 15% for each type of school and must not comprise more than 15% of all students of a given type of school. Schools already participating are excluded from these calculations.
- No infringement of the rights of any private school providers. No amendments to the Private Schools Act. Possibility for private schools to participate if they so wish.
- Equal distribution of federal and provincial teachers and students of all levels of achievement throughout the individual schools in the model regions. (All children who have successfully completed primary school; children with special needs only have to have attended primary school or a special needs school.)
- Availability of support staff and/or multi-professional teams to ease the burden on teaching staff. Possibility to deploy teaching staff as support staff.
- Consultation of school partners.
- A pedagogically inclusive concept (Strength-orientation, systematic involvement of parents in education, individualised learning for students, inclusion (optional), internal differentiation, skills orientation, vocational orientation, specific advanced teacher training in pedagogy, establishment of professional learning communities for teachers in the region, promotion of talent, advanced courses, permeability for advanced educational careers).
- No funding cuts for schools facing particular challenges (e.g. students whose first language is not German, students requiring special support).
- Development of regional networks for education between schools and all other education partners.
- Comprehensive scientific support and evaluation, nomination of experts by the Federal Ministry of Education and Women's Affairs, the Federal Ministry of Science, Research and Economy and the provinces.
- Government-level working group tasked with developing, in consultation with the provinces, proposals for the prerequisite legislative changes for establishing a model region.
- Legislative implementation via the introduction of a new legal provision for model regions in the School Organisation Act (SchOG).
- No additional federal funds for the entire model region.

5) School organisation, education directorates

- The highest education authority is the federal minister.
- Each province has an education directorate as a joint federal-provincial authority. Provincial legislation may stipulate that the provincial governor or the responsible member of the provincial government can take on the role of president of the authority.

- The education directorate is headed by the director of education as a federal employee nominated by the responsible federal minister upon recommendation by the provincial governor. The director of education undertakes the general and specialist supervision of all employees of the education directorate. The director is appointed for a period of five years.
- This authority is responsible for the performance of the federal teachers, the provincial teachers, the external school organisation (cost-neutral), the federal administrative staff and the school inspection.
- The education directorate has all the powers presently held by the province education board or the education departments of the provinces.
- School principals are appointed in accordance with a national standardised selection procedure which is to be devised by the federal government together with the provinces.
- All teachers are to be paid via the Federal Computing Centre (*Bundesrechenzentrum*, BRZ) and integrated into the teaching information system (details to be agreed upon).
- Abolition of the executive president, the vice president and the collegiate boards.
- The internal organisation of the education directorates is governed by federal law in co-operation with the provinces.
- Title: Education directorate for "the federal state".

6) Innovation in education

- Comprehensive Internet access for schools by 2020.
- Establishment of a national education foundation.

ANNEX 1.A2

The Austrian Education System

Figure 1.A2.1. **The Austrian Education System**

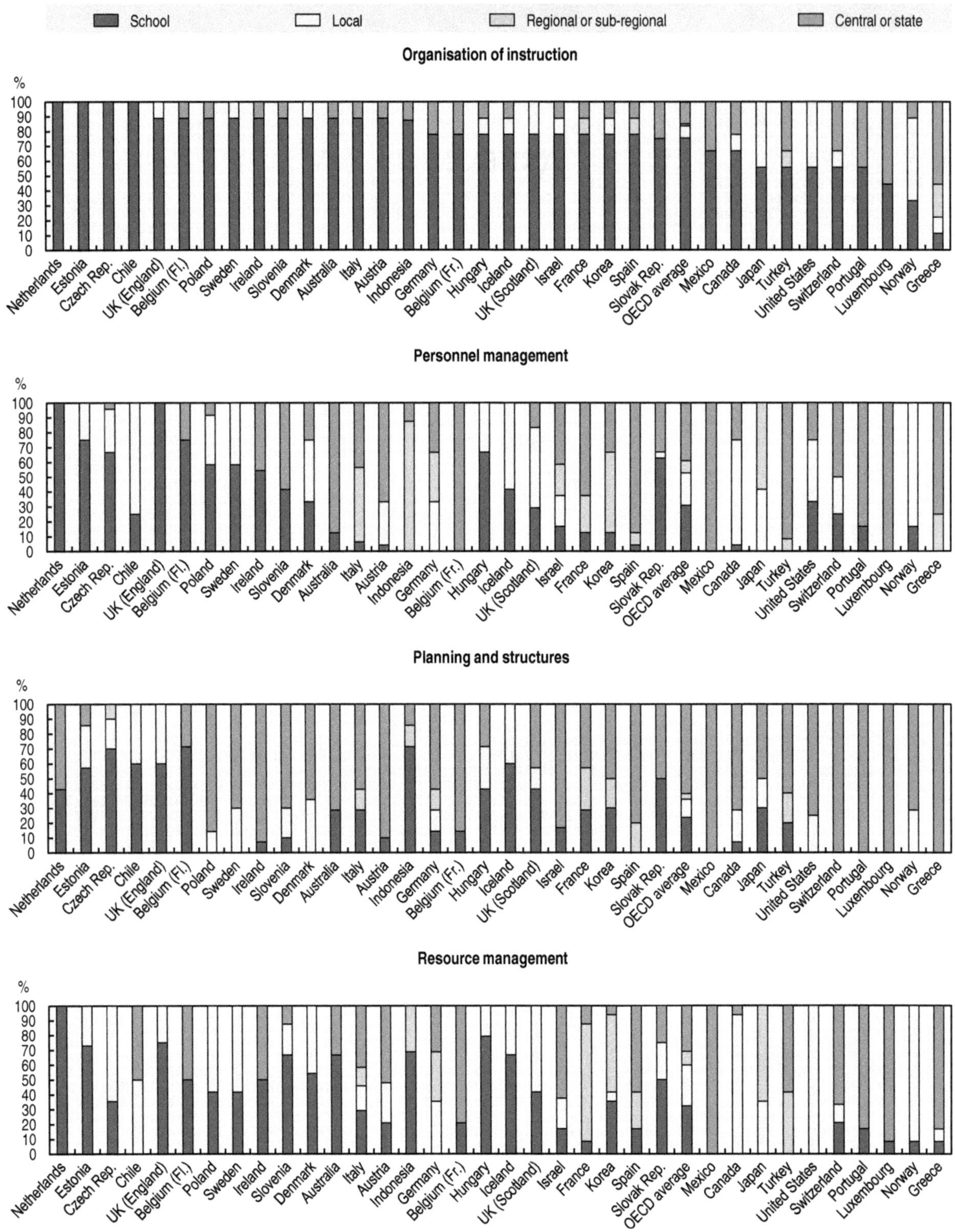

Source: OECD (no date), *Education GPS*, *http://gpseducation.oecd.org*.

ANNEX 1.A3

Distribution of decision-making in public lower secondary education

Figure 1.A3.1. **Percentage of decisions taken at each level of government in public lower secondary education, by domain, 2011**

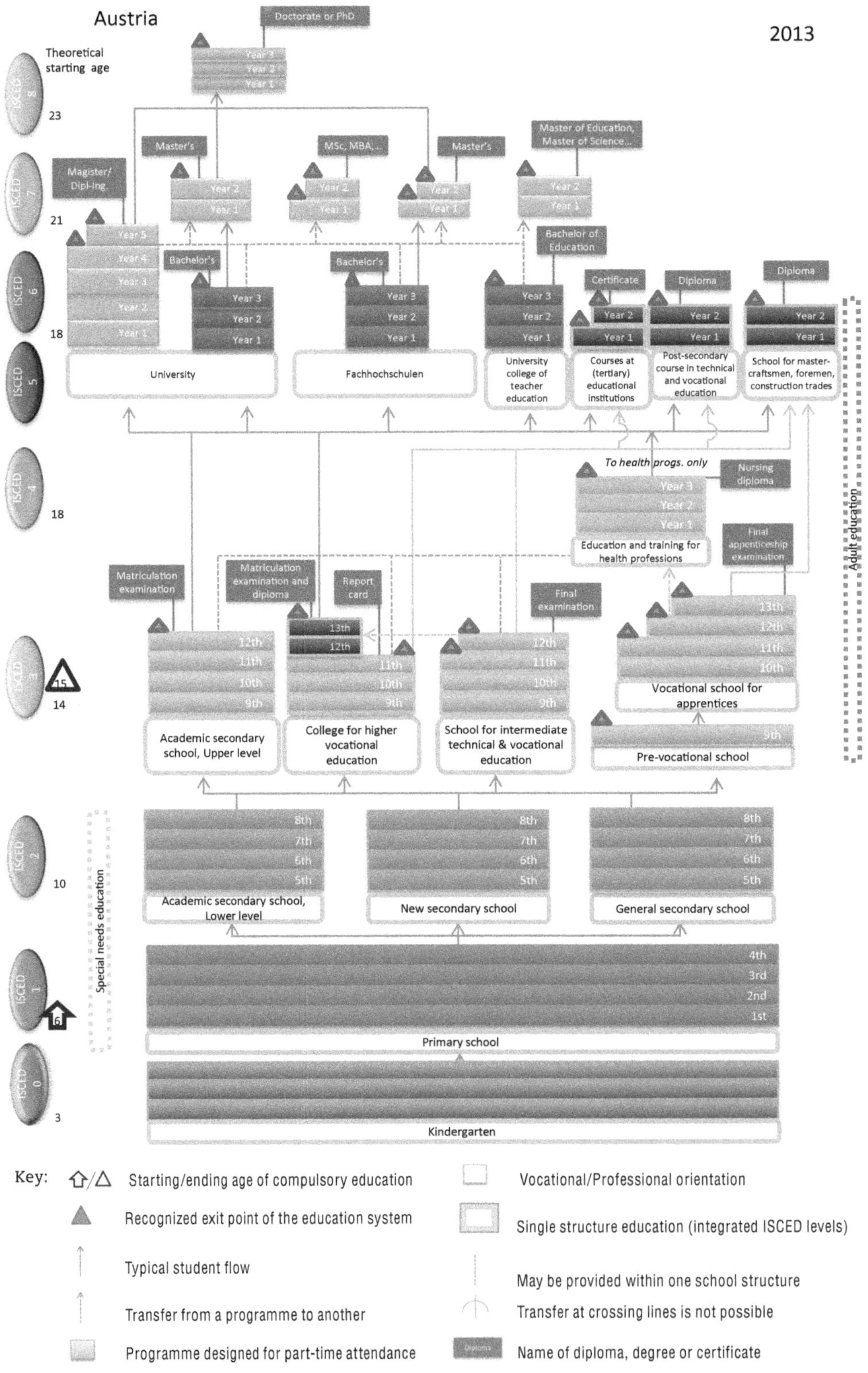

Note: Countries are ranked in descending order of the percentage of decisions about organisation of instruction taken at the school level.

Source: OECD (2012), *Education at a Glance 2012: OECD Indicators*, *http://dx.doi.org/10.1787/eag-2012-en*, Table D6.2a and D6.2b. See Annex 3 for notes.

Chapter 2

Funding and governance of school education in Austria

This chapter is about the funding and governance of primary and lower secondary education in Austria. It analyses the overall budget for education and the distribution of funding across levels of education, provinces, school types and resource categories. It looks at the complex distribution of responsibilities for governing, financing and administering different school types between the federal, provincial and municipal levels and the extent of school autonomy taking recent reforms and proposals for further reform into account. It considers the strengths and challenges inherent in the current system highlighting the problematic incentives, the lack of transparency and trust, and the inefficiencies the complex system of governance generates and makes policy recommendations to address these issues through a reform of governance and funding mechanisms.

The statistical data for Israel are supplied by and under the responsibility of the relevant Israeli authorities. The use of such data by the OECD is without prejudice to the status of the Golan Heights, East Jerusalem and Israeli settlements in the West Bank under the terms of international law.

Context and features

Goal-oriented budgeting and goals for the education system

The Austrian government has undertaken significant steps in recent years to promote goal-oriented budgeting. Building on a comprehensive reform launched in 2009, new budgeting principles were introduced in 2013. These principles promote an orientation towards the outcomes of policy making rather than the inputs as well as efficiency and transparency. More concretely, the federal budget comprises a set of policy goals associated with particular quantitative and qualitative indicators. These indicators can serve as a guideline for policy making at different levels of government as well as a transparent measure to assess the performance of the government. The 2015 budget contains two policy targets (with three indicators each) related to education: "raise the level of education of students" and "improve equity and gender-equality in education" (Bruneforth et al., forthcoming: 20). These targets are associated with detailed indicators (e.g. the graduation rate of students in upper secondary education or the share of new entrants in higher education) and then translated into the framework for monitoring quality in education (see below). Since goal-oriented budgeting was introduced only recently, its effect on educational practices and outcomes still remains to be seen.

Overall budget for education

Table 2.1 displays national trend data from the national statistical office on the absolute amount of spending on different sectors of the Austrian education system for the time period 2000-11. These data are not comparable to the international data presented further below, but provide a good picture of recent trends in public spending. Total public education spending (including post-secondary and tertiary education) increased from a level of EUR 11 654.6 million in 2000 to EUR 17 343.2 million in 2011 (Statistik Austria, online database). Similar figures are reported in Bruneforth et al. (forthcoming: 52). Their time period of analysis stretches further back in time until 1995, and they find a relative increase in spending (in nominal terms, i.e. without taking into account inflation) of 64%, which is equivalent to an increase in spending in real terms of 33%. The national trend data show that the bulk of the spending increase took place since 2005. Looking at the distribution of spending across different sectors, there are some notable differences. The strongest expansion of spending occurred in pre-primary education (ISCED-97 level 0). Between 2000 and 2011, spending on this sector increased by over 100%, while spending on primary education and lower secondary education (ISCED-97 levels 1 and 2) increased by 30% and on upper secondary education (ISCED-97 level 3) by 54%.

The picture looks slightly different when looking at total public spending on education as a percentage of GDP (the last column of Table 2.1). This measure takes into account changes in economic output during the time period of observation. The national data show that the spending effort actually declined from a level of 5.5% of GDP in 2000 to 5.2% in 2007. It then increased in line with the significant expansion of absolute spending to a

Table 2.1. **Overall public spending on education in different sectors of the Austrian education system (absolute numbers in EUR million and as a percentage of GDP, based on ISCED 97), 2000-11**

Year	Early childhood education	Primary education (Years 1-4)	Lower secondary education (Years 5-8)	Upper secondary education (Year 9 and higher)	Total public spending on education (including tertiary and post-secondary education)	Total public spending on education as percentage of GDP
2000	880.5	2 297.7	2 959.5	2 608.1	11 654.6	5.5
2001	834.8	2 368.9	2 860.8	2 584.5	12 008.6	5.5
2002	886.4	2 432.5	2 958.7	2 663.1	12 254.3	5.4
2003	926.3	2 560.7	3 181.4	2 990.7	12 617.7	5.5
2004	938.8	2 435.2	3 035.4	3 040.1	12 850.3	5.3
2005	989.2	2 533.5	3 181.4	2 945.4	13 337.3	5.3
2006	1 028.5	2 599.2	3 324.4	3 195.7	13 998.0	5.3
2007	1 108.1	2 635.2	3 415.1	3 349.9	14 616.1	5.2
2008	1 290.9	2 758.6	3 616.0	3 540.1	15 463.5	5.3
2009	1 515.0	2 876.5	3 779.0	3 934.7	16 505.6	5.8
2010	1 742.0	2 889.9	3 752.7	3 729.7	16 867.5	5.7
2011	1 773.8	2 964.8	3 834.9	4 032.3	17 343.2	5.6

Source: Statistik Austria (no date), online database, *www.statistik.at/web_de/statistiken/menschen_und_gesellschaft/bildung_und_kultur/formales_bildungswesen/bildungsausgaben/index.html.*

high of 5.8% of GDP in 2009, but declined again to 5.6% of GDP in 2011. In interpreting these figures, it is important to keep in mind that the global financial and economic crisis was associated with a significant contraction of economic output. A shrinking denominator, therefore, leads to an increase in spending as percentage of GDP, even when absolute numbers stay constant. In general, the data presented in Table 2.1 simply document a significant increase in absolute public spending, but roughly constant public spending as percentage of GDP. This suggests that the economic and fiscal crisis did not yet have a strong impact on the education budget in Austria, even though some budget cuts were introduced in 2014 and 2015 and the education budget seems to face increasing pressure to make savings from the Ministry of Finance.

By international comparison, Austrian public spending on education from primary to tertiary education as a percentage of GDP in 2012 is above the OECD average, but there are a number of OECD member countries such as Belgium, Finland, New Zealand and Norway with a significantly higher share of public spending on education (Figure 2.1). Private spending on education is very low in Austria (0.0% of GDP) compared to some other countries.[1] In this respect, Austria is very similar to other countries in continental Europe. Higher levels of private spending on education are primarily caused by differences in the financing of higher education, in particular the importance of tuition fees as a source of funding (Wolf, 2009). When both public and private spending are considered, Austrian expenditure on education from primary to tertiary education as a share of GDP is lower than the OECD average (4.9%, compared to 5.3% in 2012), but still significantly higher than in the neighbouring Czech Republic, Germany, Italy and the Slovak Republic (OECD, 2015).

Over time, the relative position of Austria compared to other countries has slightly declined. When combining both public and private spending on education, Austrian spending on educational institutions for all levels of education as a percentage of GDP was slightly above the OECD average in 2000 (5.5% of GDP vs. an OECD average of 5.4%), but fell below the average in 2011 (5.7% vs. 6.1%), the latest year for which trend data are available for Austria (OECD, 2014a, Table B2.2).[2]

Figure 2.1. **Public and private spending on educational institutions, primary to tertiary education, based on ISCED 2011, 2012**

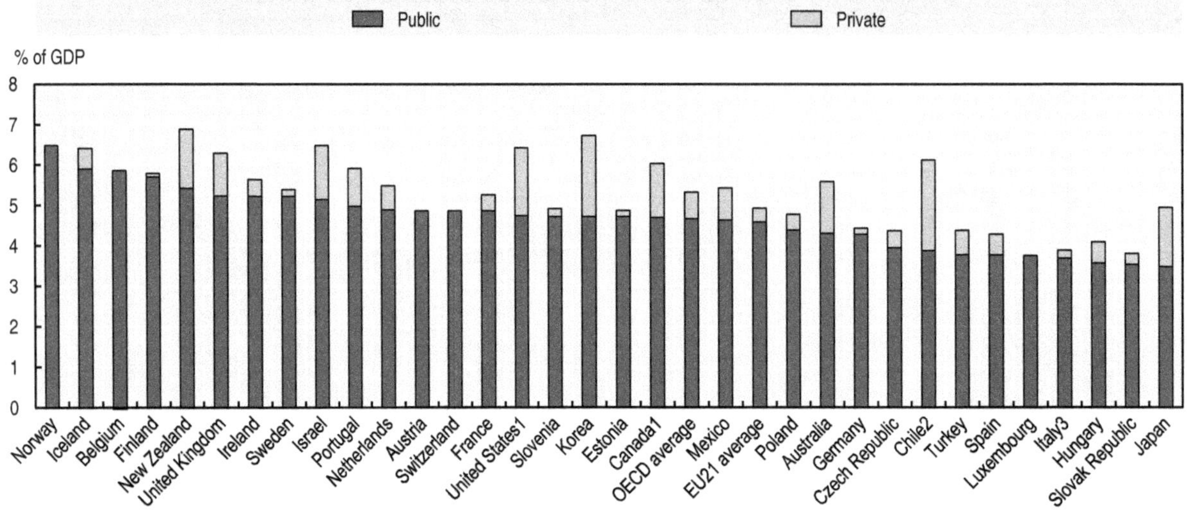

Note: Public spending includes public subsidies to households attributable for educational institutions, and direct expenditure on educational institutions from international sources. Private spending is net of public subsidies attributable for educational institutions.
1. Year of reference 2011.
2. Year of reference 2013.
3. Excludes short-cycle tertiary programmes.

Source: OECD (2015), *Education at a Glance 2015: OECD Indicators, http://dx.doi.org/10.1787/eag-2015-en*, Table B2.3.

When looking at absolute spending and spending as a percentage of GDP, it is difficult to tell whether total spending increases are associated with an increase in spending per student or an increase in the number of students due to demographic developments. It is, therefore, important to look at educational investments as per-student expenditure, which allows taking changes in the size of the school-age population into account. Per-student expenditure is typically influenced by the economic well-being of a particular country, with more wealthy countries being able to spend more on each student, while still devoting a smaller share of its GDP to education. Table 2.2 shows that, by international comparison, the Austrian education system enjoys high levels of public spending per student. In 2012, Austria spent 13 189 purchasing power equivalent USD per student from primary to tertiary

Table 2.2. **Annual per student expenditure on education in equivalent USD converted using PPPs, Austria and neighbouring countries, based on ISCED 2011, 2012**

	Pre-primary education (for children 3 years and older)	Primary education	Lower secondary education	Upper secondary education	Primary to tertiary (including R&D activities and undistributed programmes)
Austria	**7 716**	**9 563**	**13 632**	**14 013**	**13 189**
Czech Republic	4 447	4 728	7 119	7 469	7 684
Germany	8 568	7 749	9 521	12 599	11 363
Hungary	4 539	4 370	4 459	4 386	5 564
Italy	7 892	7 924	8 905	8 684	8 744
Slovak Republic	4 694	5 415	5 283	5 027	6 072
Slovenia	7 472	9 015	9 802	6 898	9 031
Switzerland	5 457	13 889	16 370	17 024	17 485
OECD average	**8 008**	**$8 247**	**9 627**	**9 876**	**10 220**
EU21 average	8 146	$8 372	10 040	10 011	10 361

Source: OECD (2015), *Education at a Glance 2015: OECD Indicators, http://dx.doi.org/10.1787/eag-2015-en*, Tables B1.1a and C2.3.

education, which is significantly above the OECD average of USD 10 220 (OECD 2015, Table B1.1a). There are only a few OECD countries that surpass Austria in this regard (see Annex 2.1). Looking across the different levels of the education system, it can be observed that, while spending levels per student in Austria are above the OECD average for all levels of education, the difference is particularly striking at the lower and upper secondary levels.

Distribution of funding across school types, provinces and resource categories

In 2012, 28% of all education spending went to general compulsory schools (*Allgemeine Pflichtschulen*, APS), 10% to general academic secondary schools (*Allgemeinbildende Höhere Schulen*, AHS) and 17% to vocational schools and colleges (*Berufsbildende Mittlere Schulen*, BMS, *Berufsbildende Höhere Schulen*, BHS, and *Berufsschulen*, BS). The rest of the budget is spent on universities, vocational tertiary institutions, early childhood education and administration (see Bruneforth et al., forthcoming: 71).

Figure 2.2 presents the most recent data on per-student expenditures in different school types of the Austrian education system. Since these data are compiled by the Austrian authorities and provided in EUR rather than PPP USD, they are not directly comparable to the international data discussed above. According to these national data, per-student spending was comparatively high in general secondary schools (*Hauptschulen*, HS, and *Neue Mittelschulen*, NMS), amounting to EUR 10 762 in 2013, compared to EUR 8 906 in academic secondary schools (AHS) and EUR 7 072 in primary schools (Statistik Austria, 2015a: 85). Looking at spending trends between 2011 and 2013, the data reflect a small increase in per-student spending in all school types except special needs schools, which is commensurate with the trends observed above. These data do not yet fully reflect the recent spending increase on the newly established New Secondary Schools (NMS), which are discussed in greater detail below.

Figure 2.2. **Per-student expenditure in different types of Austrian schools, 2011-13**

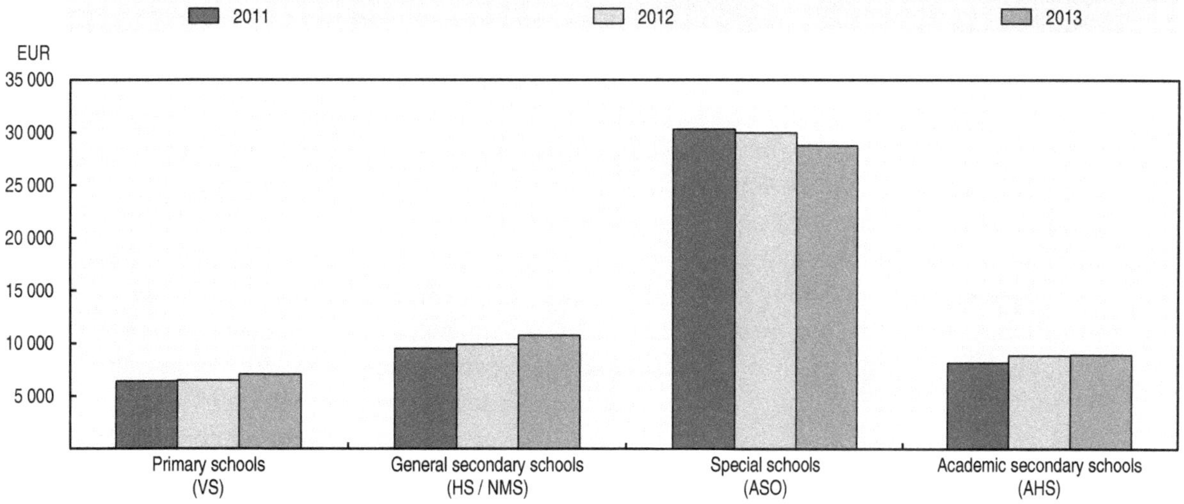

Source: Statistik Austria (2015a), *Bildung in Zahlen 2013/14: Schlüsselindikatoren und Analysen [Education in Figures 2013/14, Key Indicators and Analyses]*, Statistik Austria, Vienna, p. 85.

The data in Table 2.3 confirm that, on average, per-student spending in general secondary schools (HS, NMS) is higher than in the academic secondary schools (AHS), in particular in the case of the New Secondary Schools (NMS). Moreover, the table also reveals

Table 2.3. **Variation of per student spending across school types and provinces, 2012**

Province	School type					
	VS	HS	NMS	ASO	PTS	All compulsory schooling combined
Burgenland	7 345	9 397	11 465	36 886	13 300	**9 293**
Carinthia	6 958	10 609	10 604	51 698	11 023	**8 938**
Lower Austria	6 319	10 350	11 095	25 593	11 553	**8 563**
Upper Austria	6 153	9 387	10 044	19 087	9 038	**7 898**
Salzburg	6 094	9 046	10 113	31 476	14 693	**8 214**
Styria	7 006	11 037	10 881	36 113	10 745	**8 951**
Tyrol	6 151	8 689	9 672	23 916	10 303	**7 895**
Vorarlberg	6 547	8 433	9 877	26 672	8 707	**8 432**
Vienna	5 851	8 760	10 152	56 300	7 634	**8 310**
Austria	**6 346**	**9 679**	**10 448**	**33 401**	**10 195**	**8 402**

	Academic secondary school (AHS)			Lower secondary combined	
	AHS-U lower secondary	AHS-O upper secondary	AHS	HS + NMS	AHS-U, NMS, HS
Burgenland	8 463	8 964	**8 688**	11 141	10 291
Carinthia	8 301	8 960	**8 586**	10 605	9 793
Lower Austria	8 392	8 850	**8 580**	10 724	9 896
Upper Austria	8 294	8 688	**8 471**	9 695	9 298
Salzburg	7 983	9 320	**8 639**	9 410	8 946
Styria	8 079	8 919	**8 491**	10 949	9 992
Tyrol	8 070	8 921	**8 505**	9 285	8 963
Vorarlberg	7 944	9 475	**8 701**	9 781	9 328
Vienna	8 017	8 976	**8 432**	9 471	8 707
Austria	**8 161**	**8 949**	**8 516**	10 106	9 414

Note: For this purpose expenditure for the different programmes are aggregated using a weighted average with the number of students in the programmes as weight.
Source: Bruneforth, M. et al. (forthcoming), *OECD Review of Policies to Improve the Effectiveness of Resource use in Schools: Country Background Report for Austria*, Bundesministerium für Bildung und Frauen, Vienna, p. 55.

a significant degree of variation in per-student spending across provinces. This variation is more pronounced in the case of the general compulsory schools (APS) than in the academic secondary school sector (AHS), which is most probably related to differences in the governance arrangements (see below). General compulsory schools are the responsibility of the provincial governments, whereas the federal government is in charge of academic secondary schools. Therefore, differences in political, institutional and socio-economic conditions between the provinces are more likely to influence per-student spending in the compulsory school sector than the academic secondary school sector. In the academic secondary school sector, per-student spending is lowest in the province of Vienna (EUR 8 432) and highest in Vorarlberg (EUR 8 701). In the case of general compulsory schools, the province of Tyrol spends the least (EUR 7 895), whereas the Burgenland spends the most (EUR 9 293).

As in other OECD countries, the bulk of spending on primary, secondary and post-secondary non-tertiary education is invested in personnel. Almost three quarters of funding at these levels are spent on staff salaries, 20% are devoted to other current spending and a mere 2% is earmarked for capital investment (Bruneforth et al., forthcoming: 69). "Other current spending" includes expenditure on sub-contracted services such as support services (e.g. maintenance of school buildings), ancillary services (e.g. school meals) and rental of school buildings and other facilities. In comparison to other OECD countries, the share of spending on teacher salaries relative to spending on other staff (e.g. administrative and other support staff) is higher in Austria (ibid.: 69), which is related to the fact that teachers often take over responsibilities unrelated to teaching, which are more typically taken on by administrative or specialised staff in other countries (see below and Chapter 4).

Annex 2.2 provides an overview of the distribution of spending at different educational levels across different resource categories. In primary education, the shares of spending devoted to the compensation of both teachers (62.0%) and other staff (13.3%) in Austria are actually below the OECD averages (62.5% and 15.6% respectively), whereas the share devoted to other current expenditure is significantly above the OECD average (24.7% vs. 20.7%). In secondary education, however, the share of expenditure for teacher compensation is well above the OECD average (66.9% in Austria compared to an average of 62.4%) whereas the spending share devoted to other staff is strongly below average (6.9% vs. 15.1%). The spending share on other current expenditure is above the OECD average (26.2% vs. 21.8%). Annex 2.2 also shows the comparatively low levels of capital spending in Austria. According to the OECD data, the share of capital spending as a share of total spending is a mere 2.2% in primary and 1.9% in secondary education, which is significantly below the OECD averages of 7.1% and 6.8% respectively (OECD, 2015, Table B6.1).

Spending on teacher salaries

In absolute terms, teacher salaries in Austria are significantly above the OECD average. For instance, in 2013 the salary costs of teachers per student were USD 5 191 (PPP) for teachers in lower secondary education compared to an OECD average of USD 3 350 (OECD, 2015, Table B7.1). However, since Austria's GDP per capita is also above average, the relative position of Austria changes once this is taken into account. Teacher salary costs per student as a percentage of GDP per capita are still above the OECD average (11.9% relative to an average of 9.4% for lower secondary education), but there are a number of other countries with significantly higher teacher salary costs in relation to GDP per capita, namely Belgium, Finland, Germany, Luxembourg, Portugal, Slovenia and Spain. A detailed disaggregation of the cost components of teacher salaries reveals that small class sizes and relatively low teaching loads for teachers contribute significantly to above-average salary costs in Austria (OECD, 2015: 300-301; Bruneforth et al., forthcoming: 103, see also Lassnigg et al., 2007: 165).

In terms of relative actual salaries, Austrian primary school teachers earn 77%, lower secondary teachers 89% and upper secondary teachers 97% of the salaries of other full-time workers with a tertiary education (OECD, 2015, Table D3.2a: 442). This is comparable to a number of other OECD countries (Figure 2.3) and must be seen in the context of high wage levels of private sector employees with a tertiary education in Austria. In England (United Kingdom), for example, primary teachers earn 75% of the salaries of similarly-educated workers, lower and upper secondary teachers earn 82% of the salaries of similarly-educated workers. In the Netherlands, teachers' relative salaries amount to 69% (primary education) and 85% (lower and upper secondary education). And in Finland, teachers' salaries compare at 74%, 81% and 91% for primary, lower secondary and upper secondary education respectively. In a few countries with available data, the ratio of the actual salaries of teachers to similarly educated workers is, however, higher than in Austria, notably Luxembourg, Denmark and France (OECD, 2015, Table D3.2a). Previous

Figure 2.3. **Teachers' salaries relative to earnings for similarly educated workers, 2013**

Salaries of lower secondary teachers teaching general programmes in public institutions

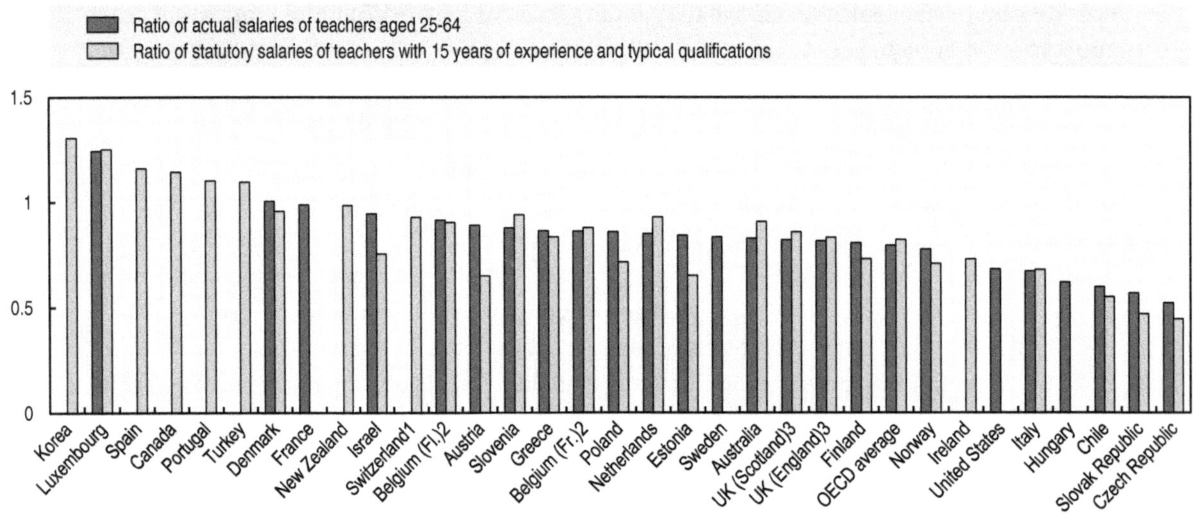

Note: The definition of teachers' typical qualification is based on a broad concept including the typical ISCED level of attainment and other criteria. For further details on the different metrics used to calculate these ratios, please refer to the methodology section in *Education at a Glance 2015*.

1. Statutory salaries of teachers with 11 years of experience and minimum qualification instead of 15 years of experience and typical qualifications.
2. Data on earnings for full-time, full-year workers with tertiary education refer to Belgium.
3. Data on earnings for full-time, full-year workers with tertiary education refer to the United Kingdom.
4. Countries are ranked in descending order of the ratio of teachers' salaries to earnings for full-time, full-year workers with tertiary education aged 25-64.

Source: OECD (2015), *Education at a Glance 2015: OECD Indicators, http://dx.doi.org/10.1787/eag-2015-en*, Table D3.2a and Table D3.2b.

calculations of relative teacher wages (e.g. OECD, 2014: 469) suggested less favourable relative salaries, but these were based on statutory salaries, whereas the most recent figures from the OECD are based on actual salaries.[3] Whereas statutory salaries as reported for the OECD Education at a Glance publication remain relatively low by international comparison, real average salaries of Austrian teachers are thus likely to be higher thanks to additional allowances for various functions that teachers might perform and compensation for overtime (Bruneforth et al., forthcoming: 103).

In comparison to other countries, the present slope of the teacher salary scale is much steeper in Austria (Figure 2.4). For example, the starting salary of a teacher in lower secondary education is 34 143 in PPP-equivalent USD in 2013 (compared with an OECD average of 31 013). The salary at the top of the scale is almost twice this amount (66 378 PPP-equivalent USD vs. OECD average of 50 414 PPP-equivalent USD) (OECD, 2015, Table D3.1a and D3.6a). Given that the average age of the Austrian teaching force is also above the international average, this results in above-average spending on teacher salaries. However, a new teacher service code that is being implemented as of September 2015 and will be mandatory for all new teachers by September 2020 changes teachers' salary progression significantly. Statutory salaries for beginning teachers will start at a higher level and the slope of the salary scale will be compressed while roughly maintaining lifetime earnings. Adequate levels of teacher remuneration seem essential considering the need to attract high quality individuals to the profession and a pending retirement wave of teachers in the near future.

Like other workers in Austria, teachers can retire early after having contributed to the pension system for at least 40 years. As provincial teachers traditionally entered the

Figure 2.4. **Lower secondary teachers' salaries at different points in teachers' careers, 2013**

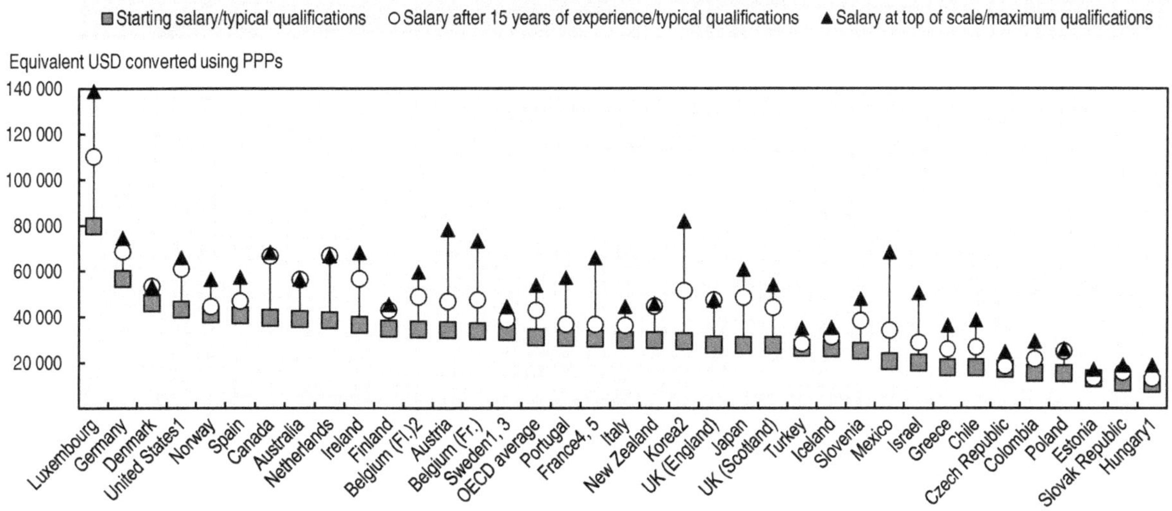

Note: Annual statutory salaries in public schools measured in equivalent USD converted using PPPs for GDP.
1. Actual base salaries.
2. Salaries at top of scale and typical qualifications, instead of maximum qualifications.
3. Salaries at top of scale and minimum qualifications, instead of maximum qualifications.
4. Includes average bonuses for overtime hours.
5. The typical qualification of starting teachers differ substantially from the typical qualification of all the current teachers.

Countries are ranked in descending order of starting salaries for lower secondary teachers with typical qualifications.

Source: OECD (2015), *Education at a Glance 2015: OECD Indicators*, *http://dx.doi.org/10.1787/eag-2015-en*, Tables D3.1a and D3.6a.

profession after a relatively short education of three years, they benefitted from this possibility in large numbers. According to calculations from the Austrian Court of Audit, large early retirement rates of teachers in the period between 2008 and 2013 led to additional costs of EUR 2 billion (Rechnungshof, 2015a: 17). Of course, it is important to bear in mind that pension benefits are based on contributions throughout an individual's working life.

Governance arrangements

The nature of Austrian federalism is different from federalism in its neighbouring countries of Germany and Switzerland. In Austria, the provincial governments have limited capacities to raise their own tax revenues and – in the case of education policy – many legal competencies remain in the hands of the federal government. The Austrian variety of federalism has been called "distributional federalism" as about 90% of all tax revenue are collected at the federal level and then redistributed to the provinces according to the regulations of the Fiscal Adjustment Act (*Finanzausgleichsgesetz*) (Bruneforth et al., forthcoming: 15). In Germany, a similar redistribution mechanism (*Finanzausgleich*) exists to compensate for inequalities in socio-economic conditions between the different *Länder*, but the German redistribution mechanism is based on binding statutory regulations regarding the distribution of tax revenues. By contrast, in Austria, the adjustment is in principle renegotiated every four years between the federal government, the provinces and the municipalities. In the more recent period, the key for distributing resources has not been re-negotiated, but extended from previous years owing to anticipated political struggles in finding a new compromise.

A key characteristic of the Austrian distributional federalism is the disconnect between the responsibility to raise revenues and the ability to spend: the provincial governments were responsible for collecting only 4% of tax revenue in 2014, but their share in expenditures amounted to 22%. Municipal governments collected 9% of revenues, but were responsible for 21% of expenditures (Bruneforth et al., forthcoming: 16). Besides the question about which level of government is responsible for collecting taxes, federalist countries also differ in the extent to which different levels of government are allowed to change tax rates and other regulations. For instance, Swiss cantons or states in the United States can set tax rates according to their own individual needs, which is not the case in Austria or Germany.

Distribution of responsibilities

The distribution of governance and funding responsibilities for the different types of schools is complex. The general academic secondary schools (AHS) and upper secondary vocational schools and colleges (BHS/BMS), which together are also referred to as "federal schools" (*Bundesschulen*), are directly financed by the federal government. The general compulsory schools (APS), which are also referred to as "province schools" (*Landesschulen*), are financed by the individual provinces and the municipalities. However, a significant share of provincial spending originates from the federal government and is transferred according to the regulations of the Fiscal Adjustment Act (*Finanzausgleichsgesetz*). Financial transfers for teachers of general compulsory schools (APS) are earmarked and based on a key related to the numbers of students. As shown in Figure 2.5, this is primarily relevant for the general compulsory schools (APS) and to a certain extent for the part-time vocational schools (BS), which are part of dual apprenticeship training schemes (not to be confused with upper vocational schools and colleges [BMS/BHS], which are financed by the federal government). The federal share in the financing of APS amounts to 71% before transfers, but decreases to 1.4% after transfers to other levels of government have been taken into account. Vice versa, the share of the provinces in spending on APS is merely 6.2% before transfers, but 75.8% afterwards.

Figure 2.5. **Distribution of spending on different school types before and after fiscal transfers, 2012**

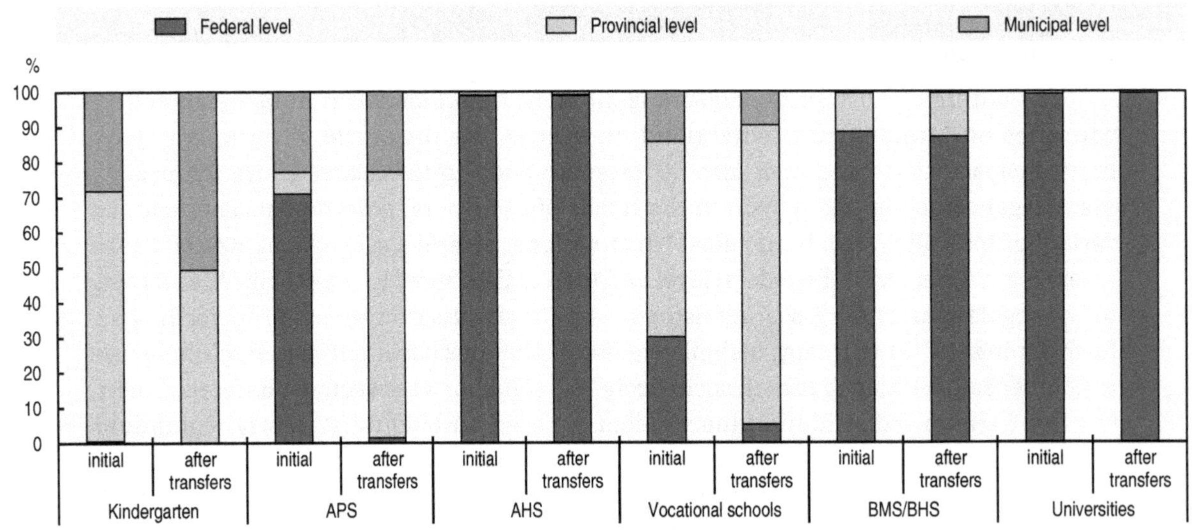

Source: Own calculations based on Bruneforth, M. et al. (forthcoming), *OECD Review of Policies to Improve the Effectiveness of Resource use in Schools: Country Background Report for Austria*, Bundesministerium für Bildung und Frauen, Vienna, p. 58.

In 2013, spending on general compulsory schools, in particular, amounted to EUR 5.137 billion, of which roughly 68% were earmarked transfers from the federal government to the provinces used to pay for teaching personnel at general compulsory schools (and officially counted as province expenditure) (Statistik Austria, 2015a: 84). Municipalities are in charge of financing operating and maintenance costs at general compulsory schools, including costs for administrative personnel, but major repairs and school construction are usually co-financed by the municipal and the provincial governments (Bruneforth et al., forthcoming: 58). In the case of general academic secondary schools and upper secondary vocational schools and colleges, the federal government is responsible for financing teaching and other personnel, maintenance costs and capital investments.

Figure 2.6 depicts the governance of funding flows in Austria. There are two key institutions which are in charge of distributing resources to schools: the school departments of the offices of the provincial governments (*Schulabteilungen in den Ämtern der Landesregierung*) and the provincial school boards (*Landesschulräte*).

The school departments of the provincial governments (referred to as "Land government" in Figure 2.6) are in charge of administering the general compulsory schools (APS), which include both primary and lower secondary schools. The provincial resources originate from a mix of earmarked transfers (for teachers) from the federal level and the general provincial share of federal taxes as explained above. The provinces are responsible for paying the teaching staff as well as remedial language teaching and other specific educational needs. In the case of large capital investments for school construction, costs are often shared between the municipal and the provincial level, although in principle the provision of school infrastructure is a responsibility of municipalities. As mentioned above, municipalities are also responsible for paying non-teaching staff (secretaries, facility managers, etc.) as well as costs for maintenance and teaching material. The Federal Ministry of Families and Youth (*Bundesministerium für Familien und Jugend*) is responsible for financing school textbooks and transportation for students.

The provincial school boards, on the other hand, are by law federal agencies located in the different provinces. They are in charge of distributing funds in the general academic secondary schools (AHS), which span both lower and upper secondary education, as well as upper secondary vocational schools and colleges (BHS/BMS). As can be seen in Figure 2.6, funding for teachers and non-teaching staff (secretaries, facility managers, etc.) as well as operating and maintenance costs originate from the federal level, but are distributed via the provincial school boards (in Figure 2.6, these are referred to as "Regional Education Boards"). Funding for infrastructure investments (building construction and repairs) comes directly from the Federal Ministry of Education and Women's Affairs (BMBF). In 2008, the federal government decided to invest a total of EUR 1.6 billion in school infrastructure (the *Schulerhaltungs- und Schulentwicklungsprogramm, SCHEP-NEU 2008*, BMUKK, 2009). As in the general compulsory sector, the Federal Ministry of Families and Youth is in charge of expenditures on schoolbooks and transport.

Despite the formal separation of responsibilities between the school departments of the provincial governments and the provincial school boards, there are multiple connections between the two types of institutions. The head of the provincial government (*Landeshauptmann/-frau*) is also the president of the provincial school boards (despite the fact that these are formally federal agencies). The day-to-day management of the provincial school boards is delegated to an executive president (*amtsführende/r Präsident/in*) representing the provincial government, but also supervised by a collegiate board (*Kollegium*), which includes both political stakeholders from the provincial level and representatives of teachers and parents. The members of the collegiate board are nominated by the political parties relative to their number of seats in the provincial parliaments. Furthermore, in five out of

Figure 2.6. **Funding streams and responsibilities in the Austrian school system**

Primary and general secondary schools (*Hauptschulen* and Neue *Mittelschulen*)

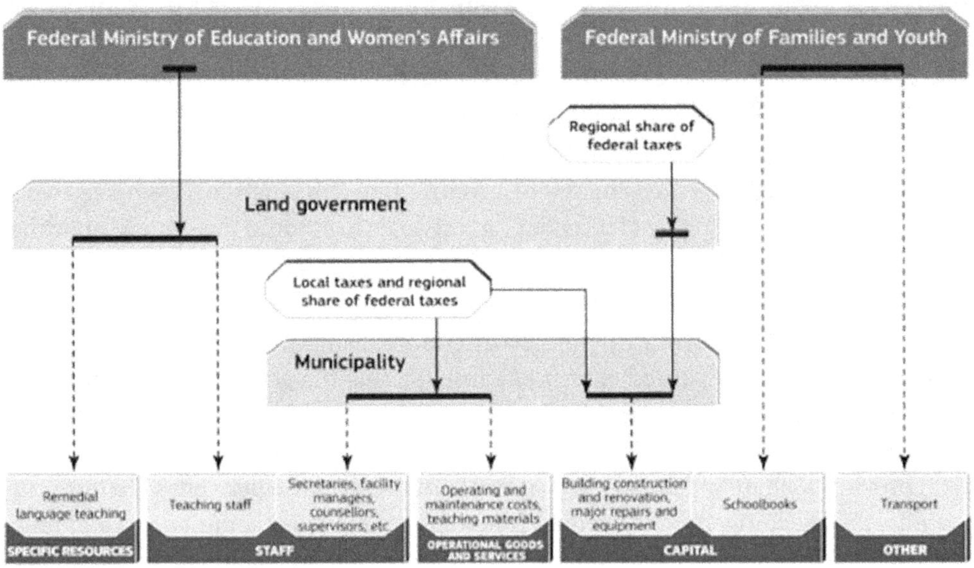

Secondary schools (*allgemeinbildende höhere Schulen*)

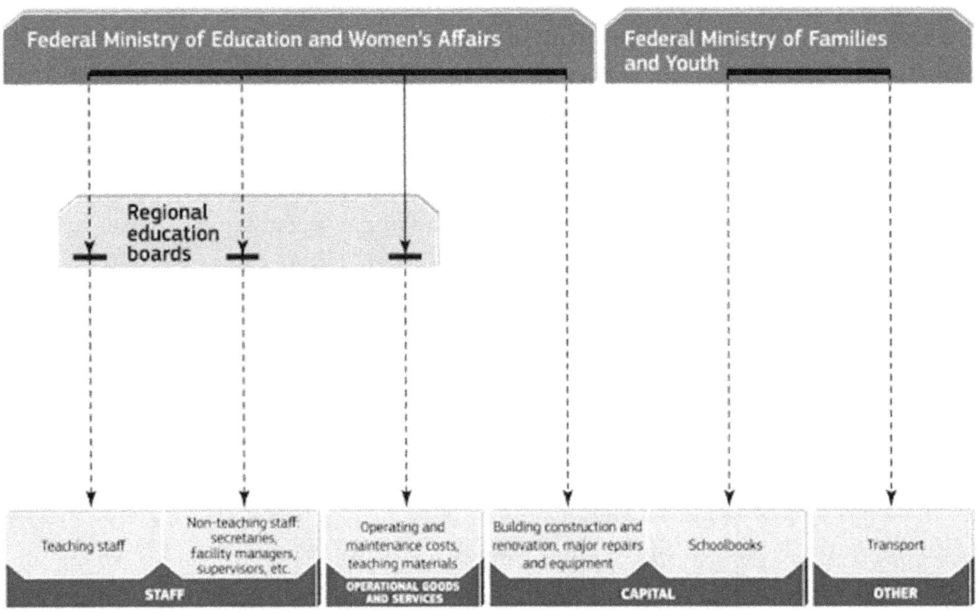

Source: European Commission, EACEA, Eurydice (2014), *Financing Schools in Europe: Mechanisms, Methods and Criteria in Public Funding*, Eurydice Report, Publications Office of the European Union, Luxembourg, pp. 73-74.

nine provinces, the provincial governments have delegated their policy-making and monitoring responsibilities to the provincial school boards in order to partially overcome the split of administrative responsibilities. The underlying statutory regulations, however, have remained unchanged in these cases.

Financial transfers in the general compulsory school sector for teaching personnel from the federal government to the provinces are based on staff plans that are negotiated between the provinces and the Federal Ministries of Education and Women's Affairs (BMBF) and Finance (BMF). 90% of transfer funds for pedagogical staff are regulated simply by student-teacher ratios, adjusted for school type (i.e. 14.5 students per teacher in primary schools, 10 students per teacher in general secondary schools, etc.). The remaining 10% are earmarked for special-needs students (but these funds are capped) and other education priorities such as language education (Bruneforth et al., forthcoming: 71). Even though transfers are based on agreed staff plans, the federal government has no control on the use of funds after the transfer has occurred. Therefore, provincial governments can and do use these funds to pursue individual policy priorities such as supporting small rural schools. This may lead to overspending on the part of the provinces, which is partly compensated by the federal government (see below for a detailed discussion). In the case of the general academic secondary schools and upper secondary vocational schools [BMS/BHS], funds are distributed from the federal ministry via the provincial school boards. Again, funding formulae are mostly based on class size and the number of students enrolled in particular schools. Special needs are taken into account to a limited degree only, and criteria vary across the nine provinces (ibid.: 72).

Governance reforms

In recent years, attempts have been made to reform and streamline this complex governance structure. In 2013, a law on reforming school governance structures was passed (*Schulbehörden-Verwaltungsreformgesetz*). This law abolished the district education boards, which had been in charge of school inspections below the provincial level. The law also created the possibility of establishing management authorities in charge of managing schools in different locations and gave school principals greater responsibilities. In total, the law is believed to have contributed to reducing the number of school inspectors and to widen the geographical areas for which individual inspectors are responsible (Bruneforth et al., forthcoming: 37-38). The Austrian Court of Audit has been critical of the reform due to the limited impact it is expected to have (Rechnungshof, 2013a). In particular, the law does not fundamentally change the dual structure of governance regimes, nor does it change the basic distribution of responsibilities between the federal and provincial levels. There have been a number of other significant reforms, such as the introduction of the New Secondary School (NMS) as a new school type (Chapter 3), the reform of initial teacher education and the reform of the teacher service code (Chapter 4). While these reforms are discussed in more detail in Chapters 3 and 4, their implications for school governance are discussed below.

In 2015, an expert commission with representatives from the federal and provincial governments as well as different federal ministries developed a comprehensive proposal for governance reform (BMBF, 2015), which resulted in a comprehensive reform proposal by the government in November 2015 (BMBF and BMWFW, 2015, see Annex 1.1 in Chapter 1 of this report for details). Among other things, this reform proposal envisions a merger between the provincial school boards and the school departments of the provincial governments by establishing new hybrid education directorates (*Bildungsdirektion*) in each province. In contrast to the current model, the new directorates would be in charge of both the APS and the AHS schools. What is more, the government proposes to strengthen the autonomy of schools while at the same time enhancing quality monitoring and assessment structures at the federal level (see below for a more detailed discussion). Further proposals from other experts and stakeholders point in a similar direction (Lassnigg and Vogtenhuber, 2015;

Schmid, 2015). The November 2015 proposal entails many promising ideas. At the time of drafting the report, however, it remained unclear how many of the reform proposals would be implemented since the political debate was still ongoing.

Resource autonomy at the school level

In general, there is only a limited degree of school autonomy for resource management in the Austrian system (for a discussion of autonomy for pedagogical issues, see further below and Chapter 4). The bulk of public spending is devoted to financing teaching staff, based on staff plans. Individual schools have limited leeway in changing resource allocation within these staff plans. They are also not free to select their own teaching personnel (except for a few pilot projects that give schools a more active role in selecting staff, even though the final decision rests with the responsible agency), as teaching staff is allocated by the provincial school boards or the school departments of the provincial governments (see Chapter 4). There are some differences between the general compulsory schools and the general academic secondary schools with regard to individual schools' autonomy to manage operating costs. Compulsory schools in general do not have individual accounts and, therefore, depend on municipal and provincial governments to finance operating costs and minor capital investments, such as IT or teaching material. General academic secondary schools have limited budgetary autonomy, and they are also allowed to rent out school facilities and keep the revenue in order to reinvest in their school infrastructure.

Figure 2.7 presents some data on the autonomy of schools from the OECD Programme for International Student Assessment (PISA) 2012, which also surveyed school principals about their degree of autonomy regarding decisions about the local school environment. Figure 2.7 presents an index based on principals' responses regarding their autonomy in selecting teachers for hire, dismissing teachers, establishing teachers' starting salaries, determining the teachers' salary increases, formulating the school budget and deciding on budget allocations within the school (OECD, 2013a: 131). As the figure shows, the autonomy of Austrian schools for resource allocation decisions is indeed quite low by international comparison. Within the OECD area, school autonomy in resource allocation was only lower

Figure 2.7. **School autonomy in resource allocation in OECD countries, 2012**

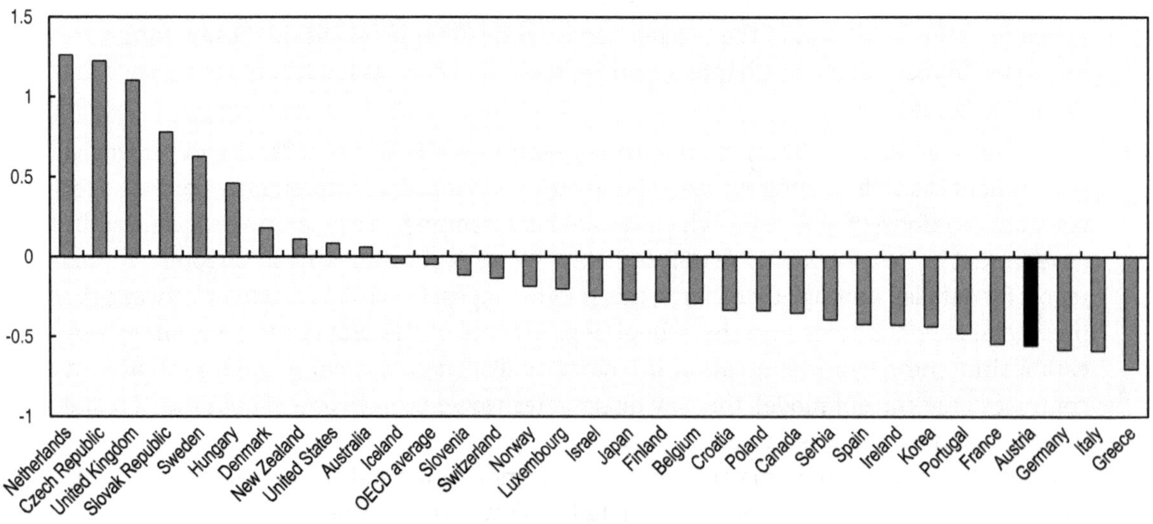

Source: OECD (2013a), *PISA 2012 Results: What Makes Schools Successful (Volume IV): Resources, Policies and Practices, http://dx.doi.org/10.1787/9789264201156-en*, p. 131.

in Germany, Italy and Greece. On the opposite end of the spectrum, schools in the Netherlands, the Czech Republic, the United Kingdom, the Slovak Republic and Sweden have the highest degree of autonomy in resource allocation.

Evaluation and assessment arrangements

In recent years, Austria has further developed its evaluation and assessment arrangements (also see Chapter 1). In particular, in 2009, Austria implemented a set of educational standards as a central reference for teaching, learning and assessment. These standards define expected student learning outcomes for mathematics and German at the end of Year 4, and for mathematics, German and English at the end of Year 8. They provide central guidance regarding the knowledge and skills that students should have acquired at key stages of education. In 2011/12, Austria also introduced national standardised assessments to assess student performance in relation to these standards (German and mathematics in Year 4 and German, English and mathematics in Year 8). These assessments are intended for strictly formative purposes and have no effects on student grades or certification. In addition, diagnostic tools are available for schools and teachers to assess the competencies of their students in Years 3, 6 and 7 ("Informal Competence Measurement"). Various provinces have, furthermore, developed their own additional assessments (Bruneforth et al., 2015; OECD, 2013b; Specht and Sobanski, 2012).

Box 2.1. **Introducing school development planning and self-evaluation: the School Quality in General Education process (SQA)**

In 1999, the Quality in Schools Initiative (*Qualität in Schulen*, QIS) was launched to stimulate schools to develop voluntary school programmes, which should include development targets, measures and evaluation. As part of the project, an Internet platform supplied schools with information and tools for both evaluation and data analysis and provided a forum for presenting the results. In autumn 2012, the Federal Ministry for Education, Arts and Culture (BMUKK) replaced the Q.I.S model with the School Quality in General Education process (*Schulqualität Allgemeinbildung*, SQA) which aims to foster individualisation and competence orientation in teaching and learning. This new key programme for general primary and secondary education built on a similar initiative for vocational education and training (*Qualitätsinitative Berufsbildung*, QIBB) and has strong links to the educational standards which were introduced in 2012. The 2012 reform of the Federal Law on School Inspection (*Bundeschulaufsichtsgesetz*) made school development and self-evaluation compulsory. Based on law, a national quality framework for schools was developed and is being implemented by SQA.

As part of the SQA process, schools establish clearly defined development plans which have to cover several years and need to be updated every other year. The school principal is responsible for the development of the plan together with the teachers. This process includes self-evaluation, whereby the results of education standards provide one important input, but schools are also encouraged to seek external advice on their own initiative. For example, external guidance can be requested from specially trained school development advisors (*Entwicklungsberatung in Schulen*, EBIS). In periodical dialogue, the school principal and the responsible school inspector (in principle every year) conclude binding target and performance agreements for the school (*Ziel und Leistungsvereinbarungen*). These must be in line with the regional, provincial and national SQA targets and country wide budget framework targets. The underlying principle is dialogue based leadership to induce a culture

Box 2.1. Introducing school development planning and self-evaluation: the School Quality in General Education process (SQA) *(cont.)*

of trust, feedback and consensus. External inspection is still possible, but limited to cases where such an intervention appears the necessary intervention tool. The implementation of the SQA process is being supported by 'SQA co-ordinators' in all schools and provinces, training programmes for principals, school inspectors and managerial staff and information and comprehensive support are also available online.

Source: Bruneforth, M. et al. (forthcoming), *OECD Review of Policies to Improve the Effectiveness of Resource use in Schools: Country Background Report for Austria*, Bundesministerium für Bildung und Frauen, Vienna; Specht, W. and F. Sobanski (2012), *OECD Review on Evaluation and Assessment Frameworks for Improving School Outcomes: Country Background Report for Austria*, Bundesministerium für Unterricht, Kunst und Kultur (BMUKK), Vienna, *www.oecd.org/edu/evaluationpolicy*. For further information, see *www.sqa.at* and *www.qibb.at* (accessed 24 March 2016).

In addition, over the last 15 years, Austria has worked to establish and support a culture of school development planning and self-evaluation (Box 2.1). In 1999, the Quality in Schools Initiative (*Qualität in Schulen*, QIS) was launched to stimulate schools to develop voluntary school programmes, which should include development targets, measures and (self-)evaluations. In 2012, the Q.I.S model was replaced by the initiative School Quality in General Education (*Schulqualität Allgemeinbildung*, SQA). This new initiative has strong links with the educational standards and standardised assessments, involves school development planning and self-evaluation, and aims to foster more individualised and competency-oriented teaching and learning. Following the reform of the Federal Law on School Inspection (*Bundeschulaufsichtsgesetz*) in 2012, school development and self-evaluation became compulsory. With the introduction of SQA, the role of the school inspection has changed from traditional school evaluation and supervision to include strong elements of quality management and development.

The school inspection for all schools is a federal responsibility and all school inspectors are employed by the provincial school boards. While all school inspectors are thus federal officials, they focus on different areas of the school system, including different levels of the education system and different school types. As inspectors for provincial schools are appointed by the federal minister based on a proposal of candidates proposed by the collegiate boards of the provincial school boards, they may, in reality, have greater proximity to the provincial authorities and be influenced by political networks in the provinces. The framework for monitoring the quality of the provision of school education thus somewhat mirrors the split of responsibilities between different levels of government and school types. At the national level, the Federal Institute for Educational Research, Innovation and Development of the Austrian School System (*Bundesinstitut für Bildungsforschung, Innovation & Entwicklung des österreichischen Schulwesens*, BIFIE) is responsible for system monitoring and reporting (e.g. managing international comparative studies such as OECD PISA or the IEA's PIRLS). In the context of the implementation of national educational standards a regular census of school performance is undertaken by BIFIE which provides reports on assessment results to all schools as well as higher levels of administration.

Strengths

The Austrian school system benefits from sustained high investment in education

As discussed above, the Austrian school system still benefits from high levels of public investment by international comparison. The recent economic and financial crisis did not yet have a strong impact on the education budget as shown above, although some budget cuts were also implemented in the field of education and there seem to be increasing budgetary pressures (Bruneforth et al., forthcoming: 57). There is still a general political willingness – confirmed in various interviews conducted during the country visit – to spare education from large-scale budget cuts. In fact, the recent reform of the teacher service code adopted in 2013 will likely lead to significant increases in spending in the coming years as it will increase the starting wages of new teachers. Furthermore, the federal government is in the process of implementing a long-term infrastructure and investment programme (*Schulerhaltungs- und Schulentwicklungsprogramm*, SCHEP-NEU 2008) with a total of EUR 1.662 billion (BMUKK, 2009). Thus, in sum, the Austrian school system does not suffer from a lack of resources. Extrapolating from interviews and school visits, the review team gained the impression that the quality of the school infrastructure (with some exceptions, see below) is good or even very good. Teachers overall seem satisfied with their working conditions, which is also confirmed by the results of the OECD Teaching and Learning International Survey (TALIS) 2008 (more on this in Chapter 4). Average class sizes as well as the ratio of students to teaching staff are low by international comparison (OECD, 2015, Tables D2.1 and D2.2).

While Austria has sustained a high investment in schooling over many years, there is concern that this significant resource commitment has not sufficiently been translated into educational improvements as measured through international surveys. In OECD PISA 2012, the mean performance of Austrian students is only slightly above the OECD average and below the level of other European countries such as Belgium, Finland, Germany and Switzerland (OECD, 2014b: 188). Hence, as will be discussed below, it appears that the main resource challenge for Austria may not be the need to expand educational investments, but to use existing resources more effectively and efficiently in order to improve the quality and equity of the system as a whole (Lassnigg et al., 2007; Lassnigg and Vogtenhuber, 2015; Rechnungshof, 2011a; Schmid, 2015). Nevertheless, it needs to be kept in mind that some education reforms (such as the introduction of the new teacher service code and the New Secondary School) require some significant investments up front. The impact of these investments naturally takes time before they can be fully evaluated, and, depending on the results of these reforms, they may require changes and adaptations.

There is a political commitment to direct additional resources to student groups in need

There are a number of ways in which the Austrian approach to school funding seeks to promote equity in education and offset educational disadvantage by directing more resources to student groups at risk of underperformance. The significant investment of public resources in New Secondary Schools (NMS) (see Chapter 3) is an example of this political commitment to allocate additional resources to schools enrolling students with lower initial performance.

The recent transformation of the general secondary schools (HS) into New Secondary Schools (NMS) aims to mitigate the negative side effects of early tracking on educational equality (Petrovic and Svecnik, 2015: 14). The introduction of the NMS has been accompanied by a significant political commitment to increase public spending for this type of school and to fund more cost-intensive pedagogical approaches (see Chapter 4). As a consequence, per student spending in the HS and NMS amounted to EUR 10 672 in 2013 compared to per student spending of EUR 8 906 at the AHS (Statistik Austria, 2015a: 85). In total, the amount of additional yearly educational investment related to the introduction of the NMS is estimated to be between EUR 164 and 250 million.[4] This additional spending is used to introduce new pedagogical methods, in particular team teaching, in order to respond to the heterogeneity of the student population in the NMS (Altrichter et al., 2015). While the existing evidence on the effectiveness of these measures is mixed so far (Eder et al., 2015), available evaluations were limited to the schools in the pilot phase and the NMS as a new school type has not yet been evaluated on a full scale (Chapter 3).

The political commitment to spend more on students with particular needs is also indicated by the joint willingness of the provincial and the federal governments to devote additional teacher resources to the education of special needs students as well as other educational priorities, such as special language courses in German for children with a migration background. However, resources for special needs students are capped. Federal transfers work with the assumption that a maximum of 2.7% of students would have special needs, even if the actual percentage is higher. If the provinces decide to hire more teachers to support students with special needs, these costs are covered first by the federal level and then refunded by the provinces at a reduced rate (more on this below).

Political discussions have been taking place in order to introduce and develop a new and more elaborate funding formula for the distribution of resources across schools, which would take into account differences in the socio-economic background of a schools' student population (Bacher, 2014; Bruneforth, 2014; Lassnigg et al., 2007: 176-177; Kuschej and Schönflug, 2013; Schmid, 2015: 14-15). More specifically, the model initially developed by Bacher for Upper Austria would take into account the educational and occupational background of students' parents, migrant status and whether German is the primary language spoken at home (Bruneforth et al., 2012). Proponents of this approach argue that the current funding arrangement does not sufficiently consider the fact that schools with a large share of students from disadvantaged socio-economic backgrounds need more resources compared to other schools (Bruneforth et al., 2012: 217).[5] The social partners (employers' associations and trade unions) jointly support the introduction of an index-based funding formula that would distribute a certain share of resources according to socio-economic criteria (Sozialpartner Österreich, 2014: 7). During the country visit, the review team gained the impression that political opposition to the introduction of formula-based funding would mainly come from provinces with a large share of rural schools. A needs-based funding formula is likely to result in a redistribution of resources from rural to urban schools (in particular in Vienna), since students from disadvantaged socio-economic backgrounds are concentrated in large cities (see Bacher, 2014; Bruneforth, 2014). Even though additional resources might be desirable, the Bacher proposal would also work by simply redistributing the current amount of resources available to schools in need, which are identified based on the criteria above.

A high degree of centralisation can facilitate educational steering

Compared to other federal countries such as Canada, Germany and Switzerland, legal competencies for education policy are more centralised at the federal level in Austria. For instance, statutory regulations related to the employment conditions and salaries of teachers as well as teacher education are passed as federal laws. The provinces can pass additional legislation to further elaborate and interpret federal legislation in certain areas such as the external organisation of schools, which can create differences in the implementation of policies and legislation across the country. But compared to Germany or Switzerland, where the *Länder* and the cantons respectively have a lot of legal leeway in setting policies, the role of the Austrian provinces is more limited.

From a steering perspective, the centralisation of policy-making competencies at the federal level in Austria is an advantage as it limits the number of potential veto players. This increases the probability that significant reforms can be passed even against vocal opposition from powerful minorities and special interests (see Tsebelis, 2002, for a general theory on veto players). For sure, the provincial governments (in particular the *Landeshauptmänner/-frauen*) play a very important role in the politics of the Austrian republic and, therefore, exert considerable political influence on the policies of the federal government. However, this influence is primarily *political* – though still effective – and to a lesser degree rooted in formal legal competencies of the provinces – at least in comparison to other federal countries.

Some of the recent reforms exemplify that the federal government has been able and willing to make use of its policy-making competencies. Furthermore, these reforms are significant steps towards developing a more comprehensive and unified system, partially overcoming the legacy of a stratified school system. Major milestones in this regard are the enactment of the new teacher service code, which abolishes differences in employment conditions and pay scales between different school types for all teachers newly entering the school system, and the reformed initial teacher education, which aims to harmonise the training standards and curricula for teachers at different education levels rather than school types (Chapter 4). The transformation of the HS into the NMS as mentioned above and elaborated in Chapter 3 is a further example. Even though the effects of this reform are still debated and unclear, and will take time to take effect, there is no doubt that it signifies a significant change of the Austrian school system, which has been promoted from the central level. This stands in stark contrast to Germany, even if one has to bear in mind that some of the German *Länder* are significantly larger in terms of population than Austria as a whole. Similar to Austria, different *Länder* have also promoted reforms of the school structure, often by merging two types of lower secondary schools (the *Hauptschule* and the *Realschule*), while leaving the academic secondary schools (the *Gymnasium*) untouched (see Helbig and Nikolai, 2015 for a comprehensive overview of changes in the school structures of German *Länder*). However, depending on political conditions, these reforms have progressed with varying speed and intensity, resulting in an even more fragmented and complex structure of the overall education system with different school types being developed in the different *Länder*. In comparison, the Austrian reforms of school structure, initial teacher education and the teacher service code have produced (or will produce in the future) a more unified and integrated system across the country.

Besides the comparatively high degree of centralisation of policy-making competencies at the federal level, the Austrian system is also characterised by strong corporatist institutions (Graf et al., 2012). Organised interests such as trade unions, employers' associations, chambers and other stakeholders are continuously and intensively involved in policy making. On the one hand, this can make significant policy innovations less likely as the involvement of many stakeholders also increases the number of potential veto players interested in blocking reforms. On the other hand, the inclusion of different stakeholders in policy formulation can increase the potential for co-operation in the later stages of policy implementation by building trust and legitimacy. This increases the probability that new policies are effectively implemented and, therefore, contribute to lasting and politically sustainable institutional change. Thus, decision-making processes in corporatist and consensus-oriented policies may take longer than in majoritarian democracies, where governments decide without a strong involvement of corporatist actors (Lijphart, 1999). But once a decision has been reached, it will likely lead to lasting policy change. In Austria, furthermore, social partners seem to agree relatively often, as for example on the further development of early childhood education and care.

Despite the advantages discussed above, a high degree of centralisation of competencies also carries some risks. First of all, the extent to which the system as a whole is able to produce policy innovation crucially depends on the willingness and political ability of the top of the hierarchy to promote such innovation. In centralised systems, the top of the hierarchy is more vulnerable to be captured by organised interest groups bent on preventing change. For instance, a case study of education reforms in France shows how teacher unions in this country have gained privileged access to policy making in the ministry and, therefore, block more far-reaching attempts to decentralise the provision and financing of education (Dobbins, 2014). This kind of filtering of policy reform proposals at the top depending on the prevailing political interests can prevent the implementation of more wide-reaching policy innovations. Second, the large complexities of multi-level governance in education might contribute to "information overload" on the part of the central government, contributing to bureaucratic bottlenecks and inefficiencies. The challenge of governing complex education systems often requires "new modes of governance" that combine some form of centralised steering with decentralisation in the provision, financing and administration of education (Wilkoszewski and Sundby, 2014).

In the Austrian case, specific elements of the Austrian governance and decision-making structure reduce the risk of these potential disadvantages. The country's strong tradition of corporatism – despite its own weaknesses in possibly prolonging decision-making processes – ensures a balancing out of the competing interests of relevant stakeholders and precludes one particular set of organised interests from monopolising access to policy making. By establishing a strong linkage between the state and the civil society, corporatism also prevents problems of "information overload" of the central government since intermediary associations such as employers' associations and trade unions supply decision-makers with policy-relevant information (Streeck and Schmitter, 1985).

There is political will to improve the efficiency of the administration and to strengthen outcome-oriented steering

The Austrian government has undertaken first steps towards improving the efficiency of the administration. In 2013, the government abolished the district school boards as an administrative layer between individual schools and the provincial school boards. And in five provinces, administrative structures and responsibilities have been partially unified and consolidated with the merger of the school departments of the provincial governments and the provincial school boards. The government's reform proposal of November 2015 goes even further by proposing to create education directorates (*Bildungsdirektionen*) as hybrid provincial and federal agencies for the country as a whole, similar to the administrative structure already developed in the five provinces.

What is more, Austria has strengthened outcome-oriented modes of steering. On a general level, the budget process has been reformed to include a set of policy targets and associated indicators that provide guidance and enhance the legitimacy and accountability of policy making by defining concrete and measurable goals. On education more specifically, a number of reforms have enhanced the outcome-orientation of the system: the establishment of BIFIE as well as national education standards and – more recently – partially centralised school leaving exams for university entrance qualifications. Furthermore, the actual impact of reforms is now more often scrutinised in scientific evaluations.

Despite this progress, there is still some way to go (see next section). In particular, it is important to make sure that administrative reforms do in fact trigger real change. Based on the interviews conducted during the review visit to Austria, the OECD review team formed the impression that in some instances, old and established administrative routines and practices persisted despite changes in formal structures. For instance, during its field visits, the review team was told that the abolishment of the district school boards sometimes merely amounted to a "change in the door plate" and did not significantly affect the amount of personnel resources devoted to school inspections or their administration. Schmid (2015: 2) confirms this impression arguing that the formal abolishment of the district school in 2013 was an incremental change at best as the former district school inspectors are now simply employed as inspectors for compulsory schools by the provincial school boards. In a similar vein, the Austrian Court of Audit criticised that this reform would only make a "small" contribution instead of being an encompassing reform (Rechnungshof, 2013a: 2). Many of the recent reforms in budgeting and outcome-oriented steering have only been implemented recently and their effect remains to be seen. However, taken together these reforms and reform debates indicate a significant political commitment for improving the efficiency of the governance of education.

Schools (mostly federal ones) have some autonomy over their own budget and in pedagogical matters

By international comparison, Austrian schools have a low degree of autonomy, but there are important exceptions. Austrian schools (as well as individual teachers) have a relatively high degree of autonomy in pedagogical matters, i.e. in choosing preferred teaching methods and in developing new subjects (for more detail, see Chapter 4). In addition, federal schools, in particular, have a certain degree of budgetary autonomy as they are able to rent out school facilities to generate additional discretionary revenue. In contrast to provincial schools, federal schools also have control over their own accounts, i.e. they are given a school budget. As a downside, this freedom might promote inequities between schools, depending on their location (i.e. whether there is a strong demand from associations and other private actors to rent school facilities), the state of their infrastructure, for which they are only partially responsible, and the individual business acumen of the school principal. Furthermore, given the discretionary character of this source of revenue, there is little transparency across schools in how much own revenue is generated and how it is used, even if the extent of these additional revenues is likely to be small and the purpose for which these funds can be used are rather narrowly defined.

As one of its central elements, the November 2015 government proposal on school reform foresees to grant individual schools more autonomy over budgetary, personnel and other matters (BMBF and BMWFW, 2015). As explained in Box 2.2, there is evidence from cross-country studies that expanding school autonomy is likely to have beneficial effects on educational performance, in particular in the Austrian context with the recent establishment of an accountability system based on national education standards and the standardisation of teachers' employment conditions through federal legislation. Such accountability mechanisms are likely to mitigate potential negative side effects of school autonomy as discussed in Box 2.2. A further important element in ensuring a positive impact of school autonomy on education processes and outcomes is to strengthen leadership and management capacity at the school level (for further details, see Chapter 4).

Box 2.2. **Expanding school autonomy: evidence from cross-country studies**

Expanding the autonomy of schools in the management of funding, human resources, curriculum design and other areas has been a major trend across European countries since the 1990s (Eurydice, 2007). International comparative research on school autonomy has shown that school autonomy has some beneficial effects on the average performance of students measured by international assessment programmes such as PISA (Wößmann, 2003; Hanushek et al., 2013; Schlicht-Schmälzle et al., 2011). Wößmann (2003) finds that beneficial effects can be observed in particular when school autonomy in personnel and process (management) decisions is combined with centralised examination and accountability mechanisms such as the ones established recently in Austria. Based on a large-scale analysis of PISA data, Hanushek et al. (2013) add the important caveat that school autonomy only had beneficial effects in relatively wealthy countries, whereas the effects turned out to be negative in poorer countries with less developed institutions. This study indicates that the beneficial effects of the delegation of management responsibilities to the level of schools depend on the schools' institutional capacities to deal with and make use of the expanded room for manoeuvre. Studying the effects of school autonomy on both the quality and equity of education, Schlicht-Schmälzle et al. (2011) confirm a weak positive effect of school autonomy on average performance, but they also find a negative effect on equity. School autonomy also increases the risk of increased stratification between rich and poor schools. Thus, the expansion of school autonomy should be accompanied by mechanisms that prevent this kind of stratification as well as the establishment of comprehensive accountability systems.

Source: Eurydice (2007), *School Autonomy in Europe: Policies and Measures*, Eurydice, Brussels; Hanushek, E.A., S. Link and L. Wößmann (2013), "Does school autonomy make sense everywhere? Panel estimates from PISA", *Journal of Development Economics*, 104(2013), pp. 212-232; Schlicht-Schmälzle, R., J. Teltemann and M. Windzio (2011), "Deregulation of education – What does it matter for efficiency and equality?", *TransState Working Paper*, 157/2011; Wößmann, L. (2003), "Schooling resources, educational institutions and student performance: The international evidence", *Oxford Bulletin of Economics and Statistics*, 65(2), pp. 117-170.

There has been notable progress in monitoring the quality of teaching and learning in Austrian schools

Austria has made important steps towards the development of an evaluation and assessment framework for schooling in the past few years with the introduction of educational standards, national standardised assessments and different diagnostic tools. This signifies a shift of attention from teaching to learning and has the potential to improve both quality and equity in education. As the *OECD Review of Evaluation and Assessment in Education* highlighted, assessment helps focus attention on the learning progress and outcomes of each student and has strong potential to raise achievement and reduce disparities if students are at the centre of the process. Educational standards and standardised assessments can help clarify learning expectations for all schools, motivate teachers and students to work towards high standards, and inform teaching and learning (e.g. through greater differentiation of instruction, greater collaboration among colleagues and better identification of students' learning needs) (OECD, 2013b).

At the same time, the review team noted that schools in Austria do not seem to have shifted to an evaluation culture yet. The review team saw only limited evidence for the systematic and joint analysis and use of student assessment results for improvement, for example, and some teachers stated during school visits that assessments may not provide timely information to influence teaching strategies. Data from OECD PISA 2012 suggest that there is potential in Austrian schools to further capitalise on evaluation and assessment to improve student learning.[6] Evaluation and assessment need to have a strong formative dimension to improve classroom practices and make a difference to student learning and to be useful for teachers and students. Yet, it is also important to hold schools accountable for the performance of their students (OECD, 2013b). This is particularly the case if schools are to be granted greater autonomy (more on this below). In Austria, it was not clear to the OECD review team from its school visits to what extent this was the case for teachers and school principals. Data from OECD PISA 2012 again substantiate these impressions. Only 39.1% of students were in a school whose principal reported that assessments were used to make judgements about teachers' effectiveness (OECD average: 50.4%), and only 58.8% of principals were in a school whose principal reported that achievement data was tracked over time by an administrative authority (OECD average: 72.1%) (OECD, 2013a).

The recent initiatives to embed a culture of school development planning and self-evaluation in the Austrian school system constitute a further strength for quality monitoring in Austria. As Bruneforth et al. (forthcoming) highlight, these developments constitute a true change of paradigm in the Austrian system of school quality development. The schools visited as part of the review visit typically found the SQA a useful process. It seemed to help school principals to reflect and to develop awareness that they can be leaders that provide a vision and strategy for their school. In various schools, it also provided an opportunity for teachers to take on leadership as co-ordinators of the SQA process in their school. Authorities and inspection services in the provincial school board also reported positive experiences in the implementation of SQA so far. The impact of SQA was being evaluated by BIFIE at the time of drafting this report. If this culture change takes further hold in the Austrian education system, it could also provide the basis for greater school autonomy.

Challenges

There are concerns about the efficient use of resources in the school sector

The international comparison of spending data above indicates that general levels of public investment in education in Austria are still relatively high. The school infrastructure is good (Chapter 3), and teachers are generally satisfied with their employment conditions (Chapter 4). In terms of performance, however, Austria merely occupies a mid-field position (Chapter 1). Related to the legacy of a stratified school structure with early tracking there are continued concerns about equity. This, in turn, implies that the main challenge for Austria is not to increase levels of spending as such, but to improve the efficiency of resource use (see also Lassnigg et al., 2007: 151; Lassnigg and Vogtenhuber, 2015: 20-21; Rechnungshof, 2011a: 58; Schmid, 2015 for a similar assessment).

However, there is concern that some of the recent reforms in fact imply quite substantial spending increases. While reforms necessarily take time and may require possible adjustments, it remains, furthermore, somewhat unclear whether these additional investments will pay off or may be subject to budget cuts after all, also considering apparently increasing budget pressures. For instance, considerable resources are and have been invested in decreasing class size, even though the empirical evidence on whether smaller classes are associated with better performance is mixed at best (Bruneforth et al., forthcoming: 117; Lassnigg and Vogtenhuber, 2015, see also Chapter 3 for a more detailed discussion). The introduction of the NMS has been accompanied by significant spending increases and there is still limited evidence on the impact of this policy (Eder et al., 2015; Chapter 3). Some have argued that the expansion of resources related to the introduction of the NMS needs to be accompanied with changes in teaching and learning practices in order to produce significant improvements (Lassnigg and Vogtenhuber, 2015: 25). A further challenge is to keep up the motivation of teachers for implementing these changes in the long term. The scientific evaluation of the NMS has shown weak to medium-strong positive effects of the NMS on educational quality, student support and learning climate, though not necessarily on learning outcomes. The positive effects are strong in those schools that have implemented the NMS concept more rigorously (Eder et al., 2015: 455).[7] Finally, the introduction of new teacher salary structures will likely create further resource pressures in the future. The starting salaries of young teachers under the new scheme will be significantly higher compared to the previous scheme. At the same time, older teachers, who have a right to stick to the old scheme, will receive higher salaries too thanks to the steep age-related wage profile of the previous salary schemes. It is difficult to pinpoint exactly the size of the spending increase, since an expected retirement wave of older teachers will free up some resources. Currently, 42% of teachers are aged 50 years or above, compared to an OECD average of 38% (OECD, 2015: 462) Also, younger teachers under the new scheme are required to teach more hours, which partly compensates for their higher salaries.

Nevertheless, the Austrian school system faces the challenge to continue to provide the resources needed to implement and follow through with the enacted reforms, in particular the introduction of the NMS, so as to reap the expected benefits in terms of improving overall performance and equity of learning outcomes, while avoiding cutbacks in other sensitive parts of the system.

Complex governance arrangements lead to a lack of transparency on resource flows in the system

As discussed above, the governance structure of the Austrian school system is very complex, creating inefficiencies in the use of resources by obfuscating the flow of resources in the system (see also Lassnigg et al., 2007: 150-151). The federal government is the main funder of school education by directly financing the general academic secondary schools and by giving transfers to the provinces. However, current governance arrangements set incentives to over- and misspend as clear lines of accountability are lacking and existing monitoring systems are not yet sufficiently developed. This has also been repeatedly criticised by the Austrian Court of Audit (e.g. Rechnungshof, 2011a: 58-59; Rechnungshof, 2012).

In the compulsory school sector, the federal government has very limited means to control the use and distribution of resources at the provincial level. Teachers in general compulsory schools (*Landeslehrer*) are employed by the provinces according to the agreed staff plans. However, the provinces are free to hire more teachers than foreseen in the staff plan, and the federal government initially covers all costs. Towards the end of the year, the federal government can reclaim the additional costs (*Refundierung*) if actual spending exceeds the level of spending foreseen in the staff plan. In 2013/14, the federal government was entitled to re-claim about EUR 70 million from the provincial governments (Rechnungshof, 2015b: 117). Between 2006 and 2010, the number of positions at general compulsory schools that were not included in the initial budget almost doubled from 1 039 to 2 063 positions (Rechnungshof, 2012: 11). Furthermore, the calculation of reimbursements agreed between the federal and the province governments is based on the low starting salaries, whereas actual expenditures are related to real salaries, which are significantly higher. This arrangement, therefore, allows provinces to hire more teachers and to secure at least a significant share of the additional expenditures from the federal government. This results in an estimated additional spending of EUR 30 million per year by the federal government (Bruneforth et al., forthcoming: 72).

Recent attempts by the federal ministry to change and confine this practice – even though backed by a recommendation to do so from the Austrian Court of Audit (Rechnungshof, 2015d: 116) – were met with strong political opposition from the provincial governments and stakeholders (such as unions and parental associations who opposed cutting back on teaching resources). Reform attempts, therefore, failed. From the perspective of the provinces, in fact, the resources provided through the general transfer scheme may not be sufficient to address all educational needs. This holds, in particular, in more rural provinces with many small schools (Chapter 3). In principle, it is possible to take into account specific education needs in the transfer payments, but these would have to be included in the general transfer scheme of the overall fiscal adjustment arrangements (*Finanzausgleich*). This is one of the reasons for the expansion of the number of earmarked education funding schemes covered in the fiscal adjustment agreements in recent years, contributing to further complexity.

Besides being unable to prevent provinces from hiring additional teachers, the federal government has no direct way of controlling or influencing the actual distribution of compulsory school teachers to individual schools, including the criteria that are applied in the selection and distribution of teachers (Bruneforth et al., forthcoming: 83; Rechnungshof, 2011a, 2012). As indicated by interviews with stakeholders at the provincial level, there seems to be little information sharing between the provinces on this point. In the academic secondary school sector, the degree of control over the distribution of teaching resources to individual schools should be higher since the provincial school boards are federal agencies. De facto, however, the influence of the federal ministry is limited here as well, also because the provincial school boards are connected to provincial politics via the collegiate boards and the heads of the provincial governments.[8] To give some examples, a recent report from the Austrian Court of Audit revealed a significant degree of overspending, even misuse of funds for official cars and representation purposes in the provincial school boards of Upper Austria and Tyrol (Rechnungshof, 2015b: 122). Furthermore, the collegiate boards of the provincial school boards effectively pre-selected the potential candidates for the executive leadership of the board so that the federal ministry only had a limited overview over the field of potential candidates (ibid.: 124). The federal ministry is not able in practice to determine the internal bureaucratic organisation and processes of the provincial school boards despite the fact that these are nominally federal agencies (ibid.: 125). Of course, there are systems in place to monitor the distribution of teachers, but these are rather fragmented and decentralised (more on this below), even if some of the monitoring systems at provincial levels have recently been somewhat harmonised. Both of these problems are addressed in the education reform package of November 2015 (BMBF and BMWFW, 2015), the final implementation of which, was, however, still in progress at the time of drafting this report.

Another example for the lack of transparency resulting from the split of regulatory competencies between the federal and provincial governments is related to the secondment of federal teachers (i.e. those employed in the academic secondary schools) to the New Secondary Schools as part of team teaching. In these schemes, teachers of both school types are supposed to team up in teaching within the New Secondary Schools, particularly in the basic subjects of German, mathematics and English. The salary costs for seconded federal teachers, however, are not included in the budget of the New Secondary Schools, but in those of their home school, which is typically an academic secondary school (Bruneforth et al., forthcoming: 101). This creates significant potential for obfuscation, a lack of transparency in resource use, and, as a result, a potential for misallocation.

In sum, giving authorities at the provincial level the authority to distribute resources across individual schools according to their own preferences has advantages and disadvantages. On the one hand, it can be argued that provincial agencies and offices have a better knowledge of local conditions and needs and are, therefore, better able to direct resources to where they are needed. Hence, there might only be a limited need for the federal government to get involved in the actual distribution of teacher resources. On the other hand, however, the lack of transparency on the use of resources creates mistrust among stakeholders, in particular when one actor – the federal government – is responsible for the financing, whereas the other – the provinces – is in charge of expenditures. This mistrust creates worries about the misuse and waste of resources at different levels of the administration. In addition, existing research on fiscal federalism shows that giving lower levels of government the power to spend without forcing them to raise their own revenues (by granting them autonomy in setting tax rates) sets strong incentives for overspending (Busemeyer, 2008). An example from the Austrian school system is the case of vocational schools, where the responsibility for financing is shared equally between the federal and the provincial governments and, as a consequence, overspending is much less of a problem (Rechnungshof, 2015d: 117).

The ambivalent role of the provincial school boards raises concerns

As a result of the split between federal and provincial schools, the governance and administrative structure of the Austrian school system is overly complex. The overlapping roles between the provincial school boards and the school departments of the provincial governments may fuel conflicts about the distribution and proper management of resources (e.g. in the case of federal teachers being seconded to New Secondary Schools) and prevent a more unified and integrated approach in the governance of the school system (Lassnigg et al., 2007: 171-172; Lassnigg and Vogtenhuber, 2015; Rechnungshof, 2011a; Schmid, 2015). It also leads to the establishment of unnecessary parallel structures in personnel management.

The hybrid character of the provincial school boards as formally federal agencies with connections to provincial politics in many ways enhances complexity further (Schmid, 2015: 3). As mentioned above, the formal head of the provincial school board is the head of the provincial government (*Landeshauptmann/-frau*), who is represented by an executive president (*amtsführende/r Präsident/in*). It is obvious that the collegiate board, which oversees the activities of the provincial school board, has a political function as well, with its members being nominated by the political parties relative to their number of seats in the provincial parliaments. Even though general assessment and aptitude tests have become more important in teacher and school leadership selection in recent years, there is a risk that appointments of teachers and, in particular, school principals is politicised, as was mentioned repeatedly in the review team's interviews (see also Rechnungshof, 2015b, and Chapter 4). The newly proposed education directorates also have a hybrid character and might suffer from similar complexities. However, the advantage of the new system as proposed in the reform package of November 2015 is that there would not be a parallel agency on the provincial level (the school departments of the provincial governments) which creates inefficiencies and duplications (e.g. in the case of teacher remuneration) as is the case now.

The provincial school boards are required to report both to the provincial parliaments and the federal ministry. On the one hand, this double role could help promote co-operation and co-ordination between the different levels of government. On the other hand, it is probably better understood as reflecting a certain lack of trust between the different levels of government. This lack of trust has led actors in the school system to establish and make use of a broad range of checks and balances, which sometimes reduce the flexibility of policy making.

The delegation of responsibilities from the school departments of the provincial governments to the provincial school boards, as is done in five out of nine provinces, promises to reduce the administrative complexity somewhat in the long term.[9] In the short term, however, it has the opposite effect. It increases the diversity of governance and administrative arrangements across provinces, further contributing to fragmentation and a lack of transparency. And despite the delegation of administrative responsibilities, the statutory regulations underpinning the dual structure have remained in place.

Current governance arrangements hinder coherent policies for the lower secondary level

The split in administrative and fiscal responsibilities between federal and provincial schools poses significant problems (Schmid, 2015: 2-3). The split is especially problematic for lower secondary schools, where the curriculum is very similar across school types, but schools are run by different levels of the administration. As long as the split between federal and provincial schools is maintained, a full-scale integration of lower secondary education into a comprehensive system – which however also requires shared political willingness among all stakeholders – seems unlikely. This is problematic as empirical educational research has repeatedly shown that education systems with early tracking of students into separate school types at the lower secondary school level, as is done in Austria, exhibit higher levels of educational inequalities (Hanushek and Wößmann, 2006; Pfeffer, 2008) (see Chapter 3 for a more detailed discussion). The NMS was not introduced in a comprehensively reflected manner in order to deal with the problem of stratification related to early tracking, but it remained a political compromise as the introduction of a fully comprehensive secondary school was not feasible for political reasons (Altrichter et al., 2015: 24). In that sense, it practically replaced the previous general secondary school (HS) and, as mentioned above, the evidence of its effects is mixed so far. Furthermore, a unified system for strategic planning or infrastructure management is lacking, since the federal government holds responsibility for the academic secondary schools and provinces and municipalities do so for general compulsory schools (see Chapter 3 for a more detailed discussion). The government proposal on education reform from November 2015 foresees the possibility of establishing fully comprehensive schools in pilot regions through collaboration between different school types limited to 15% of students and to 15% of schools in this province. This proposal has triggered a significant degree of political controversy since (BMBF and BMWFW, 2015).

There are risks for resource inequalities between municipalities and schools

As mentioned above, municipalities are responsible for financing maintenance and infrastructure costs (the latter generally with support from the provinces) in the general compulsory school sector. They are also responsible for providing additional resources for administrative personnel, janitors, and other support staff for these schools. However, based on the interviews conducted, the OECD review team formed the impression that many general compulsory schools lacked administrative staff support, which resulted in teachers and principals having to take over additional management and secretarial responsibilities. This is the result of municipalities holding the financial responsibilities for administrative staff. Municipalities may, however, have a considerable interest in supporting the maintenance of the school infrastructure (e.g. pay for janitors), but less of an interest for further expenditures that would be necessary to support pedagogical aspects of schools (see Chapter 4 for a more detailed discussion).

As a consequence of the central role of municipal governments in funding infrastructure, maintenance and administrative supportive staff, the wealth of municipalities appears to have an influence on the amount of resources available in schools, as became clear during the school visits conducted as part of the OECD review. While the involvement of provincial governments in large-scale infrastructure investments has a certain equalising effect, there are no general schemes that would equalise the amount of resources across municipalities. In the current arrangements, it is not fully transparent how funds provided by the provinces to the municipalities in addition to the funds provided by the federal level via the Fiscal Adjustment Act are distributed between municipalities. Although no exact data are available, differences in economic well-being between different municipalities (and provinces) seem to be reflected in different levels of educational investment.

Since teaching resources are distributed by the provinces and teachers are paid centrally, inequalities between schools depending on the municipality they are located in are more likely to develop in infrastructure and maintenance spending. In the medium to long term, however, these inequities can spill over and have an impact on teacher quality. Schools with a better infrastructure (including opportunities for all-day schooling and care, which is also partly financed by the municipalities) may be better able to attract high performing teachers and students, in particular when inequalities persist as the autonomy of schools to select their staff is enhanced as proposed by the government (BMBF and BMWFW, 2015).

Besides differences in economic well-being, local governments might also have different degrees of political commitment to supporting their schools. Furthermore, in particular in very small and rural schools, the availability of resources for maintenance and other support might depend on personal (or even political) connections between school leaders and the local administration. On the one hand, this might have certain advantages in the sense that the flexibility that social networks provide can compensate for the formal rigidities of the system. Also, giving municipalities a central role in supporting and financing "their" school could mobilise more resources compared to a situation when school funding entirely depends on central decisions. More importantly, these arrangements introduce a certain element of arbitrariness and unpredictability, which might in the long run contribute to aggravating inequities in resource distribution between municipalities.

There are concerns related to school autonomy

In general, Austrian schools have little financial flexibility (see Chapter 1 as well as BMBF, 2015; Lassnigg and Vogtenhuber, 2015; Schmid, 2015). They cannot save up and transfer funds from one year to the next, let alone take out loans. General compulsory schools, in particular, cannot generate additional income as is possible for academic secondary schools through renting out their facilities, for example. General compulsory schools do not have their own accounts and, therefore, depend entirely on the municipality for support in maintenance and operating costs.

Schools also have very little autonomy in choosing their staff since teacher selection is largely in the hands of the provincial school boards and the school departments of the provincial governments. In the general academic secondary school sector, the model project "Get Your Teacher" introduced in 2014, allows school leaders some influence on the selection of their teachers, but nothing similar has been introduced for the general compulsory school sector yet. As indicated by our interviews, individual school leaders can and sometimes do influence the decision-making processes at the higher level through personal connections with the provincial authorities. This is problematic, however, since it increases the lack of transparency and arbitrariness of decision-making.

The limited degree of autonomy has partly been compensated by the establishment of "pilot" or "model" projects in schools (*Schulversuche*), but at a risk of increasing the degree of fragmentation in the whole system. According to research from the Court of Audit, 50% of Austrian schools undertake some form of pilot project, either by introducing new pedagogical concepts and teaching subjects or by trying out organisational innovations (Rechungshof, 2015c: 231). Many of these "pilot" projects have become institutionalised for a longer time period (up to several decades), which is an obvious contradiction to the original purpose of model projects. The Court of Audit found that the BMBF did not have a complete oversight over all pilot projects and, therefore, also did not know how much was spent on them. Furthermore, there was very little systematic evaluation of the success of the different pilot projects. This example demonstrates both the deficiencies in controlling resource use as well as the negative side effects of a limited degree of school autonomy. Even though pilot projects can be a useful instrument to promote innovations, the extensive use of this instrument in the case of Austria clearly points to serious structural weaknesses in the governance of the system. Schools make use of the instrument of "pilot projects" in order to compensate for the rigidity of formal regulations.

In the current debates about governance reform in Austria, the concept of school autonomy is not well-defined and not all stakeholders appear to be talking about the same aspects of autonomy. In general, autonomy seems to be mostly regarded as an issue related to administrative rather than pedagogical autonomy. However, this may also be a consequence of the fact that the Austrian system actually does allow a rather high degree of teacher autonomy in choosing teaching methods and for schools and teachers to develop new teaching subjects (Chapter 4).

There are also concerns among teachers that increasing school autonomy might strengthen the role of school principals *vis-à-vis* teachers, which is problematic in a context in which policies have not yet been successful in building professional pedagogical leadership. In addition, some school leaders the review team interviewed were rather sceptical of school autonomy in administrative terms, as they feared this would further increase their workload and overburden them with additional tasks. This indicates that strengthening school autonomy would also require a shift in the culture of school leadership. School leaders need to be better qualified and prepared in order to be able to use the full potential of school autonomy, and require sufficient support to fulfil their role and dedicate themselves to their role as pedagogical leaders (e.g. through support staff and teacher leaders) (see Chapter 4).

Information and quality assurance systems are fragmented across provinces and school types

As hinted at above, there are multiple information and quality assurance systems in place, which make a comprehensive approach to monitoring the quality and the performance of the system difficult. First of all, due to split competencies, there are two different systems for monitoring teaching staff in the federal schools and the provincial schools respectively. The monitoring system for federal schools (*Unterrichts-Personalinformationssystem*, UPIS) is different and separated from the system used in provincial schools. The monitoring of teacher resources at the provincial level is set out in the Regulation on Controlling for Provincial Teachers (*Landeslehrer-Controlling-Verordnung*), which contains stipulations on the kind of data to be delivered to the federal government. However, each of the provinces uses different software in order to monitor the use of teacher resources and, based on the interviews conducted, the OECD review team formed the impression that there was little co-ordination across provinces on this point. Furthermore, the controlling software for the use of teacher resources is not systematically connected to the other elements of the quality assurance and monitoring system. For federal schools, it could be expected that controlling processes would be more integrated. The Austrian Court of Audit, however, found in a report from 2011 a large degree of heterogeneity in the organisation of controlling processes across the provincial school boards and a lack of central co-ordination from the federal ministry (Rechnungshof, 2011b: 191-194). The report states that even in federal schools, seven different software programmes were used to administer students.

The BIFIE collects information about students (e.g. their performance in national educational standards, socio-economic and parental background, migration status and language). It also collects data on teachers and resources by means of background questionnaires. Thus, there is a lot of data available in the system. While there is co-operation between different institutions, there is room for deepening the collaboration between the work of BIFIE, the work of Statistics Austria, and the statistical section of the Federal Ministry of Education and Women's Affairs. What is missing is an institutional broker or agency which would better connect and analyse the different streams of data. There are also concerns about the difficulty of sharing information about students' transitions from one school type to another, in particular, but not only, at the transition from early childhood education to primary schools. In a follow-up to its 2011 report, the Court of Audit welcomes the recent changes in the controlling system, in particular the introduction of the SQA process and the installation of a unified IT structure in federal schools (Rechnungshof, 2014: 339-341). Despite these advances, the Court still sees many deficiencies such as the lack of written performance agreements between the ministry and its subsidiary agencies.

Thus, there is a clear and ongoing need for developing one integrated system that brings together data on teachers, students and learning outcomes. This is necessary in order to get a measure of the effectiveness of the use of resources, i.e. an indicator of how resource use is related to output and performance and whether particular groups of students are disadvantaged. In general, the culture of transparency, evaluation and accountability needs to be further developed in Austria, also to promote the better use of all the information that is already available for decision-making at different levels of the system and by different stakeholders, including schools.

The school inspectorate could pay a stronger role in improving the quality of education

For all schools, the school inspection is under the responsibility of the federal authorities and organised by province. School inspectors are federal officials located in the provincial school boards, but, as mentioned above, there are different school inspection regimes for the general compulsory schools, on the one hand, and the academic secondary schools, on the other, and school inspectors are appointed for these specific school types. There is only one "layer" of provincial school inspectors (*Landesschulinspektor*) for academic secondary schools. In the case of general compulsory schools, there is an additional layer of inspectors (inspectors for compulsory schools, *Pflichtschulinspektoren*) below the level of the provincial school inspectors. This is related to the legacy of the former district school boards (abolished in 2013). Inspectors for compulsory education are usually located in so called "education regions" which replaced the former district-level inspectorates and are organised differently depending on the provincial school board. Also, even though resources for the school inspection are limited overall, the number of schools per inspector is much larger in the compulsory school sector compared to the academic secondary school sector (Eurydice, 2015).

According to the review team's interview partners, resources for school inspections are too few to allow for regular school visits. One inspector might be responsible for as many as 100 schools. Hence, school visits only occur when there are concrete reasons for inspection. Therefore, the school inspectorate mainly provides external advice and consulting services in case of concrete problems. It does not conduct thematic reviews on specific themes or aggregate the information collected from individual schools to conduct system-wide analyses as is done in various other countries. As the *OECD Review on Evaluation and Assessment Frameworks* pointed out, external school evaluation mechanisms have the possibility to collect a rich set of evidence on different qualitative aspects of schooling (OECD, 2013b). In Austria, qualitative information collected by the inspectorate (e.g. during the SQA process) is not well connected to quantitative data provided by Statistics Austria, the Ministry and the BIFIE. Thus, a systematic and comprehensive analysis of the relative performance of individual schools is difficult (see also Schmid, 2015: 5). Furthermore, there are no systematic mechanisms in place that would trigger certain policy reactions depending on the findings from quality monitoring systems (e.g. giving additional resources to low-performing schools). In general, the school inspectorate could play a stronger role in improving the quality of the Austrian school system (see also Rechnungshof, 2011a: 59).

Policy recommendations

Monitor resource flows and make sure resources are used efficiently

A prime objective of the reform of education governance and financing should be to enhance the transparency of resource flows in the system. The division of labour between the federal and the provincial governments in the financing of school education sets problematic incentives. The current funding arrangements allow province governments to spend more than budgetary planning actually allows for, with little consequences. Decentralisation of spending powers to provincial and municipal levels, as it currently exists in Austria, needs to be combined with adequate accountability and reporting mechanisms. In the current system, this is achieved only partially. In particular, there is insufficient reporting at the provincial level on the use of federal resources, also in relation to expected performance.

On the other hand, the province governments feel constrained by the existing regulations. From the perspective of the provinces, the current fiscal arrangements grant them little flexibility in devoting more resources to particular priorities as identified by local stakeholders since all earmarked funding for specific educational needs has to be formally agreed upon in the fiscal adjustment negotiations. The factor that could most likely contribute to breaking this vicious circle is the development of mutual trust between the federal and the provincial governments, allowing the provinces more flexibility in resource use while establishing improved accountability and controlling instruments at the same time, which would enhance the transparency of resource flows.

One concrete instrument to achieve this is to bring together the different information systems and merge them into an integrated system that links data on students, teachers, schools and resource flows. The current system is fragmented between different departments and institutions (the Ministry of Education and Women's Affairs, Statistics Austria and BIFIE), different levels of government (federal and provincial) and different school types. An integrated system would overcome this kind of fragmentation by connecting information on educational performance and students (currently collected by BIFIE) with data on the use of teacher resources (currently monitored by two different systems in federal and provincial schools, of which the latter is further hampered by the fact that each province uses a different software) as well as the rich qualitative information available through the quality assurance system (SQA for general schools, QIBB for vocational schools). Such an integrated system would allow drawing conclusions about the effective use of resources and, therefore, the relative performance of particular schools, which in turn facilitates more targeted policy reactions (see also Rechnungshof, 2011a: 58-60, 170-171). As a recent *OECD Review on Evaluation and Assessment Frameworks* highlighted, making the best use of the evidence generated by different evaluation and assessment activities depends to a large extent on the development of a coherent information management system. This should include the collection of data on students, teachers, schools and their performance over time and make adequate arrangements for sharing this information with multiple stakeholders to meet different information needs. Bringing together the different data in one single platform would also help to facilitate the analysis of this information for improvement (e.g. by facilitating independent research and analytical studies). The development of a brokerage agency, or equipping an existing institution with this function (e.g. BIFIE), constitutes one option to facilitate the process of sharing information and data. Such an agency could also help to promote the use of data, evidence, research and evaluations for decision-making (OECD, 2013b; OECD, 2007).

The unification and centralisation of the framework conditions for the school system would further support the transparency of resource flows. Policy makers in Austria have already taken important steps in this regard in recent years, e.g. with the introduction of national education standards, the reform of the teacher service code, the reform of initial teacher education and the establishment of systematic education monitoring. These initiatives have to be sustained and further developed. At the same time, responsibilities for the implementation of these measures need to be further clarified at the provincial level and further possibilities for expanding school autonomy should be explored (see below). The administratively complex system of dedicated allowances for school-level staff, which lacks transparency, also needs to be reconsidered (Chapter 4).

Efficiency of resource use can also be promoted by establishing systematic processes of evidence-based policy evaluation. The recent introduction of goal-oriented budgeting as a general principle in fiscal policy is already a significant step in this direction. For the most part, however, the institutions and processes that could be used to monitor the effectiveness of resource use are weakly developed. A negative example for this is the wide-spread use of school pilot projects which are not systematically evaluated.

Explore different ways to introduce needs-based formula funding

Funding should be distributed according to clearly defined criteria (OECD, 2012: 75). In the system currently in place in Austria, the bulk of funding is distributed according to student numbers. A significant (and growing) share of funding is devoted to particular educational needs, but total funding for these needs is capped at a relatively low level and needs to be (re-)negotiated in the complex fiscal adjustment arrangements (*Finanzausgleich*). Being confronted with the relative rigidity of the existing financing arrangements, provincial and local governments have found ways to work around the confines of the existing system to a certain extent. The provincial governments' overspending on teacher resources and partial refunding from the federal government is an example of such a "workaround". Ultimately, these mechanisms hurt the principle of transparency of resource flows and contribute to the development of mistrust between different levels of government.

To address these challenges, policy makers should explore different possibilities to introduce more elaborate needs-based formula funding for the distribution of teaching and other resources. A previous OECD study describes the introduction of needs-based funding formulae as a highly efficient and transparent method of funding schools when tackling inequities in the provision of education (OECD, 2012: 72; see also Fazekas, 2013). There are a number of examples from other countries where formula-based funding has been introduced successfully, e.g. in Hamburg, the Netherlands, the Swiss cantons of Berne and Zurich as well as in Toronto (Canada) (see Box 2.3 for details).

In the Austrian context, a number of proposals for the design and implementation of index-based formula funding have already been developed and are being discussed (Bacher, 2014; Bruneforth, 2014; Kuschej and Schönpflug, 2014). Common to these proposals is the idea that the funding formula according to which resources are distributed between schools should contain elements in addition to simple student numbers that take into account the characteristics of the student population, e.g. by considering the socio-economic composition of the local population in terms of education and income, the share of children with a migration background or the share of non-German-speaking children (for overviews see Fazekas, 2013; Kuschej and Schönflug, 2013). In principle, the funding formula can be extended to include other elements, e.g. a factor that would give rural schools additional funding if this is seen as a political priority. As the review by Fazekas (2013: 16-18) shows the choice of variables included in the funding formula is crucial with regard to its impact on equity of funding. However, the degree of redistribution and equalisation between different types of schools (rural vs. urban, socially disadvantaged

Box 2.3. The international debate on formula-based funding

In its study on equity and quality in education, the OECD recommended – among other things – the introduction of "formula funding using a needs-based group of variables" (OECD 2012: 75) as the most effective and transparent way of tackling inequalities in the provision of resources between schools with different student populations. Additional resources provided through formula-based funding should be used to "provide further help for pupils such as additional teaching time, specialised learning material and in some cases smaller classes" (ibid.: 75). The concrete set of variables to be used in the funding formula depends on the availability of data in a particular country as well as political priorities. There are some examples from other countries where needs-based funding formula have been introduced.

The Netherlands have introduced formula-based funding for both primary and secondary education. The funding formula contains two elements: the first provides extra funding for students whose parents have a weak educational background, the second is dependent on the socio-economic profile of a particular school community. Thus, the index has a micro- as well as a macro-level component. This is an example of an encompassing index-based system, although the share of index-based funding as percentage of total education funding is low (about 4.5%, see Kuschej and Schönflug 2013: 43).

Toronto (Canada) applies a "Learning Opportunities Index" (LOI) to govern the distribution of resources across schools in the municipal school district. The funding needs of schools are evaluated based on six variables: 1. Median income in the students' residential area; 2. the share of low-income families in a particular area; 3. the share of families receiving social assistance; 4. the share of adults without high school diploma; 5. the share of adults with a university degree; and 6. the share of single parents. Students are matched to neighbourhoods based on postal codes. Similar to the Netherlands, the share of resources distributed according to the needs-based formula only amounts to about 5% of total education spending.

The Swiss canton of Zurich uses a social index to distribute teaching resources across schools since 2004/05. The social index contains three elements based on official statistics: first, the share of foreigners (not counting foreigners from Austria, Germany and Liechtenstein), the share of children receiving social assistance, the share of tax payers with a low income. Different from the other indices, this index does not provide additional resources for disadvantaged students, but uses the index to distribute regular teaching resources.

Source: Fazekas, M. (2012), "School Funding Formulas: Review of Main Characteristics and Impacts", *OECD Education Working Papers*, No. 74, *http://dx.doi.org/10.1787/5k993xw27cd3-en*; Forum Wien Welt Offen (2014), *Themendossier Sozialindizierte Stärkung von Bildungsstandorten: Österreichische Beiträge & Positionen sowie internationale Modelle [Thematic Dossier Social-index-based Improvement of Schools: Austrian Contributions and Positions as well as International Models]*, *http://wienweltoffen.at/wp-content/uploads/2014/09/Dossier_ Sozialindizierung.pdf*; Kuschej, H. and K. Schönpflug (2013), *Indikatoren bedarfsorientierter Mittelverteilung im österreichischen Pflichtschulwesen: Vorläufiger Endbericht, Studie im Auftrag der Kammer für Arbeiter und Angestellte für Wien [Indicators for Needs-based Resource Distribution in the Austrian Compulsory School Sector: Preliminary Final Report, Study Commissioned by the Chamber of Labour Vienna]*, Institute for Advanced Studies, Vienna; OECD (2012), *Equity and Quality in Education: Supporting Disadvantaged Students and Schools*, *http://dx.doi.org/10.1787/9789264130852-en*.

vs. privileged, etc.) is fundamentally a political and societal discussion and cannot be decided by scientific criteria. Furthermore, there is a trade-off between "transparency-simplicity and sensitivity to local conditions-complexity" (ibid.: 21). Simple funding formulae, which include only few indicators, are transparent and easy to administer, but do not necessarily pay sufficient attention to the peculiarities of local needs.

Furthermore, a shift towards a formula-based funding system would also require a decision on the share of school funding that comes from formula-based funding relative to basic funding. Obviously, a significant share of the total funding needs to be based on student numbers in order to ensure the stability of basic funding from year to year, topped up by additional funding as determined by needs-based funding formulae. Bacher (2014) proposed that individual schools should be able to decide freely on how to spend this additional funding, while local stakeholders such as parents, teachers, local governments and students should have a greater say on how these funds should be spent. This would strengthen the connection between local schools and communities, in particular parents, and it would disburden higher levels of governments from administrative oversight.

In general, formula-based funding has the advantage that the criteria used to distribute funds across schools are made explicit and, therefore, subject to political scrutiny (Fazekas, 2013; OECD 2012: 72). This is a significant improvement in terms of transparency compared to a regime with more implicit than explicit criteria for distribution. As part of the discussion about funding formulae, current differences in spending per student across provinces, different geographical areas and school types should be made transparent as well. Transparency is a central precondition for informed debate and priority-setting.

Align financing and spending responsibilities in one hand

A major challenge in the current governance and funding arrangements is the division of responsibilities between the federal and the provincial governments in financing schools (Lassnigg et al., 2007: 174-175; Lassnigg and Vogtenhuber 2015; Rechnungshof, 2011a; Schmid, 2015). This is particularly problematic in the case of lower secondary education, where all school types actually follow the same curriculum and – as part of the New Secondary School – are encouraged to co-operate with each other. The complex administrative dual structure of provincial school boards and provincial school departments creates inefficiencies in the management of resources, contributes to obfuscating funding flows and nourishes a culture of mistrust and struggles over competencies.

Ideally, the governance and funding for all levels of education should be placed under the same regulatory regime, which would imply ending the formal divide between federal and provincial schools (as well as between federal and provincial teachers) (see also Rechnungshof, 2011a: 60-61). The dual structure of provincial school boards and school departments in the provincial governments should be transformed into a unitary structure, which will, out of necessity, have a hybrid character with shared responsibilities. While the federal government has the formal competencies to pass major legislation in education policy (with the provinces being limited to interpretive regulation), there is a need for regional flexibility in the implementation of federal laws. In this context, the expert commission on school reform (BMBF, 2015: 20-22) proposed to create a new type of education directorate (*Bildungsdirektion*) (see Schmid, 2015: 19ff. for a similar proposal). These directorates would be directly responsible to the heads of provincial governments and indirectly responsible to the federal government. Thus, they would also be a hybrid organisation, similar to the current provincial school boards. These proposals have largely been included in the government reform package of November 2015 (BMBF and BMWFW, 2015). Given the complex and hybrid nature of the education directorates, there is still a certain danger of administrative inefficiencies and politicisation, and a risk that the new structure fails to effect real change. However, there would be only one agency (instead of two) in charge of both federal and compulsory schools and teachers in each province which would be a significant advantage of the new system compared to the current one.

In principle, it is less important whether the newly created institutions are formally provincial or federal agencies, which is ultimately a political decision. Some argue clearly in favour of putting the federal government in charge of the overall governance system (Lassnigg et al., 2007: 176; Schmid, 2015). The proposals of the expert commission on administrative school reform also pointed in this direction (BMBF, 2015: 17). However, given the legacy of Austria's school system, it will always have a partially hybrid character. The abolition of the traditional provincial school departments would go along with the reform of the provincial school boards, which are then put in charge of both federal and provincial schools. These new education directorates would still be federal agencies, but would incorporate personnel and political leadership from the provincial level, similar to the provincial school boards before. The most important point is that a unitary governance structure is created, which is able to overcome the formal division between federal and provincial schools, which hinders integrated and strategic policy making, especially at the lower secondary school level. Employment conditions as well as educational curricula should be governed by the same regulatory regime independent of level of education and school type. Absent any new legal reforms, there will be at least three such regimes in the coming years, because the new teacher service code will take a considerable amount of time to be implemented. The new education directorates should be responsible for teacher recruitment, while giving schools some autonomy in choosing their personnel (see below, and also Chapter 4), as is also proposed in the government's reform package of November 2015 (BMBF and BMWFW, 2015). This would help align financing and spending responsibilities through involvement of the federal level in the joint allocation of all teacher resources in the new institutions.

To increase transparency and effectiveness of funding flows, all teachers should be employed by the same employer (e.g. the new education directorates) according to the same standards. The recent reforms of initial teacher education and the teacher service code have already set important legal preconditions in this regard. The distribution of teaching (and other) resources should be based on funding formulae, which take into account additional factors besides student enrolment such as socio-economic need or – if politically desired – topography (see above and Chapter 3). The distribution of resources across different schools needs be made more transparent. All funding for teachers should be provided directly by the federal government via the new education directorates. The complex transfer arrangement of teacher funding through provincial administrations would then become unnecessary.

Municipalities and provincial governments could continue to be involved in financing maintenance costs and infrastructure investments, but to facilitate strategic planning for each educational level this involvement should not depend on school type. One option could be to ensure that municipal governments are more strongly involved in the financing of primary schools, the provinces in lower secondary education and the federal government in upper secondary education. This option has the advantage of maintaining the strong connection between municipalities and "their" primary schools, often accompanied by the believe of municipal leaders that maintaining primary schools would have a positive influence on the demographic development of a local community. As became obvious during the visit of the OECD team, primary schools in rural areas occupy a central place in local communities as meeting places for students, parents and all kinds of associations. Municipal governments might be more engaged in mobilising fiscal and other resources for schools when they still have a formal role to play in their funding compared to a situation when all funding decisions are made at a higher level of government. However, if municipalities continue to play a strong role in the provision and financing of education, it would be important to establish some kind of fiscal equalisation scheme on the provincial level (e.g. an investment fund) and to make the distribution of provincial funds to municipalities more transparent to prevent fiscally weaker municipalities from falling behind.

Alternatively, the federal government could devolve *all* funding responsibilities for infrastructure and maintenance to the provinces and concentrate on teacher funding only. In this new division of labour between the provincial and the federal governments, both provincial and the federal governments would continue to be involved in the funding of schools, but the former would be in charge of all infrastructure and maintenance expenditures, whereas the latter would be responsible for financing and allocating all teacher resources. While the funding and organisation of the school offer and infrastructure would require co-ordination between the different provinces, the division of labour would be better defined compared to the current situation in which both levels do a little bit of both, depending on the school type. Given the history of political struggles between the federal and the provincial governments, any future arrangement will most likely have to be a political compromise in the sense that both levels will have to be involved to a significant degree, i.e. the whole-sale delegation of funding for both teachers and infrastructure to either the federal or the provincial government will be politically difficult. Given this state of affairs, a clear division of labour, e.g. putting provincial governments in charge of all investments and maintenance and the federal government in charge of the funding and allocation of all teachers, could be a feasible compromise.

Rebalance funding across different types of school staff

The overarching goal should be to bring more consistency and transparency to the funding of staff. If a unified system of teacher funding along the lines sketched out above should not be feasible and the current system of federal and provincial teachers is maintained, some of the unintended incentives that this system produces should be corrected. For one, if the system of provincial refunds for overspending on teachers (*Refundierung*) is maintained, the refunding of teacher costs to the federal government should be based on actual salary costs rather than nominally low salaries. Alternatively, it would be possible to introduce an equal split between the federal and provincial governments in funding teachers for all general compulsory schools as is done in the case of vocational schools, where no or very little overspending occurs (Rechnungshof, 2015d: 117). This is likely to reduce incentives for overspending. Ideally, however, as discussed above, the responsibility for financing and allocating all teachers should be in one hand through the new education directorates, independent of the school type or level of education.

A related problem, which is also discussed in Chapter 4, is that, in the current system, the responsibility for hiring teachers and school leaders, on the one hand, and administrative staff, on the other, is fragmented between the municipal, the provincial and the federal level. The availability of administrative staff appears inadequate as teachers and school leaders have to take on many administrative responsibilities in addition to their regular teaching load. In some cases, these administrative responsibilities are counted towards fulfilling their teaching requirements. In other cases they are entirely voluntary. In principle, administrative staff should be hired and employed by the same institutional entity that is in charge of hiring teachers. This would help prevent shortages of such staff in schools and avoid inequities in the distribution of personnel resources, which are too dependent on local fiscal and political conditions in the current system (in the sector of compulsory schools).

It is crucial to ensure that schools are provided with adequate administrative staff so that school leaders and teachers can focus on improving teaching and learning. Schools in the academic secondary sector seem to receive more dedicated funding for administrative support. In the general compulsory schools, the local and provincial governments would need to provide these additional resources, which leads to a lack of administrative staff as well as an unequal distribution of personnel. Policy makers should strive to harmonise and equalise the funding conditions for administrative staff across school types and levels of education. It would be worthwhile to consider the introduction of minimum regulations on administrative staff and to centralise the responsibility for recruitment of administrative staff to the same level as teacher recruitment (e.g. in the hands of the new education directorates).

Besides administrative staff, there is a clear need to increase the availability of professionals who can support schools in their work with young people, i.e. social pedagogues, psychologists and social workers. In line with changing educational needs, family patterns and increasing diversity and heterogeneity in schools and within classes, these professionals play an important role in supporting the teaching staff. The current need to integrate a large number of young refugees and asylum seekers into the education system might aggravate the current shortcomings further in the near future. Hence, policy makers should review the possibilities to create more positions for these types of professionals working in schools, even if it would imply decreasing the number of regular teachers (see Chapter 4). It will be important to ensure that the kind of professionals that are made available meet schools' needs and that schools have some level of influence over such allocation decisions. Schools that need such professionals the most should be given priority in allocation decisions. Furthermore, schools can and should be encouraged to reach out to and collaborate with relevant agencies outside of schools.

Review the role of municipalities in education

Municipalities play an important role in providing for and financing general compulsory schools, and primary schools, in particular. These schools, in turn, can be a focal point for local activities and associations. Nevertheless, the current arrangement of over 2 000 municipalities each managing their own schools is very resource-intensive, as these schools often operate below their optimal size. For a more detailed discussion regarding the organisation of the school offer, see Chapter 3. With regard to governance and funding of education, a consolidation of the number of small schools could be achieved by supporting the establishment of larger associations of municipalities (*Gemeindeverbünde*), which are jointly responsible for the management and financing of a particular school. This would also imply larger catchment areas, in particular for lower secondary education. Associations of municipalities would help to simplify the complex system of transfers between municipalities when children from one municipality choose to attend school in a different one. This would be an important precondition for successfully increasing school autonomy. Very small schools might be overburdened with the management requirements associated with greater school autonomy. But if associations of municipalities (or schools) are in charge of resource management instead of individual schools, even very small schools can benefit from greater autonomy.

A consolidation of the local school landscape can and should go along with a redefinition of the role of municipalities as school providers. Such a consolidation frees up resources, which can be reinvested in newly expanding sectors of the schooling system, i.e. early childhood education and care as well as afternoon care and all-day schooling, which are increasingly demanded by parents.

Enhance school autonomy while creating the conditions for autonomous schools to perform well and while taking steps to prevent inequalities from emerging

It is important to ensure that schools become learning-centred organisations, which take responsibility for both improving educational results and reducing the impact of socio-economic background on learning. Enhancing the autonomy of schools can be an important tool that helps to achieve both goals provided that the right conditions are in place (Lassnigg et al., 2007: 172; Hanushek and Wößmann, 2010; Hanushek et al., 2013; see also BMBF, 2015; Rechnungshof, 2011a: 61-62; Schmid, 2015). The effect of delegating more autonomy to schools depends on schools' ability to make use of this autonomy in a constructive way and thus requires a strengthening of school leadership and management structures (see Chapter 4). Furthermore, autonomous schools need to be embedded in a comprehensive regulatory and institutional framework in order to prevent further inequalities between schools.

By international comparison, Austrian schools have little autonomy, particularly for resource management. A reform of school governance should give schools more autonomy in selecting their personnel, i.e. teachers. Being able to select teachers according to particular criteria (e.g. teaching methods, extracurricular activities, etc.) would allow schools to more effectively shape their profiles. One option would be to allow schools to select part of their teaching force while institutions above the school level (i.e. provincial authorities) remain in charge of recruiting and assigning the remaining part of the teaching force in order to ensure that common standards are applied and that particular schools are not systematically disadvantaged. In Germany, the use of such a mixed system is quite common.[10] Schools are allowed to advertise for positions at their own institutions in databases managed by the *Land* government. This is only possible for a certain share of the open positions in a given year, often related to particularly urgent needs or special profiles of the school. The remainder of the positions is assigned by bureaucratic agencies above the school level, similar to Austria. Applicants for teaching positions can, therefore, choose between applying directly for open positions at schools and submitting an application to the general large pool of applicants. Giving schools the full autonomy in hiring teachers carries the risk of amplifying differences between schools, since the more attractive schools will be able to attract the better teachers. Vice versa, not allowing schools any influence on the selection of teaching personnel can lead to misallocations and frustrations and prevent schools from developing a particular profile. Schools should also receive more autonomy in financial matters. Allowing the general compulsory schools a degree of financial autonomy similar to the academic secondary schools would be an important first step in mitigating inequalities between different school types. General compulsory schools would, then, be able to tap into own sources of revenue as well as to maintain their own accounts and operational budgets.

Increased school autonomy needs to be accompanied by effective accountability mechanisms (Lassnigg et al., 2007: 172-173; Hanushek and Wößmann, 2010: 26-27; Hanushek et al., 2013; Schmid, 2015: 15). The quality assurance framework (SQA) established in 2011 is a good starting point in that respect, but if school autonomy increases, the role of external school evaluation – in a reformed school inspectorate – would also need to be strengthened. In the OECD PISA 2012 study, only 20.3% of 15-year-olds were in a school whose principal reported that their school had participated in an external evaluation (OECD average: 63.2%) (OECD, 2013a, Table IV.4.32). Information generated through the quality assurance system needs to be systematically connected with resource management decisions and accompany the process of giving schools greater autonomy. This would allow concentrating additional support to schools that are identified as underperforming in the quality monitoring system or to schools struggling with their new autonomy. The proposal of the expert commission on school governance reform envisioned the establishment of a central quality assurance office as well as a joint political group and a joint steering group of experts (BMBF, 2015: 19, 23). These three institutions would jointly supervise and accompany the gradual transformation of existing into autonomous schools. Depending on the concrete design of monitoring processes and institutions, in particular the central quality assurance office, this could be one feasible way of enhancing the autonomy of Austria's schools.

Besides accountability, there are other factors that need to go along with school autonomy. First of all, expanding school autonomy requires a redistribution of resources, in particular higher investment in administrative personnel and school leadership capacity (see Chapter 4 for a more detailed discussion). For obvious reasons, a critical school size is also necessary in order for schools to be able to effectively use their autonomy. If schools are too small, delegating more responsibilities to the school level may simply overwhelm school leaders with additional work tasks. Hence, considerations about increasing school autonomy should go together with discussions about increasing the average school size (more on this in Chapter 3). As an alternative to increasing school size, different kinds of providers (*Träger* or *Schulerhalter*) could be put in charge of schools: For instance, one provider (such as a regional education centre, a larger municipality or an association of local governments) could be put in charge of administering several schools (see above).

Notes

1. In contrast to Germany, the spending of private businesses on vocational training is not included in the official education budget.
2. The methodology changed from *Education at a Glance 2014* to *Education at a Glance 2015*. While spending on educational institutions covered all levels of education for *Education at a Glance 2014* including pre-primary education and undistributed programmes based on ISCED-97, *Education at a Glance 2015* covers primary to tertiary education only, excluding pre-primary education and undistributed programmes, based on ISCED 2011.
3. Actual salaries for teachers aged 25-64 refer to the annual average earnings received by full-time teachers aged 25-64, before taxes. It includes work-related payments, such as annual bonuses, results-related bonuses, extra pay for holidays and sick-leave pay. Income from other sources, such as government social transfers, investment income, and any other income that is not directly related to their profession, are not included. Statutory salaries refer to scheduled salaries according to official pay scales. The salaries reported for the OECD *Education at a Glance* publication are gross (total sum paid by the employer) less the employer's contribution to social security and pension, according to existing salary scales. Salaries are "before tax", i.e. before deductions for income tax.
4. Personal communication with Stefan Vogtenhuber and Lorenz Lassnigg, October 20, 2015. See also Rechnungshof, 2013b.
5. In part, this is, of course, taken into account in the NMS reform. Compared to the AHS, per-student spending at the NMS is significantly higher, and the NMS is a school type in which children from disadvantaged socio-economic backgrounds are over-represented. However, the distinction

between the two school types of NMS and AHS is very crude and neglects differences in the socio-economic profile of students between rural and urban areas.

6. Data from OECD PISA 2012 point to the need to support schools further to make better use of assessment data (OECD, 2013a, Figure IV.4.11 and Table IV.4.30). Only 62.6% of students were in a school whose principal reported that assessments were used to monitor the school's progress from year to year compared to an OECD average of 81.2%, only 39.1% of students were in a school whose principal reported that assessments were used to make judgements about teachers' effectiveness (OECD average: 50.4%), and 69.5% of students were in a school whose principal reported that assessments were used to identify aspects of instruction or the curriculum that could be improved (OECD average: 80.3%).

7. Since the NMS reform has only been implemented recently, these preliminary findings need to be confirmed in the future. The NMS concept requires a long-term cultural change from teachers and school principals and it might, therefore, take some time before effects can be observed.

8. Furthermore, there is some limited leeway for redistribution between schools for specific purposes, which is granted on purpose.

9. In a recent report, the Austrian Court of Audit provides a comparative estimate of costs for administering one teacher position in these two different regulatory regimes (Rechnungshof, 2015b). The report compares administrative procedures in the province of Tyrol which has maintained the dual structure, and the province of Upper Austria where the provincial office has delegated the bulk of its responsibilities to the provincial school board. The report finds differences in administrative costs for federal teachers, although this should be the same since they are administered by the provincial school board in both cases: Upper Austria spends about 20% more than Tyrol (EUR 247 compared to EUR 206). However, with regard to provincial teachers, the situation is reversed: In this case, administrative costs per teacher were EUR 237 in Tyrol compared to EUR 215 in Upper Austria (ibid.: 22). The Court of Audit states that part of these differences may be explained by differences in the age structure of personnel. However, it could also be related to different administrative structure, indicating that administrative costs might be lower in provinces that have delegated responsibilities to the federal agencies. Of course, this comparison is merely based on two cases and can, therefore, not be generalised.

10. See *https://verwaltung.hessen.de/irj/Verwaltung_Internet* (accessed 8 October 2015) for the case of Hesse and *www.lehrer-online-bw.de/,Lde/Startseite/Stellen* (accessed 8 October 2015) for the case of Baden-Württemberg, for example.

References

Altrichter, H. et al. (2015), "Ziele und Merkmale der Neuen Mittelschule" [Goals and characteristics of the New Secondary School], in F. Eder, H. Altrichter, J. Bacher, F. Hofmann and C. Weber (Eds.), *Evaluation der Neuen Mittelschule (NMS): Befunde aus den Anfangskohorten, Forschungsbericht [Evaluation of the New Secondary School (NMS): Insights from the First Cohort. Research Report]*, Leykam, Graz, pp. 23-38.

Bacher, J. (2014), *Ein Modell indexbasierter Mittelverteilung für Österreich, Vortrag 4. Enquete: Zukunft trotz(t) Herkunft: "Arme Schulen – Reiche Schulen": Mehr Mittel für Schulstandorte mit einer hohen Zahl an sozial benachteiligten SchülerInnen [A Model for Index-based Resource Distribution in Austria, 4th Presentation for Committee of Inquiry: Future Defies Backgrounds: "Poor Schools – Rich Schools": More Resources for Schools with a High Number of Socially-disadvantaged Students]*, Institute of Sociology, Linz.

BMBF (2015), *Freiraum für Österreichs Schulen: Empfehlungen zur neuen Steuerung, Expert/innenarbeitsgruppe Schulverwaltung [Freedom for Austria's Schools: Recommendations for New Steering, Expert Working Group on School Administrations]*, Bundesministerium für Bildung und Frauen, Vienna.

BMBF and BMWFW (2015), *Bildungsreformkommission Vortrag an den Ministerrat [Education Reform Commission Presentation to the Council of Ministers]*, Bundesministerium für Bildung und Frauen, Vienna, *www.bmbf.gv.at/ministerium/vp/2015/20151117.pdf?55kaz6*.

BMUKK (2009), *SCHEP-NEU: Schulerhaltungs- und Schulentwicklungsprogramm der Bundesregierung [SCHEP-NEU: School Maintenance and Development Programme of the Federal Government]*, Bundesministerium für Unterricht, Kunst und Kultur, Vienna.

Bruneforth, M. et al. (forthcoming), *OECD Review of Policies to Improve the Effectiveness of Resource use in Schools: Country Background Report for Austria*, Bundesministerium für Bildung und Frauen, Vienna.

Bruneforth, M. (2014), *Eckdaten zur sozialen Zusammensetzung von Schulstandorten, Vortrag 4. Enquete: Zukunft trotz(t) Herkunft: "Arme Schulen – Reiche Schulen": Mehr Mittel für Schulstandorte mit einer hohen*

Zahl an sozial benachteiligten SchülerInnen [Key Data for the Social Composition of Schools, 4th Presentation for the Committee of Inquiry: Future Defies Backgrounds: "Poor Schools – Rich Schools": More Resources for Schools with a High Number of Socially-disadvantaged Students], BIFIE, Vienna, Salzburg, Graz.

Bruneforth, M., C. Weber and J. Bacher (2012), "Chancengleichheit und garantiertes Bildungsminimum in Österreich" [Equality of opportunities and guaranteed minimum education standards in Austria], in B. Herzog-Punzenberger (ed.), *Nationaler Bildungsbericht Österreich 2012, Band 2: Fokussierte Analysen bildungspolitischer Schwerpunktthemen [National Education Monitoring Report for Austria 2012. Volume 2: Focussed Analysis of Key Areas of Education Policy]*, Leykam, Graz, pp. 189-227.

Busemeyer, M.R. (2008), "The impact of fiscal decentralisation on education and other types of spending", *Swiss Political Science Review*, 14(3), pp. 451-481.

Dobbins, M. (2014), "Explaining change and inertia in Swedish and French education: A tale of two corporatisms?", *Policy Studies*, 35(3), pp. 282-302.

Eder, F. et al. (2015), "Executive summary", in F. Eder et al. (eds.), *Evaluation der Neuen Mittelschule (NMS): Befunde aus den Anfangskohorten, Forschungsbericht [Evaluation of the New Secondary School (NMS): Insights from the First Cohort. Research Report]*, Leykam, Graz, pp. 443-466.

European Commission, EACEA, Eurydice (2014), *Financing Schools in Europe: Mechanisms, Methods and Criteria in Public Funding. Eurydice Report*, Publications Office of the European Union, Luxembourg.

Eurydice (2015), European Encyclopaedia on National Education Systems: Austria, *https://webgate.ec.europa.eu/fpfis/mwikis/eurydice/index.php/Austria:Overview*.

Eurydice (2007), *School Autonomy in Europe: Policies and Measures*, Eurydice, Brussels.

Fazekas, M. (2012), "School Funding Formulas: Review of Main Characteristics and Impacts", *OECD Education Working Papers*, No. 74, OECD Publishing, Paris, *http://dx.doi.org/10.1787/5k993xw27cd3-en*.

Forum Wien Welt Offen (2014), *Themendossier Sozialindizierte Stärkung von Bildungsstandorten: Österreichische Beiträge & Positionen sowie internationale Modelle [Thematic Dossier Social-index-based Improvement of Schools: Austrian Contributions and Positions as well as International Models]*, *http://wienweltoffen.at/wp-content/uploads/2014/09/Dossier_Sozialindizierung.pdf*.

Graf, L., L. Lassnigg and J.J.W. Powell (2012), "Austrian corporatism and institutional change in the relationship between apprenticeship training and school-based VET", in M. R. Busemeyer and C. Trampusch (eds.), *The Political Economy of Collective Skill Formation*, Oxford University Press, Oxford, New York, pp. 150-178.

Hanushek, E.A., S. Link and L. Wößmann (2013), "Does school autonomy make sense everywhere? Panel estimates from PISA", *Journal of Development Economics*, 104(2013), pp. 212-232.

Hanushek, E.A. and L. Wößmann (2010), "The economics of international differences in educational achievement", *NBER Working Paper* 15949, National Bureau of Economic Research, Cambridge.

Hanushek, E.A. and L. Wößmann (2006), "Does educational tracking affect performance and inequality? Differences-in-differences evidence across countries", *Economic Journal*, 116 (March), C63-C76.

Helbig, M. and R. Nikolai (2015), *Die Unvergleichbaren: Der Wandel der Schulsysteme in den deutschen Bundesländern seit 1949 [The Incomparables: Change of the School Systems of the German Länder Since 1949]*, Verlag Julius Klinkhardt, Bad Heilbrunn.

Kuschej, H. and K. Schönpflug (2014), *Indikatoren bedarfsorientierter Mittelverteilung im österreichischen Pflichtschulwesen, Vortrag 4. Enquete: Zukunft trotz(t) Herkunft: "Arme Schulen – Reiche Schulen": Mehr Mittel für Schulstandorte mit einer hohen Zahl an sozial benachteiligten SchülerInnen* [Indicators for Needs-based Resource Distribution in the Austrian Compulsory School Sector, 4th Presentation for the Committee of Inquiry: Future Defies Backgrounds: "Poor Schools – Rich Schools": More Resources for Schools with a High Number of Socially-disadvantaged Students], Institute for Advanced Studies, Vienna.

Kuschej, H. and K. Schönpflug (2013), *Indikatoren bedarfsorientierter Mittelverteilung im österreichischen Pflichtschulwesen: Vorläufiger Endbericht, Studie im Auftrag der Kammer für Arbeiter und Angestellte für Wien [Indicators for Needs-based Resource Distribution in the Austrian Compulsory School Sector: Preliminary Final Report, Study Commissioned by the Chamber of Labour Vienna]*, Institute for Advanced Studies, Vienna.

Lassnigg, L. and S. Vogtenhuber (2015), *Challenges in Austrian Educational Governance Revisited: Re-thinking the Basic Structures*, Institute for Advanced Studies, Vienna.

Lassnigg, L. et al. (2007), *Ökonomische Bewertung der Struktur und Effizienz des österreichischen Bildungswesens und seiner Verwaltung: Endbericht, Studie im Auftrag des BMUKK [Economic Analysis of the Structure and Efficiency of the Austrian Education System and its Administration: Final Report, Study Commissioned by the BMUKK]*, Institute for Advanced Studies, Vienna.

Lijphart, A. (1999), *Patterns of Democracy*, Yale University Press, New Haven, CT.

OECD (2015), *Education at a Glance 2015: OECD Indicators*, OECD Publishing, Paris, *http://dx.doi.org/10.1787/eag-2015-en*.

OECD (2014a), *Education at a Glance 2014: OECD Indicators*, OECD Publishing, Paris, *http://dx.doi.org/10.1787/eag-2014-en*.

OECD (2014b), *PISA 2012 Results: What Students Know and Can Do (Volume I, Revised edition, February 2014): Student Performance in Mathematics, Reading and Science*, PISA, OECD Publishing, Paris, *http://dx.doi.org/10.1787/9789264208780-en*.

OECD (2013a), *PISA 2012 Results: What Makes Schools Successful (Volume IV): Resources, Policies and Practices*, PISA, OECD Publishing, Paris, *http://dx.doi.org/10.1787/9789264201156-en*.

OECD (2013b), *Synergies for Better Learning: An International Perspective on Evaluation and Assessment*, OECD Reviews of Evaluation and Assessment in Education, OECD Publishing, Paris, *http://dx.doi.org/10.1787/9789264190658-en*.

OECD (2012), *Equity and Quality in Education: Supporting Disadvantaged Students and Schools*, OECD Publishing, Paris, *http://dx.doi.org/10.1787/9789264130852-en*.

OECD (2007), *Evidence in Education: Linking Research and Policy*, Knowledge management, OECD Publishing, Paris, *http://dx.doi.org/10.1787/9789264033672-en*.

Petrovic, A. and E. Svecnik (2015), "Das Projekt NMS – Implementierung, Modellentwicklung und Umsetzung" [Project New Secondary School – Implementation, model development and implementation], in F. Eder et al. (eds.), *Evaluation der Neuen Mittelschule (NMS): Befunde aus den Anfangskohorten, Forschungsbericht [Evaluation of the New Secondary School (NMS): Insights from the First Cohort. Research Report]*, Leykam, Graz, pp. 13-22.

Pfeffer, F.T. (2008), "Persistent inequality in educational attainment and its institutional context", *European Sociological Review*, 24(5), pp. 543-565.

Rechnungshof (2015a), *Bericht des Rechnungshofes: Landeslehrerpensionen, Bund 2015/12 [Report of the Court of Audit: Pensions of provincial teachers, Vol. 2015/12]*, Austrian Court of Audit, Vienna.

Rechnungshof (2015b), *Bericht des Rechnungshofes, Bund 2015/13, Rechnungshof GZ 860.180/002-181/14 [Report of the Court of Audit, Vol. 2015/13, Court of Audit File Number GZ 860.180/002-181/14]*, Austrian Court of Audit, Vienna.

Rechnungshof (2015c), *Bericht des Rechnungshofes: Schulversuche, Bund 2015/1 [Report of the Court of Audit: School pilots, Vol. 2015/1]*, Austrian Court of Audit, Vienna.

Rechnungshof (2015d), *Bericht des Rechnungshofes: Finanzierung des Landeslehrer; Follow-Up-Überprüfung, Bund 2015/12 [Report of the Court of Audit: Financing Provincial Teachers, Follow-up Evaluation, Vol. 2015/12]*, Austrian Court of Audit, Vienna.

Rechnungshof (2014), *Bericht des Rechnungshofes: Controlling im Bundesschulwesen; Follow-up-Überprüfung, Bund 2014/10 [Report of the Court of Audit: Controlling in the Federal Schools Sector; Follow-up Evaluation, Vol. 2014/10]*, Austrian Court of Audit, Vienna.

Rechnungshof (2013a), *Stellungnahme des Rechnungshofs zum Schulbehörden-Verwaltungsreformgesetz 2013, Wien, 28. Mai 2013 [Statement of the Court of Audit about the 2013 Reform of School Governance Structures, Vienna 28 May 2013]*, Vienna, *www.rechnungshof.gv.at/fileadmin/downloads/_jahre/2013/beratung/gesetzesbegutachtungen/Stellungnahme_Schulbehoerden_Verw.reformgesetz.pdf*.

Rechnungshof (2013b), *Bericht des Rechnungshofes: Modellversuch Neue Mittelschule, Bund 2013/12 [Report of the Court of Audit: Pilot of the New Secondary School, Vol. 2013/12]*, Austrian Court of Audit, Vienna.

Rechnungshof (2012), *Bericht des Rechnungshofes: Finanzierung der Landeslehrer, Bund 2012/4 [Report of the Court of Audit: Financing Provincial Teachers, Vol. 2012/4]*, Austrian Court of Audit, Vienna.

Rechnungshof (2011a), *Vorschläge des Rechnungshofs zur Verwaltungsreform [Proposals of the Court of Audit for a School Administration and Governance Reform]*, Austrian Court of Audit, Vienna.

Rechnungshof (2011b), *Bericht des Rechnungshofes: Controlling im Bundesschulwesen, Bund 2011/1 [Report of the Court of Audit: Controlling in the Federal Schools Sector, Vol. 20111/1]*, Austrian Court of Audit, Vienna.

Schlicht-Schmälzle, R., J. Teltemann and M. Windzio (2011), "Deregulation of education – What does it matter for efficiency and equality?", *TransState Working Paper*, 157/2011.

Schmid, K. (2015), *Schulgovernance – Eckpunkte für einen Paradigmenwechsel: Ableitung eines idealtypischen Modells für Österreich anhand internationaler Evidenz, ibw-Kurzexpertise 2015 [School Governance – Key Points for a Shift of Paradigm: Development of an Ideal Model for Austria on the Basis of International Evidence, ibw-Research Brief]*, Institut für Bildungsforschung der Wirtschaft, Vienna.

Sozialpartner Österreich (2014), *Bildungsfundamente: Ziele und Maßnahmen für eine zukunftsorientierte Bildungsreform [Education Base: Goals and Measures for a Future-oriented Education Reform]*, Wirtschaftskammer Österreich, Bundesarbeitskammer, Österreichischer Gewerkschaftsbund, Landwirtschaftskammer Österreich, Vienna, *www.sozialpartner.at/wp-content/uploads/2015/08/Bildungsfundamente-2013.pdf*.

Specht, W. and F. Sobanski (2012), *OECD Review on Evaluation and Assessment Frameworks for Improving School Outcomes: Country Background Report for Austria*, Bundesministerium für Unterricht, Kunst und Kultur (BMUKK), Vienna, *www.oecd.org/edu/evaluationpolicy*.

Statistik Austria (2015a), *Bildung in Zahlen 2013/14: Schlüsselindikatoren und Analysen [Education in Figures 2013/14, Key Indicators and Analyses]*, Statistik Austria, Vienna.

Statistik Austria (2015b), *Bildung in Zahlen Tabellenband [Education in Figures Tables]*, Statistik Austria, Vienna.

Statistik Austria (no date), online database, *www.statistik.at/web_de/statistiken/menschen_und_gesellschaft/bildung_und_kultur/formales_bildungswesen/bildungsausgaben/index.html*.

Streeck, W. and P.C. Schmitter (1985), "Community, market, state – and associations? The prospective contribution of interest governance to social order", in W. Streeck and P.C. Schmitter (eds.), *Private Interest Government: Beyond Market and State*, Sage, London, Beverly Hills, New Delhi, pp. 1-29.

Tsebelis, G. (2002), *Veto Players: How Political Institutions Work*, Princeton University Press, Princeton.

Wilkoszewski, H. and E. Sundby (2014), "Steering from the Centre: New Modes of Governance in Multi-level Education Systems", *OECD Education Working Papers*, No. 109, OECD Publishing, Paris, *http://dx.doi.org/10.1787/5jxswcfs4s5g-en*.

Wolf, F. (2009), "The division of labour in education funding: A cross-national comparison of public and private education expenditure in 28 OECD countries", *Acta Politica*, 44, pp. 50-73.

Wößmann, L. (2003), "Schooling resources, educational institutions and student performance: The international evidence", *Oxford Bulletin of Economics and Statistics*, 65(2), pp. 117-170.

ANNEX 2.A1

Data for Chapter 2

Table 2.A1.1. **Comparative data on per student expenditure on education, OECD countries, ISCED 2011, 2012**

	Pre-primary education (for children 3 years and older)	Primary education	Lower secondary education	Upper secondary education	Primary to tertiary (including R&D activities and undistributed programmes)
Australia	10 298	7 705	10 574	9 581	10 347
Austria	**7 716**	**9 563**	**13 632**	**14 013**	**13 189**
Belgium	6 975	9 581	11 670	12 210	12 135
Canada	..	9 680		11 695	..
Czech Republic	4 447	4 728	4 312	7 119	5 235
Denmark	n/a	10 953	7 902	9 959	7 684
Estonia	n/a5	5 668	6 524	7 013	6 878
Finland	9 998	8 316	12 909	8 599	11 030
France	6 969	7 013	9 588	13 070	10 450
Germany	8568	7 749	9 521	12 599	11 363
Hungary	4 539	4 370	4 459	4 386	5 564
Iceland	10 250	10 003	10 706	7 541	10 287
Ireland	..	11 087	11 087	11 564	10 740
Israel	3 416	6 931	n/a	n/a	7 903
Italy	7 892	n/a	8 905	8 684	8 744
Japan	5 872	8 595	9 976	10 360	11 671
Korea	5 674	7 395	7 008	9 651	9 569
Luxembourg	19 719	20 020	20 247	20 962	22 545
Mexico	n/a	2 632	2 367	4 160	3 509
Netherlands	8 176	8 185	12 227	12 368	12 211
New Zealand	9 670	7 069	8 644	10 262	9 443
Norway	9 050	12 728	13 373	15 248	15 497
Poland	6 505	6 682	6 682	6 419	7 398
Portugal	5 713	6 105	8 524	8 888	7 952
Slovak Republic	4 694	5 415	5 283	5 027	6 072
Slovenia	7 472	9 015	9 802	6 898	9 031
Spain	6 182	7 111	9 137	9 145	9 040
Sweden	12 212	10 312	10 966	11 329	12 742
Switzerland	5 457	13 889	16 370	17 024	17 485
Turkey	..	2 577	2 448	3 524	3 514
United Kingdom	10 699	10 017	10271	9 963	12 084
United States	10 042	11 030	11 856	13 059	15 494
OECD average	**8 008**	**8 247**	**9 627**	**9 876**	**10 220**
EU21 average	8 146	8 372	10 040	10 011	10 361

Note:
.. Missing value
n/a Data not available
Source: OECD (2015), *Education at a Glance 2015: OECD Indicators, http://dx.doi.org/10.1787/eag-2015-en*, Tables B1.1a and C2.3.

Table 2.A1.2. **Data on expenditure by primary and secondary educational institutions, by resource category, OECD countries with available data, ISCED 2011, 2012**

		Primary education						Secondary education					
		Percentage of total expenditure		Percentage of current expenditure				Percentage of total expenditure		Percentage of current expenditure			
	Notes	Current	Capital	Compensation of teachers	Compensation of other staff	Compensation of all staff	Other current expenditure	Current	Capital	Compensation of teachers	Compensation of other staff	Compensation of all staff	Other current expenditure
		(1)	(2)	(3)	(4)	(5)	(6)	(7)	(8)	(9)	(10)	(11)	(12)
OECD													
Australia		81.3	18.7	62.9	15.1	78.0	22.0	88.3	11.7	59.2	16.2	75.4	24.6
Austria		**98.1**	**1.9**	**60.7**	**12.6**	**73.3**	**26.7**	**98.2**	**1.8**	**68.0**	**8.6**	**76.5**	**23.5**
Belgium	1	96.2	3.8	69.7	19.3	89.0	11.0	97.5	2.5	72.4	16.5	88.9	11.1
Canada	1, 2	92.6	7.4	62.6	15.0	77.5	22.5	92.6	7.4	62.6	15.0	77.5	22.5
Chile		..	..	..	..	..	..	..	..	..	..	..	..
Czech Republic		90.1	9.9	46.1	16.5	62.6	37.4	92.1	7.9	46.8	12.4	59.2	40.8
Denmark	1	94.7	5.3	63.4	17.0	80.5	19.5	93.0	7.0	39.0	20.7	59.8	40.2
Estonia		..	..	..	..	..	..	..	..	..	..	..	..
Finland	1	91.7	8.3	55.6	9.5	65.1	34.9	91.0	9.0	51.1	12.7	63.8	36.2
France		91.6	8.4	56.8	20.4	77.2	22.8	90.6	9.4	58.4	24.0	82.5	17.5
Germany		90.8	9.2	x(5)	x(5)	82.1	17.9	90.2	9.8	x(11)	x(11)	81.5	18.5
Greece		..	..	..	..	..	..	..	..	..	..	..	..
Hungary	3	94.1	5.9	x(5)	x(5)	72.8	27.2	93.8	6.2	x(11)	x(11)	74.7	25.3
Iceland	1	93.0	7.0	x(5)	x(5)	74.5	25.5	95.2	4.8	x(11)	x(11)	75.4	24.6
Ireland	3	92.0	8.0	76.5	12.4	89.0	11.0	94.5	5.5	70.2	8.9	79.1	20.9
Israel		91.5	8.5	x(5)	x(5)	85.2	14.8	94.0	6.1	x(11)	x(11)	83.9	16.1
Italy	3	96.6	3.4	62.4	19.0	81.3	18.7	97.2	2.8	64.7	18.7	83.4	16.6
Japan	1	88.1	11.9	x(5)	x(5)	85.8	14.2	88.6	11.4	x(11)	x(11)	86.2	13.8
Korea		87.4	12.6	54.6	14.9	69.4	30.6	86.6	13.4	56.5	12.5	68.9	31.1
Luxembourg		85.8	14.2	78.4	3.7	82.1	17.9	91.1	8.9	77.0	12.9	89.9	10.1
Mexico	3	97.4	2.6	86.4	8.2	94.6	5.4	96.8	3.2	78.8	12.0	90.8	9.2
Netherlands		88.0	12.0	x(5)	x(5)	83.6	16.4	88.6	11.4	x(11)	x(11)	81.6	18.4
New Zealand		..	..	..	..	..	..	..	..	..	..	..	..
Norway	1	89.3	10.7	x(5)	x(5)	79.8	20.2	87.6	12.4	x(11)	x(11)	79.8	20.2
Poland		94.1	5.9	x(1)	x(1)	x(1)	x(1)	95.9	4.1	x(7)	x(7)	x(7)	x(7)
Portugal	3	98.7	1.3	80.0	13.9	93.9	6.1	98.7	1.3	80.7	10.2	90.9	9.1
Slovak Republic	1	92.6	7.4	51.1	13.8	64.9	35.1	94.8	5.2	52.4	14.0	66.4	33.6

Table 2.A1.2. **Data on expenditure by primary and secondary educational institutions, by resource category, OECD countries with available data, ISCED 2011, 2012** *(cont.)*

		Primary education						Secondary education					
		Percentage of total expenditure		Percentage of current expenditure				Percentage of total expenditure		Percentage of current expenditure			
	Notes	Current	Capital	Compensation of teachers	Compensation of other staff	Compensation of all staff	Other current expenditure	Current	Capital	Compensation of teachers	Compensation of other staff	Compensation of all staff	Other current expenditure
		(1)	(2)	(3)	(4)	(5)	(6)	(7)	(8)	(9)	(10)	(11)	(12)
Slovenia	1	92.4	7.6	x(5)	x(5)	81.2	18.8	93.5	6.5	x(11)	x(11)	76.8	23.2
Spain	3	94.9	5.1	71.0	9.7	80.7	19.3	94.7	5.3	74.9	8.3	83.1	16.9
Sweden		93.5	6.5	52.7	16.7	69.4	30.6	92.3	7.7	50.7	14.9	65.6	34.4
Switzerland	1, 3	90.5	9.5	66.6	16.6	83.2	16.8	92.0	8.0	73.0	12.2	85.2	14.8
Turkey	3	96.3	3.7	x(5)	x(5)	89.3	10.7	91.9	8.1	x(11)	x(11)	84.8	15.2
United Kingdom	3	93.7	6.3	54.4	29.0	83.4	16.6	94.0	6.0	59.8	22.0	81.8	18.2
United States		91.2	8.8	54.6	26.6	81.3	18.7	91.2	8.8	54.6	26.6	81.2	18.8
OECD average		**92.3**	**7.7**	**63.3**	**15.5**	**79.7**	**20.3**	**92.9**	**7.1**	**62.5**	**15.0**	**78.4**	**21.6**
EU21 average		93.1	6.9	62.8	15.3	78.5	21.5	93.8	6.2	61.9	14.6	77.0	23.0

Note:
.. Missing value
x Data included in another category or column
1. Some levels of education are included with others. Refer to "x" code in Table B1.1a for details.
2. Year of reference 2010.
3. Public institutions only.
4. Year of reference 2012.

Source: OECD (2015), *Education at a Glance 2015: OECD Indicators, http://dx.doi.org/10.1787/eag-2015-en*, Table B6.1.

Chapter 3

Organisation of the school offer in Austria

This chapter focuses on the organisation of the school offer. It analyses the distribution of schools across the country and the size of schools and classes as well as the distribution of responsibilities for maintaining schools and their infrastructure and facilities. It examines recent reforms to change the organisation of the school offer towards greater equity with the New Secondary School reform and the expansion of all-day schooling. Furthermore, it briefly describes how the school offer seeks to facilitate the inclusion of students with special educational needs and to meet the needs of greater diversity in schools and classrooms. It considers strengths and challenges, paying particular attention to the structural obstacles for a more rational organisation for the school offer in rural areas, the remaining equity issues of early tracking and selection, and the difficulties for the introduction of integrated forms of all-day schooling. It concludes by proposing different policy recommendations to address these issues.

The statistical data for Israel are supplied by and under the responsibility of the relevant Israeli authorities. The use of such data by the OECD is without prejudice to the status of the Golan Heights, East Jerusalem and Israeli settlements in the West Bank under the terms of international law.

Context and features

From an international perspective, one of the most salient features of the school offer in Austria is the very small average school and class size. These features are particularly pronounced in rural areas, especially in the many mountainous areas. The distributed and somewhat fragmented nature of decision-making in education, combined with limited school autonomy, particularly for resource management, is another important contextual aspect influencing the organisation of the school offer in Austria (Chapter 2).

Distribution of schools

Schools in Austria are very unevenly distributed. Figure 3.1 shows that in terms of the number of schools per population there is a large gap between the Burgenland (and to a lesser extent Tyrol), on the one hand, and Vienna, on the other.

Figure 3.1. **School density**

Number of schools per 100 000 inhabitants, per province, school year 2013/14

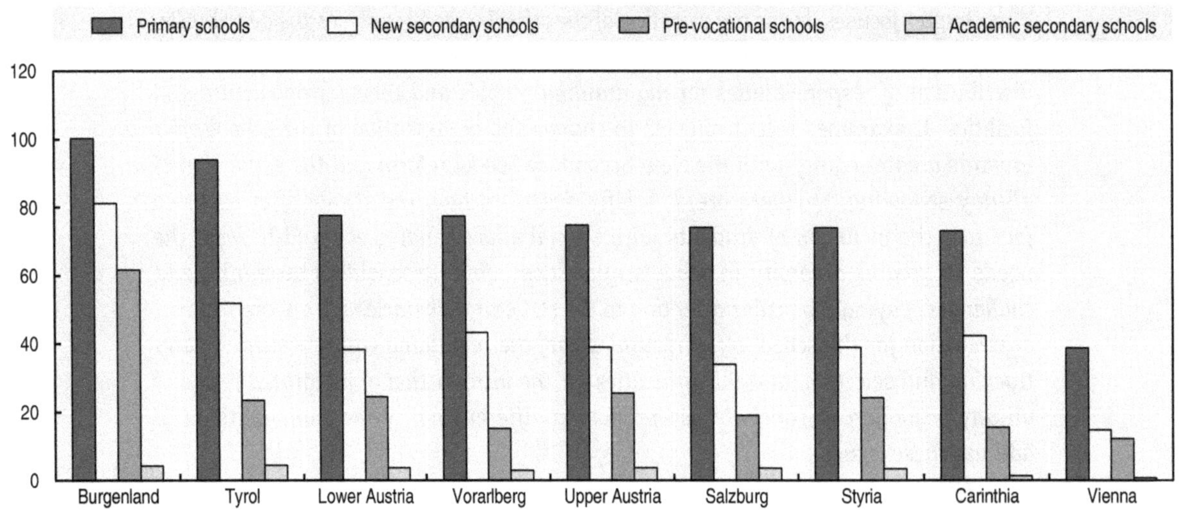

Source: Bruneforth, M. et al. (forthcoming), *OECD Review of Policies to Improve the Effectiveness of Resource use in Schools: Country Background Report for Austria*, Bundesministerium für Bildung und Frauen, Vienna.

This is reflected in a wide variety of average school sizes across the provinces (Figure 3.2). In part, this is a consequence of geographic characteristics: thinly populated areas tend to have smaller schools, particularly for primary education. Hence, while average primary school size is 107 students per school, the variation is large: average school size is 57 in Burgenland and 248 in Vienna.

When analysing the development of student numbers per school, it is clear that the differences between urban and rural areas with respect to school size are increasing due to urbanisation. Since the mid-2000s, schools in thinly populated areas show a distinct

Figure 3.2. **Average school size**

Average number of students, per province

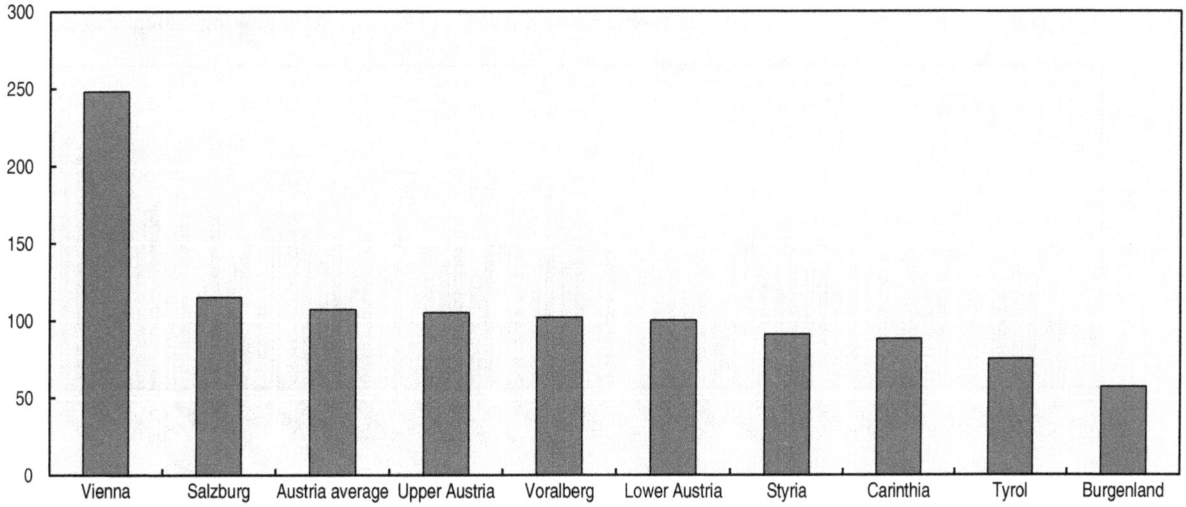

Source: Bruneforth, M. et al. (forthcoming), *OECD Review of Policies to Improve the Effectiveness of Resource use in Schools: Country Background Report for Austria*, Bundesministerium für Bildung und Frauen, Vienna.

decrease in student numbers, while schools in densely populated areas are declining less, on average, and larger schools even show increasing sizes (Bruneforth et al., forthcoming: 77). The steepest decrease can be observed in Salzburg, with a decline of 10.3 students per primary school, on average, between the school years 2006/07 and 2012/13. In Vienna, on the other hand, the number of students in primary schools increased over the same period (an increase of 8.4 students per primary school on average). These phenomena vary across the provinces: while the effect is substantial in Salzburg and Carinthia (a mountainous province characterised by strong out-migration), demographic change does not influence school sizes that much in Upper Austria, Tyrol and Vorarlberg.

Small community schools are a pressing, but sensitive issue in national and regional politics. The term "small-sized schools" ("*Kleinschulen*") is typically used to refer to those schools with at most one class per year. These are a wide-spread phenomenon in Austria's rural areas. Topographical features in connection with regional development objectives based on a belief in the broader social function of schools for their community appear to have an influence on average school size across the provinces. Large mountainous areas, notably in the central and Western parts of Austria, complicate the streamlining of the school offer, as they require students to commute to school over longer distances.

Class size and student to teacher ratios

Austria has one of the lowest student-teacher ratios among OECD countries (Figure 3.3). In primary education the average student-teacher ratio is 12, 20% below the OECD average (15 students per teacher). The average class size of 18 is also well below the OECD average (21 students per class) (Figure 3.4).

In 2007, the federal government introduced federal regulations with the aim to decrease class sizes for pedagogical reasons to a recommended level of 25 students. This was quickly interpreted as an absolute maximum class size by the provinces. Following the implementation of this regulation, between 2007 and 2013, average class size decreased from 19.9 to 18 in public primary education and from 24 to 21 in public lower secondary education.

Figure 3.3. **Ratio of students to teaching staff in educational institutions, 2013**

By level of education, calculations based on full-time equivalents

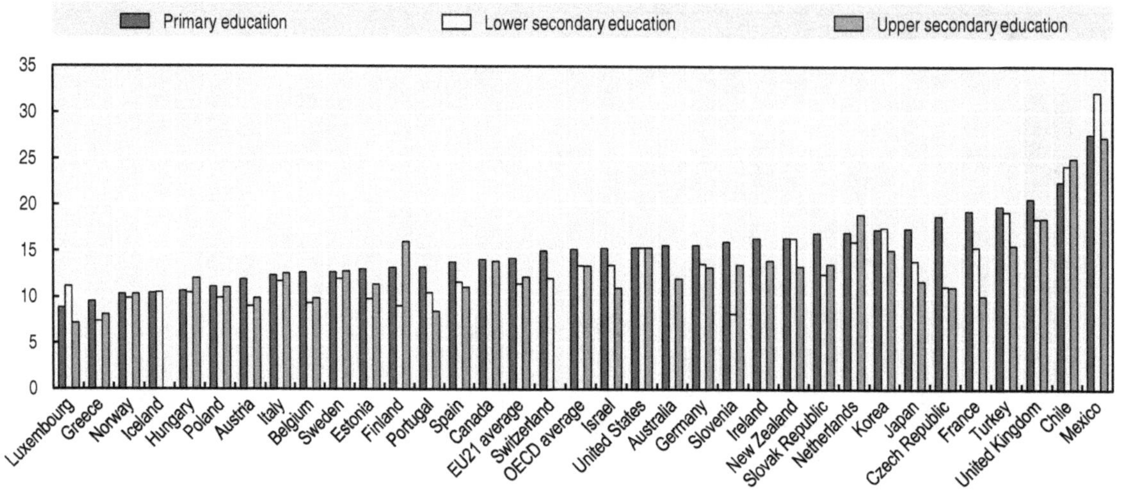

Note: Countries are ranked from smallest to lowest student-teacher ratios for primary education

1. Includes only general programmes in lower and upper secondary education.
2. Public institutions only. For Israel, public institutions only for upper secondary education. For Belgium, data do not include independent private institutions.
3. Year of reference 2012.
4. Primary includes pre-primary.
5. Includes data on management personnel.
6. Upper secondary includes programmes from post-secondary non-tertiary education.

Source: OECD (2015), *Education at a Glance 2015: OECD Indicators, http://dx.doi.org/10.1787/eag-2015-en*, Table D2.2.

Figure 3.4. **Average class size, public and private institutions, by level of education, 2013**

Calculations based on number of students and number of classes

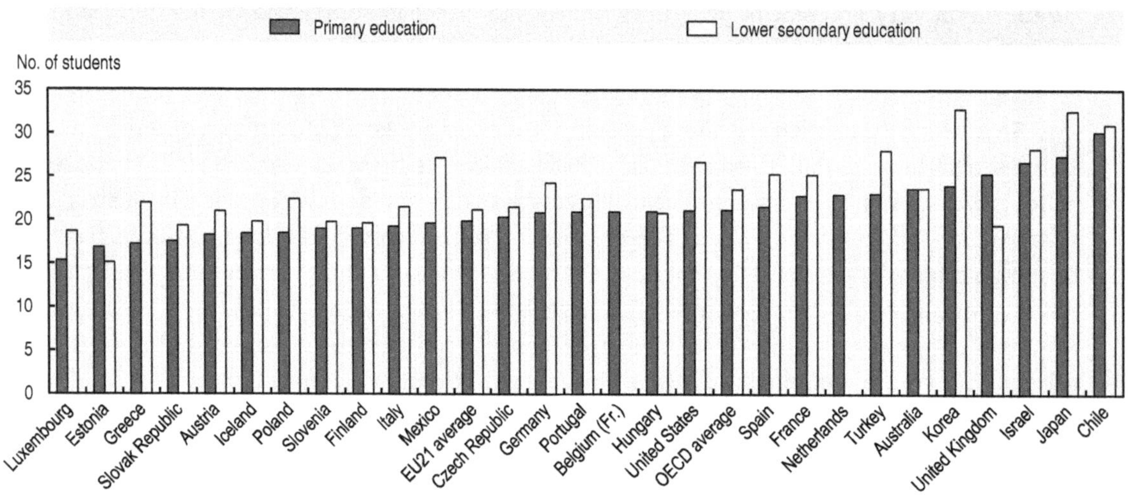

Note: Countries are ranked from lowest to smallest class size in primary education.

Source: OECD (2015), *Education at a Glance 2015: OECD Indicators, http://dx.doi.org/10.1787/eag-2015-en*, Table D2.1.

Classes in urban areas are typically much larger than in rural areas and provinces with many rural schools tend to have more schools with small classes. However, when considering student-teacher ratios the differences between urban and rural schools are less striking, suggesting that schools with bigger classes do not necessarily have much fewer human resources, but use them in a different way. This phenomenon is more pronounced for primary education than lower secondary education (Bruneforth et al., forthcoming).

Catchment areas and school size

Generally, there is little freedom of school choice at the compulsory school level in Austria. For reasons of administrative planning, families are expected to enrol their children in a school within the catchment area (*Schulsprengel*) they live in. Every public general compulsory school (*Allgemeine Pflichtschule,* APS) is assigned a certain school catchment area, which is defined by the provincial authorities. If a catchment area comprises several schools, provincial law regulates how to assign children to these schools. In Vienna, for example, the municipality in consultation with the school board assigns children to schools on the basis of criteria like the distance from their home to school and enrolled siblings.

In several places, there are developments that have loosened the system of school catchment areas in compulsory education. In Vienna, catchment areas are quite large, consisting of the municipality district the school is located in as well as the neighbouring districts. Catchment areas can have several hundreds of thousands inhabitants, and they also overlap. In Linz, the capital of Upper Austria, the catchment area principle has been entirely abolished. Families can freely enrol their children in the school of their choice, and only if there are too many applicants for a specific school, the distance from home and the presence of siblings in the school of choice are considered as factors for admission. The loosening of the catchment area regime is a reaction to demand from families. Enrolment in a school in a different catchment area or municipality is generally possible, but it requires permission from the concerned authorities, since in that case municipalities have to transfer compensation payments for the students concerned to the receiving municipality. Schools with specialised curricula, such as music or sports, are exempt from the catchment area principle.

For enrolment in academic secondary schools (*Allgemeinbildende Höhere Schule,* AHS), families can freely decide which school they want their child to enrol in within the province. In schools where demand exceeds supply, students can be assigned to another academic secondary school based on distance to school, siblings enrolled and ability. Depending on the provincial regulations, parents can indicate their preference through a list of alternatives to their school of first choice.

The introduction of a certain degree of school autonomy in the 1990s, which included partial autonomy over curriculum development, has encouraged schools to develop pedagogical priorities and specific subject-related profiles to become more attractive for (high achieving) students and their parents. As a consequence, growing competition between schools could be observed, which came along with certain selection effects (see Schratz and Hartmann, 2009). But competition is not actively facilitated by education policies. For example, while aggregate results of national assessments at the province and national level are available to the public, results of individual schools in these assessments are not published in order to avoid school rankings and potential segregation effects.

Governance of the school offer

All provinces have established minimum student numbers as a legal requirement for maintaining a school location. However, many schools continue to be operated by the municipalities even when their student numbers have already fallen below the defined threshold. The Austrian Court of Audit noted the difficulty to balance the challenges of maintaining very small schools with the interest to offer schooling within reasonable distance (Rechnungshof, 2014: 34).

The closure of a school requires a complicated administrative process that involves the municipality, the provincial government and the federal level represented by the provincial school board – all with potentially diverging interest. This requires intense political dialogue with concerned stakeholders and responsible authorities sometimes even offer financial or other incentives to municipalities to gain their consent for closure. In some cases where no consensus had been reached, the process of school closure stretched over several years due to administrative court proceedings initiated by the concerned municipality (Rechnungshof, 2014).

A closure of a school in one municipality can require also new infrastructure investments in the neighbouring municipality to adapt its school location to a larger number of incoming students. School transport is generally provided free of charge to students (apart from a small contribution) by the Federal Ministry of Family and Youth (*Bundesministerium für Familien und Jugend*) through a family compensation fund (*Familienlastenausleichsfonds*). There are no figures available on the cost of school transport which may accrue for the municipality in the context of school closures. The municipality in which a school has been closed down usually has to transfer a per-student compensation to the absorbing municipality to proportionally cover infrastructure and non-teaching staff expenditures for its students. Despite the compensation transfer, the sending municipality has no say on decisions regarding the school in the receiving municipality.

Another challenge for small communities is that there is often no clear concept for the use of redundant school facilities while the cost for basic maintenance to avoid decay of buildings may continue to burden the municipality's budget. For example, the government of Upper Austria has discussed potential use with the municipalities concerned, and solutions included infrastructure-utilisation by other schools, childcare facilities, associations or churches, while in other cases the school buildings had to be sold or demolished (Rechnungshof, 2014). Also, private initiatives are addressing this challenge and developing innovative concepts for the use of closed down school buildings.[1]

Building and renovating schools

The federal law on the maintenance of compulsory schools (*Pflichtschulerhaltungs-Gesetz*) states that the provinces are responsible for all general compulsory schools (also referred to as provincial schools, *Landesschulen*). This federal law establishes only broad framework criteria for the establishment, maintenance and closure of schools as well as the school infrastructure and the bearing of cost. All detailed provisions including the criteria for minimum sizes of schools and their geographical distribution (i.e. distance between the area of residence and the nearest school), are laid down in provincial implementing legislation and differ considerably from province to province. According to the federal law, the provinces can devolve the responsibility for school infrastructure and maintenance to the municipalities, a possibility which all provinces have opted for.

Academic secondary schools (also referred to as federal schools, *Bundesschulen*), on the other hand, are under the responsibility of the federal level. There are no legislative acts that provide for the co-ordination and creation of synergies between the infrastructure of provincial and federal schools within a same locality. Co-ordination and co-operation exist depending on local circumstances (e.g. regarding sport facilities), but are not compulsory and the extent to which they occur has not been evaluated systematically (Rechnungshof, 2014).

The establishment of a new federal school, or the renovation of an existing building, is planned and adopted by the Federal Ministry of Education and Women's Affairs (BMBF) in close co-operation with the provincial school boards, which assess the need and priorities for infrastructure investments in their regions. The federal government has adopted a long-term school development programme (*Schulentwicklungsplan*, SCHEP-NEU) for federal schools for the decade 2008-18. The focus is on the modernisation of existing infrastructure and school architecture to provide students and teachers with adequate classrooms and workplaces. In addition, important investments are made in infrastructure to allow for implementation of the educational concepts needed to expand provision of all-day schools and school-based day care.

Of the EUR 1.662 billion made available by the school development programme, EUR 577.3 million have already been spent on completed construction projects, and a further EUR 379.85 million are allocated to projects currently under construction. Between 2008 and 2018, 270 construction projects at federal schools should be finalised. This means that one-third of all federal school buildings will have been extended, completely refurbished or newly built. Investments will be transferred to the owners of the school buildings, i.e. the Federal Real Estate Company (*Bundesimmobiliengesellschaft*) and others, mainly municipalities, via (increased) rental payments. Another major investment programme aims at the expansion of all-day schooling (more on this below).

The school providers are responsible for the establishment of general compulsory schools, in consultation with the provincial school board and the school department of the provincial government. The quality and state of construction of individual general compulsory schools is monitored by the provincial authorities. The provincial governments have regional programmes to support municipalities in the construction and renovation of schools.[2] The adequacy of school infrastructure for each type of school is subject to provincial legislation and can be further broken down in detailed guidelines for school construction and room equipment. Expert commissions are established to assess the suitability of planned infrastructure.

Implementation of recent reforms for school structure

Introduction of the New Secondary School (NMS)

The New Secondary School (*Neue Mittelschule*, NMS) was introduced in 2008 as a pilot project. It was originally designed as a comprehensive school for all 10-14 year-old students (Years 5 to 8), combining the lower secondary stages of general secondary school (*Hauptschule*, HS) and academic secondary school (*Allgemein bildende höhere Schule*, AHS). The intention was to abolish early tracking in the long-run. However, due to a political compromise within the government coalition, all lower secondary stages of academic secondary schools continued to exist next to the NMS. The AHS are only invited to work with the NMS on a project basis. Since the beginning of the school year 2015/16, all HS have been transformed into NMS.

The NMS has more or less the same curricula as the AHS, with educational goals that are similar, but not identical to the AHS. This is different to the former HS, which also had more or less the same curricula, but special provisions for different instructional ability groups, and different educational goals to those of the AHS. Importantly, the NMS aims to open up better chances for their students, particularly to help them continue their education at a school providing the secondary school leaving certificate (matriculation examination, *Matura*). Better results in the NMS are sought by applying new pedagogical approaches, including more individualised and project-based learning and a competence-orientation. To achieve these objectives additional teaching resources (in particular for team teaching in core subjects) are provided for the NMS (Chapter 4).

Until the introduction of the NMS, students were tracked according to their abilities also within classes of general lower secondary school, i.e. students in one class were assigned to three different instructional ability groups (*Leistungsgruppen*) for the subjects of mathematics, German and English. The assignment to a specific ability group, based on the teacher's judgement, had important implications for the students' school career. For example, upper secondary programmes (AHS, BHS) could not be chosen by students from the third ability groups, and transition to BHS or AHS was unlikely also for students of the second group. Assignment to ability groups was based on teacher judgements regarding their students' achievement levels, but looking at actual student performance reveals a significant overlap in achievement between groups. For example, in 2008/09, about one-sixth of students in the third group exceeded the national mean achievement of the second group. Students with higher achievements were thus formally excluded from access to the BHS or the AHS (Bruneforth and Lassnigg, 2012).

With the introduction of the NMS, explicit streaming into ability groups was abolished, as the focus of the NMS is on individualisation and differentiation within classes. The additional resources that were needed for ability grouping in the HS (since ability groups were smaller than classes) are used for team teaching in the NMS. In addition, the federal government provides funding for six additional teaching hours per class (in sum) for differentiated instruction, primarily in mathematics, German and foreign language (mainly delivered through team teaching). Since 2015, schools can use additional teaching resources also for other subjects. Although there is no explicit ability grouping in the NMS, students are streamed implicitly in Years 7 and 8 as they are graded according to different grading schemes depending on their ability.

In 2012, the Austrian Parliament adopted the legal regulations for a system-wide implementation of the NMS, before the end of the initially agreed testing phase and well before the impact evaluation of the pilot trial had become available. The introduction of the NMS was subject to an audit by the Austrian Court of Audit (Bund 2013/12), which specifically criticised the premature roll-out decision and the substantially higher costs for teaching staff in NMS (EUR 7 200 per student as compared to EUR 6 600 in the HS) while there was no evidence on its effectiveness at that time (also see Chapter 2 for an analysis of the funding implications of the reform).

A summative evaluation of the impact of NMS on student achievements was published in February 2015 (Eder et.al 2015). Although it should be noted that this evaluation was limited to the schools in the pilot phase, it revealed deficits in the implementation of the reform and its pedagogical approach in the majority of the evaluated schools, resulting in average student achievements that showed no improvement compared to the HS. It did show, however, weak to medium-strong positive effects on educational quality, student support and learning climate (Eder et al., 2015). The implementation of the NMS likely requires a long-term cultural change from teachers and school principals, and it might, therefore, take some time before effects can be observed.

All-day schooling

The expansion of all-day schooling is another priority of the current federal government. Austrian primary and secondary schools were traditionally part-time schools operating in the morning only. With an increasing number of single parent families and parents working full-time, the demand for day care is on the rise. In addition, initiatives to expand all-day schooling in Austria are motivated by the aim to increase equity in educational opportunities.

Since the school year 2006/07, schools are obliged to offer all-day programmes if at least 15 parents request it. Currently, there are two forms of all-day schooling that can be introduced in schools: fully integrated all-day programmes (*verschränkte Form*) and optional afternoon care (*Nachmittagsbetreuung*). According to a 2012 survey, the latter form is far more widespread. Only around 5% of the schools with all-day offers provide fully integrated programmes.

Funding for the provision of all-day schooling is shared between the federal and provincial levels. In 2014, the federal and provincial governments agreed to make available an amount of EUR 375 million for the years 2015 to 2018 to pay for additional infrastructure necessary to facilitate all-day schooling, such as group rooms, refectories, kitchens and playgrounds. In the budget of 2015, the planned funds for the expansion of all-day schooling in general compulsory schools amounted to EUR 109 million. However, until 2015, provinces did not request all the earmarked funds, moving more slowly toward all-day schooling then hoped for by the federal ministry.

Freedom from tuition fees does not apply to the extracurricular part in all-day public sector schools. However, parental contributions for the extracurricular may not exceed the amount that covers the costs, whereby the financial capacity of parents has to be taken into account. Since 2007, the offer of all-day schooling has increased substantially. While in 2007, 76 979 students attended a form of all-day schooling, in 2014 this had almost doubled to 140 102 students. About 40% of all school locations now offer all-day schooling.

Special needs education, inclusion and diversity

Special needs education

Apart from the systemic approach to improve equity via the introduction of the NMS, there is specific support for students with special educational needs (SEN) (*sonderpädagogischer Förderbedarf*, SPF). In the Austrian context, students are considered as having special educational needs when they have been diagnosed by experts as not being able to follow instruction without special support due to physical and mental disabilities. Although regulations clearly indicate that children must not be labelled as having SEN simply due to unsatisfactory achievement, there seems to be a risk that students are diagnosed with special needs when they show general learning problems, especially in combination with a migrant background (Bruneforth and Lassnigg, 2012: 90).

Students with SEN can be enrolled in special needs schools (*Sonderschule*, ASO), in special classes in regular schools, or be integrated in regular classes ("integrative education"). The latter is co-ordinated by SEN-centres, which are special needs schools with the specific task to provide pedagogical expertise and logistical support for "integrative education" in their region. In 2013, 30 000 students were identified with SEN. According to data from the statistical division of the Federal Ministry of Education and Women's Affairs (BMBF), 38.7% of these SEN students were enrolled in special schools.[3] Even though regulations concerning special needs education are established at the federal level, there are substantial differences in implementation between the provinces, which can be illustrated by the different enrolment rates of SEN students in special needs schools, ranging from 18.8% of SEN students in Styria to 54% in Tyrol.[4] Provinces also differ significantly in the rates of students diagnosed with special needs.

To facilitate the inclusion of children with special needs and as part of a cross-sector National Action Plan 2020 of the federal government, the UN Convention on the Rights of Persons with Disabilities (Art 24) is being implemented in the area of education. "Inclusive regions" are currently being piloted across Austria with the aim to enhance inclusion in regular schooling by giving regional special needs schools a stronger co-ordination role with regard to pedagogy and resource distribution. Based on these pilots, a detailed development concept should be agreed between the federal government, the provinces and the municipalities with the aim to roll out inclusive regions across Austria by 2020. Accompanying measures aim to adapt initial teacher education and continuous professional development to a context of inclusion: inclusive pedagogy will be part of the training for all teachers under the new teacher training scheme from autumn 2015 (see Chapter 4). Another key measure of the national action plan is to widen barrier-free education offers and support, in particular in relation to learning materials and buildings (barrier-free access to federal schools).

Support for students with a migrant background

Policies in Austria do not target students with an immigrant background, but strategies focus mainly on children speaking a different language than the language of instruction (Herzog-Punzenberger and Unterwurzacher, 2009). Support for these children starts before the first year of schooling. Children facing difficulties acquiring the German language are supported in their language development in childcare institutions by targeted individual support.

The implementation of these measures is regulated by the provinces, based on an agreement between the federal and provincial governments. Compulsory standardised diagnostic tools to determine needs for additional support are a central element of the support system. The results serve as a basis to develop individually tailored, child-oriented support measures. The agreement between the federal and provincial governments also made attendance in the final year of kindergarten compulsory and free of charge for all children with language deficits, and subsequently for all children. The government programme for 2013-18, as well as the federal government's proposal for education reform presented in November 2015 (BMBF and BMWFW, 2015; see Annex 1.1 in Chapter 1), envisage the introduction of a second free and compulsory kindergarten year with a strong focus on children with language deficits, with the option to opt-out after three months.

Specific measures for students not mastering the language of instruction are also implemented at the school level (Chapter 4). Students starting school with substantial difficulties to follow instruction due to severe deficits in the language of instruction can be classified for up to two years as "non-regular students" (*außerordentliche Schüler*). As "non-regular students", they are entitled to special support while they fall under special exemptions concerning grading. This regulation also applies to students who migrate to Austria at older ages and enter the Austrian school system in higher year levels. School leaders are responsible for the assessment and "classification" of students. The procedure to assess language competence is not standardised. Schools with "non-regular students" can offer language support courses amounting up to 11 weekly hours per student, for which additional teaching resources are provided by the federal level as earmarked part within the overall staff plans. Schools can decide to offer the course in parallel to regular instructions or in form of integrated instruction. In 2012/13, 15 544 "non-regular students" were enrolled in the Austrian school system, 10 229 of which in primary education (3.2% of total primary enrolment).

Since students can be classified as "non-regular" only at the time when they enter the Austrian school system for the first time, there appears to be a structural incentive to label students pre-emptively in order to receive additional resources for language support, which would not be possible anymore once the student has entered as "regular student".

Additional language support in German as a second language can also be offered by schools for students who are not enrolled as "non-regular students" (though they often only receive 2 to 3 weekly hours). To cover the human resources needed, the federal government provides funding for specialised staff within the general staff plans, i.e. there is no earmarked contingent for such posts. Whether the provided posts are indeed used for language instruction, however, is decided at the province level and not evaluated by the federal level.

Youth Coaching

The Federal Ministry of Labour, Social Affairs and Consumer Protection (*Bundesministerium für Arbeit, Soziales und Konsumentenschutz, BMASK*) is the main actor and provider of funds for a system of career assistance (*Netzwerk Berufliche Assistenz*). Under this umbrella the nation-wide "Youth Coaching" initiative offers youth coaches who advise and accompany young people aged 15-19 at risk of dropping out from school or being marginalised.

Strengths

There is strategic and thorough infrastructure planning and maintenance, particularly for federal schools

There is an ambitious national school development programme for federal schools (*Schulentwicklungsprogramm*, SCHEP-NEU). As mentioned above, between 2008 and 2018 the systematic investment of EUR 1.662 billion should ensure that one third of the federal schools will have been extended, refurbished or newly built by 2018. Spending within this programme is based on careful planning with medium-term and long-term prognoses for infrastructure needs developed for federal schools, with bottom-up input. Furthermore, federal school infrastructure is evaluated every seven to ten years.

At the same time, the infrastructure planning for municipal and provincial schools appears to be more fragmented. There does not seem to be any system-wide planning regarding the infrastructure for primary schools and NMS. It is also unclear whether poorer municipalities are equally able to support "their" primary schools as richer municipalities and there is no system in place to redistribute funds to compensate for this (this challenge will be discussed below, also see Chapter 2 for more details about resource inequalities between municipalities).

Most stakeholder groups the review team spoke to expressed satisfaction with the state of school infrastructure, although for provincial schools the quality of infrastructure appeared to depend on the wealth of the municipality (e.g. the OECD review team observed striking differences in the quality of infrastructure across the provincial schools it visited in different parts of Austria). However, looking at data from OECD PISA 2012 suggests that school principals in Austria are less satisfied with the physical infrastructures than the OECD average (Figure 3.5) (OECD, 2013b). But it is difficult to interpret what these data mean and whether Austrian school principals have higher expectations than other school principals or whether the physical infrastructure is in a worse state than in other OECD countries.

Figure 3.5. **School principals' views on adequacy of physical infrastructure**

Score on the PISA index of quality of physical infrastructure

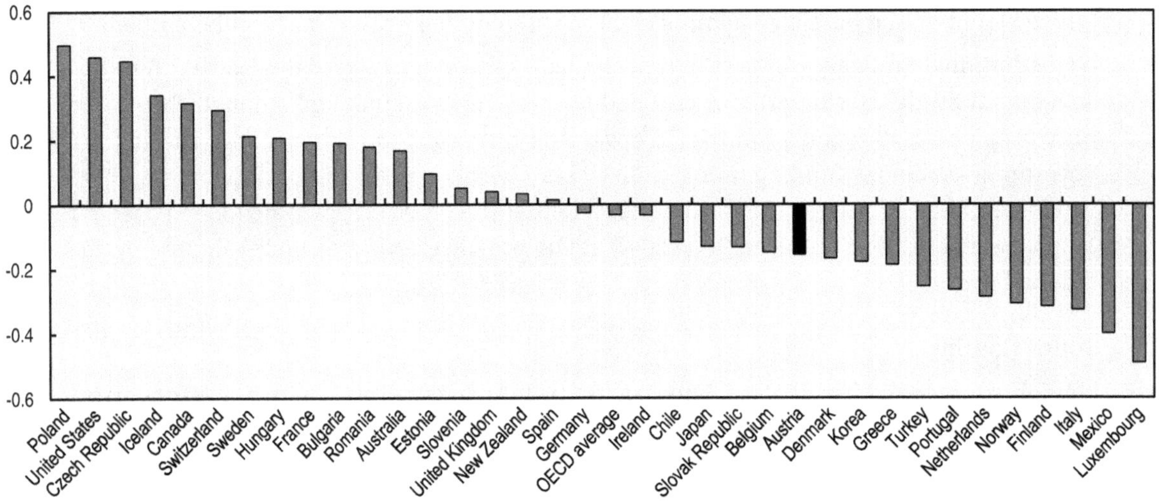

Note: Higher values on the index of quality of physical infrastructure indicate better physical infrastructure.

Source: OECD (2013b), *PISA 2012 Results: What Makes Schools Successful? Resources, Policies and Practices*, *http://dx.doi.org/10.1787/9789264201156-en*, Table IV.3.15.

Individual provinces are developing strategies for the consolidation of their school offer

In a review of research literature on school size, Ares Abalde (2014) finds that there are several potential advantages to larger school size and school consolidation from a pedagogical perspective, as small school size reduces course options within schools, may lead to isolation of teachers through to few opportunities for classroom release and professional development, and makes it harder for schools to exercise autonomy and to develop distributed pedagogical leadership. Larger schools are likely to be able to offer a larger curriculum, more specialised teachers and courses, a broader range of extracurricular activities and a higher share of administrative staff and para-professionals offering support to teachers and school leaders. Of course these benefits need to be weighed against the cost of transporting students in rural areas with low population densities (or mountainous areas), counteracting the savings from size economies – as well as broader regional and local development aspects and objectives. However, on average, the costs of supporting small schools are high and any loss in functionality or in quality represents an expensive inefficiency in the school system which drains resources away from other areas of potential investment.

While there is no overall strategy to consolidate the school offer in Austria, different provinces have been taking their own steps to rationalise the distribution of schools. For example, some provinces have developed "regional education plans", which aim to respond better to current demographic realities and to streamline the school network at regional level (Bruneforth et al., forthcoming). In addition, some provinces (Vorarlberg and Styria) have consolidated their school networks so as to organise the school offer more effectively. In four of the nine provinces, there has been a trend to set up municipal school associations (*Schulgemeindeverbände*). Under such associations, municipalities agree to pool their resources and jointly run one school. There have also been some creations of "associated schools" (*angeschlossene Schulen*), bringing together a school cluster under one school principal, which can be an alternative to closures of small schools. According to the November 2015 reform proposal, the federal government plans to further promote this model of school network consolidation in the future and to also allow for the clustering of different types of school as part of model regions to further promote longer common schooling (e.g. primary schools, NMS and AHS) (BMBF and BMWFW, 2015). Finally, provinces can create incentives for schools to group together or consolidate. In Salzburg, for example, the OECD review team was informed that schools need to have ten classes in order to receive a school principal, which provides an incentive for smaller schools to cluster together under one common leadership. This seems to be a requirement in addition to a national regulation for schools to have ten teachers for a school principal position to be created. In schools with less than ten teachers, school leadership is typically exercised by a teacher with a reduced teaching load.

Some steps have been taken to reduce the negative impact of early tracking

As described in Chapter 1, there are important concerns related to the equity of educational opportunities for students from different socio-economic backgrounds in Austria. There have been a number of policies to address this issue, particularly by aiming to reduce the negative impacts of early tracking. Most prominently amongst these is the introduction of the NMS, even if the impact of this reform is not yet clear as pointed out above. Although the NMS does not replace the lower level of the AHS, it is specifically targeted at providing more students a chance to enter higher education. The fact that there is a common curriculum for NMS and AHS and that educational goals share more commonalities between the NMS and the AHS than was the case between the HS and the AHS are an important precondition for this. Moreover, significant additional resources have been made available for the NMS to use new pedagogical approaches and to better prepare students from a variety of backgrounds for higher education (Chapter 2). While currently the NMS and the AHS operate in parallel, there is a continuing public debate in which several parties want to work towards a comprehensive school for 10-14 year-olds, with the new teacher education and service code as further steps in this direction (see Chapter 4).

There is political will to develop all-day schools as an equity strategy

As described above, the federal government has planned and invested substantial funds for the expansion of all-day schooling in general compulsory schools. In the 2015 budget, available funds amounted to EUR 109 million. Although provinces have so far not utilised the entire available federal budget to expand all-day schooling, this represents a serious effort by the federal ministry. This is reflected by the fact that the offer of all-day schooling has increased substantially since 2007. However, as discussed below, while the government has been promoting integrated forms of all-day schooling which are also favoured by some stakeholders such as the Federation of Austrian Industries (*Industriellenvereinigung*) and which promise greater returns in terms of better quality, only a small minority of schools are currently offering that option.

Several countries have been introducing all-day schooling in order to increase quality and equity (OECD, 2012). As the reasoning goes, while all students would benefit from more learning time, extracurricular activities and guidance with their homework, this should be particularly true for children of families who are less capable of supporting their children in these regards. There are some interesting studies focussing on the effects of full-day kindergartens that show positive results in terms of quality and equity (Gibbs, 2014)

There have been some steps towards the greater inclusion of students with special educational needs

As part of the cross-sector National Action Plan 2020 of the federal government, the UN Convention on the Rights of Persons with Disabilities is being implemented in the area of education (Art. 24). "Inclusive regions" are currently piloted across Austria with the aim to support the implementation of greater inclusion in regular schooling. To support the implementation of more inclusive education, regional special needs schools are given a stronger co-ordinating role with regard to pedagogy and resource distribution. Based on these pilots, a detailed concept should be agreed between the federal level, the provinces and the municipalities with the aim to roll out inclusive regions across Austria by 2020.

Challenges

Small schools (and small classes) are expensive and drain resources away from other potential investments in the school system

Although research shows that in Austria the student-teacher ratio between urban and rural areas differs much less than class sizes, student to teacher ratios must be very low in very small schools with as little as ten students, as is the minimum in the Burgenland. Such small schools are relatively expensive to run as maintaining and investing in the infrastructure (e.g. IT facilities and equipment) of many small schools is more expensive than for fewer large ones. But small schools do not only have financial implications. Small schools and small buildings make it more difficult to realise other policy objectives, such as creating comprehensive schooling and all-day provision. Also in terms of education quality there is little evidence on the effects of small schools and that schools of this size substantially improve teaching and learning, also relative to larger schools that are more cost-efficient to operate. Is it, of course, important to bear broader regional and local development objectives in mind and to recognise that the investments in these small schools can have wider returns for the communities and villages in which these schools are located (Box 3.1). Many of the local parents, teachers, school leaders and politicians the review team spoke with in small villages in the Burgenland highlighted that schools contribute to ensuring that such villages remain attractive to parents with young children. But this broader social function of small schools in rural communities may require a broader reflection about policy options and funding solutions beyond education (e.g. involving local and regional development strategies and funds).

While decisions about the organisation of the school offer are also political, some structural factors may hinder a more rational organisation of the school offer in the case of Austria. First, there is insufficient regulation of minimum school size and there appear to be many loopholes to ignore existing regulations. While all provinces have defined minimum student numbers for opening a school, schools continue to operate even if student numbers fall below this threshold. Also, in some provinces, the existing minimum numbers are very low: ten students per school in the Burgenland visited by the

Box 3.1. **The effects of small schools on rural communities**

In a recent review of the literature on school size, Areas Abalde (2014) finds three potential beneficial effects of schools on small villages: effects on social capital, effects through the other services that schools provide and effects on the local economy. In terms of social capital, schools can act as a meeting point and a place for interaction and the forging of bonds within the community, play a role in maintaining community cohesion, and contribute to maintaining and transmitting local history and culture (Berry and West, 2010). By providing a space for interaction and bonding and by promoting a community identity, schools increase the amount of social capital within the community, thereby facilitating co-operation and co-ordination for mutual benefit among community members (Nguyen et al., 2007). The social capital the school promotes is expected to have a positive impact on the life of the community, and this will especially be the case when the community supports and is involved in school activities (Moulton, 2001).

In rural and remote areas, schools frequently provide additional services apart from education. These activities can be related to education, e.g. in the form of a study centre for young people and adults, or a kindergarten, but they can also be used for other activities, as an information centre for municipal services, a work place for very small businesses, a space for the organisation of local cultural activities, or a polling station (Sigsworth, 2005; Koulouris and Sotiriou, 2006).

Lastly, schools in small villages may have an influence on the local economy, as young economically active parents will be less likely to move to cities (Koulouris and Sotiriou, 2006). Moreover, it has been argued that consolidation may lead to reduced taxes, declining property values and closing businesses (Duncombe and Yinger, 2010). A study of rural communities in the state of New York (Lyson, 2002) indicated that housing values were higher and municipal structures more developed in small villages with schools than in villages without them. However, these results do not show causality, lower housing prices may have been caused by other factors than the presence of the school. In fact, other research shows that the negative economic trends present in some consolidating districts were already in place prior to consolidation (Sell and Leistritz, 1997).

Source: Ares Abalde, M. (2014), School Size Policies: A Literature Review, *OECD Education Working Papers*, No. 106, *http://dx.doi.org/10.1787/5jxt472ddkjl-en*.

review team, for example. Second, the current governance arrangements and split in responsibilities for funding and spending between the federal government and the provinces analysed in detail in Chapter 2 may set problematic incentives. As the costs for teachers, the largest cost factors in operating a school, are covered by the federal level, provinces and municipalities have little incentive to rationally plan their school networks of general compulsory schools in rural areas.

There is no system-wide planning of school facilities based on needs

As a result of the present governance arrangements (Chapter 2), Austria has a fragmented system of school facility and network planning. Depending on the school type, different government levels are involved in the decision making process on opening, closing and maintaining schools, sometimes simultaneously. While the federal level is responsible for the planning and organisation of school facilities for academic secondary schools at the lower secondary level, the provincial and municipal level are responsible for the organisation of the school offer for general compulsory education. It is, therefore, difficult for the federal level to influence and steer the distribution and the density of primary and lower secondary school networks as a whole across the country. While the national planning of the organisation of academic secondary schools is possible through the federal government, there is no unified system for infrastructure planning for all general compulsory schools which are run by the provinces and the many (sometimes very small) municipalities. The catchment areas for schools (particularly for primary education) tend to coincide with the borders of the municipalities. Incentives for municipalities as the maintainers of general compulsory schools work against a systematic planning of the school offer as municipalities benefit from their school as an important service for the community, but do not have to bear most of the costs (i.e. teacher salaries) which are covered by the federal level. Moreover, if municipalities close down a school, they need to pay for all students going to school in an adjacent catchment area.

The separation of the allocation of means for infrastructure (i.e. the responsibility of municipalities) from education policies impedes planning and oversight. The problems of a lack of national planning are aggravated by the fact that there is a lack of data on the school and municipality level, which makes it difficult to relate data on performance (that is available) to infrastructure investments by provinces and municipalities. This makes it very difficult to assess the effectiveness and efficiency of these investments, let alone to steer and influence them.

The local responsibility for infrastructure planning of general compulsory schools also entails the risk for inequalities in investments between poorer and richer municipalities. In general, the many small municipalities receive much less resources than the provinces in the fiscal adjustment mechanism.

School consolidation appears necessary, but faces obstacles

The downward demographic trends, particularly in the rural areas of Austria are likely to increase the pressure to consolidate schools. Especially in rural areas, per student costs are going up. It was reported to the OECD review team that many parents are opposed to school consolidation as it would imply that their children have to travel longer distances to reach compulsory schools. However, several respondents pointed out that children do travel longer distances when in kindergarten and in the early years of lower secondary education. Moreover, local politicians fear the possible depopulation of municipalities and argue that municipal schools are an important element in keeping the municipality attractive for parents. School closures, so the argument, thus risk exacerbating demographic trends further. Policies to increase average school size in Vorarlberg led to an electoral defeat by the provincial authorities who supported this policy.

In addition, school consolidation faces a number of obstacles related to school governance arrangements in Austria that may prove difficult to overcome (Chapter 2). First, closing down a school requires a complicated administrative process that involves the municipality, the provincial government and the federal level – all with potentially diverging interests. Second, while the municipalities benefit from keeping schools open, they are only responsible to carry part of the costs, teacher salaries being paid at the federal level. In addition, municipalities have other strong disincentives to close their school. Municipalities have to compensate the municipality hosting their students by paying a per capita proportion of the school maintenance costs, which includes also larger investments such as renovations, without being able to influence the decision over such investments. The review team was told that due to the high transfer costs, it may in the end be cheaper for municipalities to keep small schools open rather than to send their students to a neighbouring municipality, although the overall costs for the Austrian school system are higher. Finally, most often there are no strategies for using the empty buildings when the school is closed down. Taking care of the purposeless buildings is costly and not attractive. In terms of supporting municipalities with ideas or information, there seems to be little sharing of experience across provinces. For example, Styria and Vorarlberg have introduced interesting approaches to school consolidation, but these are not widely shared.

There is an increasing lack of resources in urban areas

The high costs of small schools (and small classes) in rural areas mean that per student spending in these areas is higher than in urban areas. This disparity in per student spending between rural and urban areas is growing. Analysis of the relationship between the demographic developments and the allocation of resources in the primary school sector has shown that the schools in areas with demographic decline have earned a "demographic dividend" by increasing their resources per population, whereas Vienna suffered a "demographic penalty". For primary education in all provinces except Vienna, the student population aged 6-9 declined by 15-30% between 2000 and 2012, whereas the resources per student for primary schools increased by 20-40% in the same period. In Vienna, however, where the student population increased slightly, the resources remained stable (Bruneforth et al., forthcoming: 51).

However, it is in these urban areas where challenges and opportunities related to demographic and socio-economic diversity are most pressing. In other words, the mechanisms of resource allocation do not reflect the real needs of students and schools. Practically this means that in many urban schools there is likely to be insufficient support personnel, such as psychologists, social pedagogues and language instructors (Chapter 4). To tackle this issue, proposals of formula funding based on factors of disadvantage have been made, which aim both to increase the transparency of school funding and to enhance equity in education by channelling resources more directly to the students most in need (Chapter 2).

Challenges remain connected to the offer of lower secondary education in two different tracks

As discussed in Chapter 1, students' socio-economic background has an important influence on their performance in Austria (Figure 3.6). This means that education is contributing to social mobility less than in many other OECD countries and that education instead reinforces existing patterns of disadvantage.

One of the most prominent explanations for the unequal learning outcomes of students from different demographic and socio-economic backgrounds is that Austrian school children spend relatively few years in primary school before being tracked into different school types, as also the relatively short amount of time Austrian students spend in primary school compared to other countries illustrates (Figure 3.7). Austrian children enter primary school at the age of six and after four years they are traditionally tracked either to schools that prepare for professional education (NMS) or schools that prepare for higher education (AHS). There is substantial evidence from cross-country studies associating early tracking with a stronger effect of family background on student performance (e.g. Hanushek and Wößmann 2006; Pfeffer 2008; Chmielewski, 2014).

Figure 3.6. **The impact of socio-economic background on education performance**

Score-point difference in mathematics associated with one unit increase in the PISA index of economic, social and cultural status

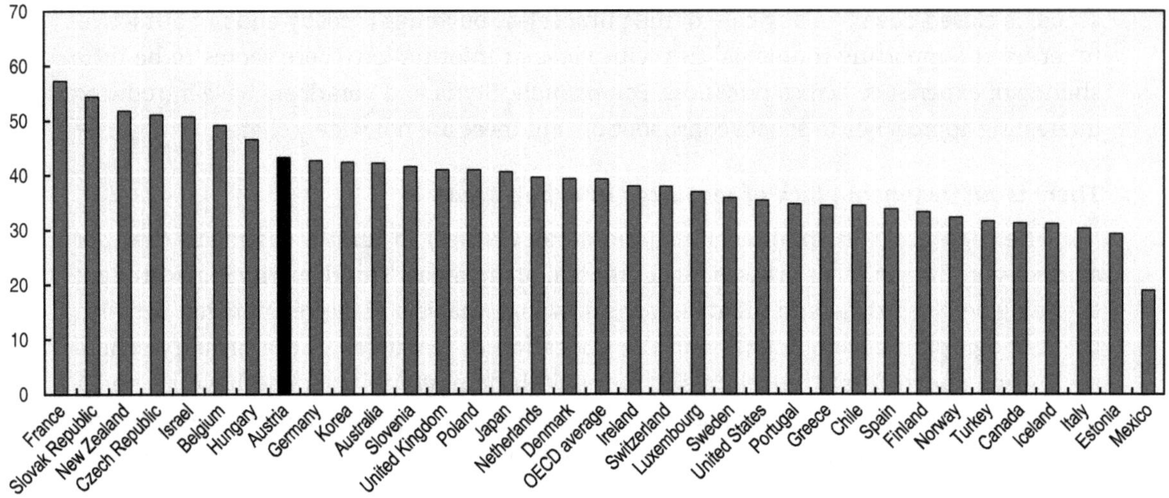

Source: OECD (2013a), *PISA 2012 Results: Excellence through Equity Giving Every Student the Chance to Succeed*, *http://dx.doi.org/10.1787/9789264201132-en*.

Figure 3.7. **Total number of hours of compulsory instruction time, 2015**

By level of education, in public institutions

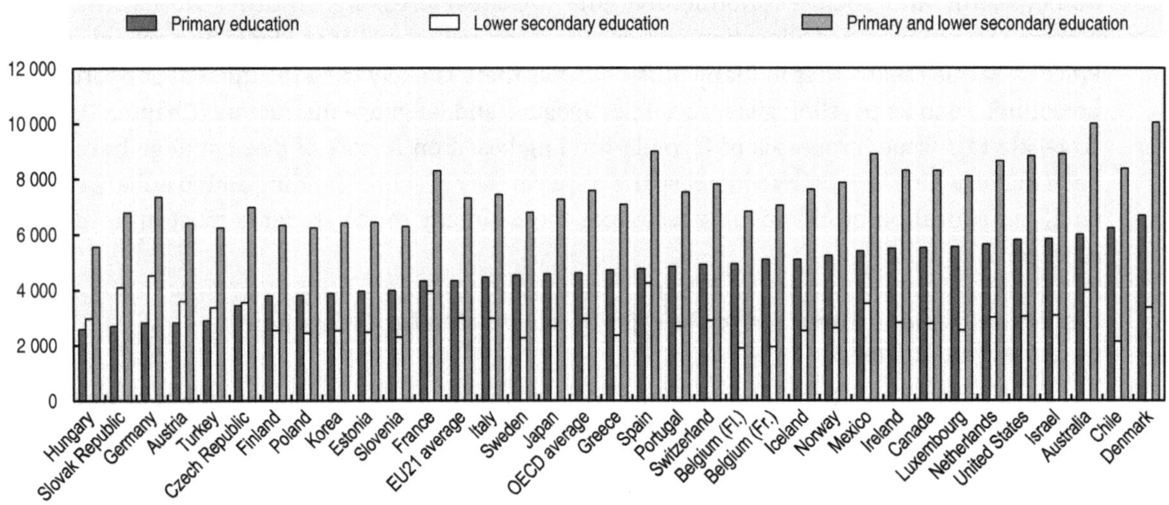

Note: Countries are ranked in ascending order for primary education.
Source: OECD (2015), *Education at a Glance 2015: OECD Indicators*, *http://dx.doi.org/10.1787/eag-2015-en*, Table D1.1.

In Austria, research shows that students' achievement is not the most important factor in their choice of school type. Families of students with the same level of achievement at the end of Year 4 make very different decisions concerning enrolment in secondary education tracks, depending mainly on their family background. In fact, only 29% of the differences in school choice can be explained by differences in student achievement (Bruneforth et al., 2012: 203).

Austria has implemented first steps to reduce the negative effects of early tracking, but due to a political compromise, the NMS has not replaced the lower secondary tier of academic secondary schools, thus leaving the system of early tracking as such in place. As mentioned in Chapter 2, one of the challenges in implementing structural change in the Austrian school system is the fragmentation of responsibilities for lower secondary education, with the federal level responsible for academic secondary schools and the provincial level responsible for the New Secondary Schools. This hampers co-ordination between the two separate tracks and the introduction of more comprehensive schooling. There are also some concerns about the implementation of the NMS reform. While new and innovative pedagogies have been introduced in the NMS, especially in the area of team teaching, more needs to be done to organise this effectively (Chapter 4). Also, explicit ability grouping within the NMS has been abolished, but children are still being tracked implicitly as they are subjected to two different grading schemes in Years 7 and 8. This means that these students still have different chances to continue education at higher levels of education. So far then, the additional funding for NMS seems to have been used by improving the quantity rather than quality of teaching resources. A first evaluation of the NMS reform confirms these impressions revealing deficits in the implementation and no significant impact on student performance yet (Eder et al., 2015). Also, there is increasing pressure on the NMS as a growing number of students choose to go to the AHS (Figure 3.8), especially in urban areas. With a decreasing number of students attending the NMS, the average achievement level of students remaining in the NMS is likely to go down. This trend is also likely to result in smaller NMS schools, which will make it more difficult to free up resources to develop and implement innovative pedagogical approaches.

Figure 3.8. **Trends in student numbers for HS/NMS and AHS**

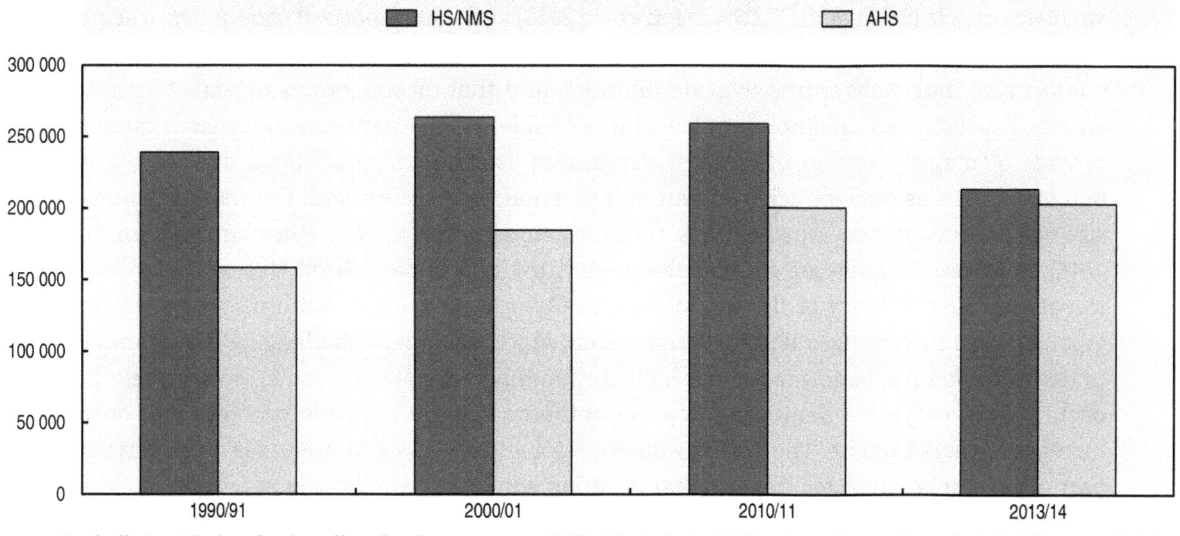

Source: Statistik Austria (no date), online database, *www.statistik.at/web_de/statistiken/menschen_und_gesellschaft/bildung_und_kultur/formales_bildungswesen/schulen_schulbesuch/index.html*.

Concerns related to the introduction of all-day schooling

The expansion of all-day schooling is a priority of the current government, with the explicit goal of improving the equity of the Austrian education system. Since 2007, the offer of all-day schooling has increased substantially (see above). However, the system-wide introduction of all-day schools is slow compared to the ambitions of the federal government, as the fact that the provinces had not requested all of the funds provided by the federal government for the expansion of all-day schooling.

Although there is widespread consensus amongst researchers and practitioners that only the fully integrated form can achieve the educational goals linked to full day programmes, optional afternoon schooling is more widespread. As mentioned above, the optional model is applied by most of the schools with all-day offers, with only around 5% of the schools with all-day offers providing fully integrated programmes. To allow for the introduction of a fully integrated all-day programme, two-thirds of parents and of teachers have to vote in favour of its implementation. As a consequence, demand for all-day schooling is rising, while most of it is implemented as optional afternoon school without an integrated curriculum, focusing on day care.

Another issue that the review team encountered in schools offering all-day schooling was a lack of reflection on how to engage parents in a system of all-day schooling. There was some concern in schools that parental engagement decreased when their children attended all-day programmes, probably based on the assumption that all educational needs of their children would now be taken care of at school. This creates some risks, as research shows that parental involvement is a key factor in improving children's educational performance and that high-quality parental involvement may help reduce performance differences across socio-economic groups (Borgonovi and Montt, 2012).

Policy recommendations

Provide incentives and support for a rational organisation of the school offer

Austria currently has a high density of schools and very small average school size. Research from different countries indicates that per student expenditure is highest in the smallest schools (Falch et al., 2008; Larsen et al., 2013) and that important economies of scale can be achieved when increasing school size up to a certain enrolment level. However, some studies also find that returns to scale diminish and that diseconomies of scale begin to emerge beyond a certain enrolment level (Ares Abalde, 2014). International research cannot provide a "magic" number of optimal school size as school size affects a diverse set of outcomes such as student achievement and parental involvement and the most adequate size will depend on contextual features, including student composition (Humlum and Smith, 2015). However, if schools are so small that their capacity is underutilised, this has a negative impact on the efficiency of the school system (Ares Abalde, 2014). With many extremely small schools in provinces like the Burgenland (which has a less challenging topography), underutilisation (i.e. large spaces and high staff numbers for few students) is very likely to occur. Given projected demographic developments (Chapter 1), this problem will only increase in years to come. The small average school and class size in Austria is an important part of the explanation for the fact that Austrian education is relatively expensive for the quality that it delivers. It is also an important driver of the inequality in per student funding between rural and urban areas.

Addressing these issues is challenging in any school system. For local governments, closing down schools poses difficulties and for parents it is difficult to see "their" school closed. However, in situations with scarce resources, it is important to consider which investments have the highest rate of return and contribute most to the public good. Of course, the broader returns of schools in terms of local and regional development need to be taken into account, but this broader function of small schools in rural communities requires a wider reflection about different strategies and funding solutions beyond education (e.g. from local development funds). In education, increasing average school size would free up resources that could be invested in other important areas that can have benefits in terms of equity such as early childhood education and care, the quality of teachers or the further development of all-day schooling, which. What is true for school size is true for class size too, as the small class size in Austria contributes to make education expensive and increasing class size could be an important way to reduce costs. It is, of course, important to maintain access to schooling for younger children at a reasonable distance from home. The current situation of children being considered to be able to travel longer distances before the age of six (when they go to kindergarten) and after age of ten (when they go to lower secondary school), but not in between, is, however, not rational.

When designing and implementing policies it will be important to learn from the lessons of Austrian provinces and other countries that have successfully increased school size. Research shows that even if consolidation is usually met with opposition, consolidation can end up being positively valued by teachers, parents and students. Studies have shown examples where nearly all students and teachers, both moving and receiving, reported experiencing benefits from consolidation (Box 3.2) and citizens from vacated communities also felt that consolidation had actually improved their community's financial situation (Nitta et al., 2010; Killeen and Sipple, 2000). At the same time, when pursuing consolidation policies, potential negative effects on student well-being related to increased transportation time, reduced individual attention to each student and fewer links to parents and the local community need to be taken into account and addressed (Ares Abalde, 2014).

Box 3.2. **Positive experiences with consolidation: an example from the United States**

In four rural locations around Arkansas, teachers and administrators in eight high schools experienced consolidation between the 2002-03 and 2006-07 school years. Despite many differences among contexts and among participants' experiences, Nitta et al. (2010) found two policy-relevant themes. First, students adapted better than teachers to the new social environment created by consolidation. Students described a relatively smooth and successful transition. Students also reported participating in more diverse social and academic opportunities. In contrast, teachers struggled with their new relationships. In fact, teachers already at receiving high schools reported more social disruption after consolidation than moving students did. The second theme that emerged was that students and educators generally experienced benefits from consolidation. Teachers experienced improved working conditions and professional development opportunities after consolidation, and as noted above, students generally adapted to their new social environments and experienced more diverse social and academic opportunities. By all accounts, not only moving but receiving students had broader course offerings, with more Advanced Placement and vocational courses.

Source: Ares Abalde, M. (2014), "School Size Policies: A Literature Review", *OECD Education Working Papers*, No. 106, *http://dx.doi.org/10.1787/5jxt472ddkjl-en.*

Increasing school and class size can be stimulated through a variety of instruments (Box 3.3 provides some examples from different countries). The most straightforward measure is to set (and enforce) minimum school and class sizes. These can be set at a level that would not require massive school closures and then increased incrementally towards a desired level over a longer period of time. In addition, allowing extra administrative and management budgets for larger schools could help provide incentives for increasing

Box 3.3. Country examples of school consolidation strategies

In the **United States**, some states have used financial compensation as an incentive for consolidation. This could take the form of direct revenue compensation to school districts that choose to consolidate, or also offering these districts the possibility to raise optional taxes (Meyer, 2000). Other options consist of offering consolidating schools compensation for the difference in financial aid received if after consolidating the schools qualify for less aid than they did separately before being merged; or on paying for the differences in teachers' salaries in case they are raised after consolidation (which occurs frequently) (Meyer, 2000). States can also offer schools with limited financial resources to carry out capital construction projects to build new consolidated schools (Howley et al., 2011).

Other incentives for consolidation may come indirectly from changes in the administrative structure of a country or region. In **Iceland**, for instance, the amalgamation of municipalities resulted in new larger municipalities, in some cases with several schools not very far from each other. This created incentives for local politicians to profit from economies of scale and close some schools down and transfer students to schools formerly belonging to a different municipality (Sigbórsson and Jónsdóttir, 2005).

Sometimes school consolidation and closure can take place as a result of a direct policy intervention, such as eliminating all districts or schools with enrolments below an arbitrary number (Howley et al., 2011). For instance, in **Korea**, in 1981 the government recommended that schools with fewer than 180 students should be either merged or closed, but the government provided only a small amount of financial support (such as a subsidy for transportation) (Im, 2009). Sometimes authorities can offer schools or school districts the possibility to avoid consolidation, but at the cost of financial penalties (PSBA, 2009). And in some occasions, when given the choice, the local districts choose to accept the financial penalty and maintain their schools (PSBA, 2009).

Source: Ares Abalde, M. (2014), "School Size Policies: A Literature Review", *OECD Education Working Papers*, No. 106, *http://dx.doi.org/10.1787/5jxt472ddkjl-en*.

school size. In terms of local and rural development, it was argued that schools can play a key role for the local community beyond their immediate educational function. However, it should be possible to develop alternative institutions to take over this function of a social hub, e.g. other cultural and social centres, as part of broader regional and local development initiatives and strategies. These institutions could, in certain cases, also use the vacated former school building.

A number of ways should be considered to remove current obstacles to school consolidation. First of all, it would be important to simplify the complex process currently required to close down and merge schools. In this context, local disincentives to school consolidation need to be addressed. Currently, while municipalities experience the benefits of maintaining even very small schools within borders, they only feel part of the cost of keeping these schools open. In addition, the creation of larger catchment areas (going beyond the borders of one municipality) in rural areas would be an important step towards consolidation. Once larger catchment areas (with multiple municipalities in it) have been established, a more rational decision can be made about which schools to keep open within the catchment area. The current system where the municipal area and the catchment area coincide means that when the last school closes in a catchment area, the concerned municipality needs to transfer funds to another municipality for each student, without controlling how that money is being spent.

Finally, and most importantly, it is key to link school consolidation to a strong quality agenda. When school consolidation is part of an agenda to improve quality and sound arguments are made why school enlargement is necessary as part of that agenda, the nature of the conversation changes. It is important to bring the school community, teachers, parents and local politicians on board in such a conversation. It is necessary to communicate a vision of quality education to persuade others of the need for change instead of on a narrow focus on cost savings. School consolidation must go in line with visible improvements in the quality of the students' school in order to make consolidation attractive to parents and students.

Pursue further strategies to increase equity in education by addressing early selection

Apart from school and class size, the second major challenge in the Austrian school offer is the early selection at age ten after four years of primary education. As the NMS reform did not result in the full integration of lower secondary education following a political compromise, early selection continues to the present day, with the NMS and the AHS still offering two separate tracks.

A recent OECD publication on Equity and Quality in Education makes a clear case against early tracking considering its effect on inequality (OECD, 2012), and as shown by international research, early selection is typically related to a stronger effect of socio-economic background on the performance of students. Student selection and, in particular, early tracking, exacerbates differences in learning between students. It has an impact on educational inequities, as any given pathway and any given school affects learning in two ways. First, the teaching environment can vary, since it depends on the curriculum, the teachers and the resources. Less demanding tracks tend to provide less stimulating learning environments. Second, students' outcomes can also be affected by students' peers (Field et al., 2007). These policies determine the way students are put together or directed to separate classrooms, pathways and schools according to their abilities, and have an impact on equity and on educational failure. Evidence shows that the track to which students are assigned has a great impact on their educational and life prospects (Shavit and Müller, 2006).

Proponents of grouping students according to their performance suggest that students learn better when grouped with others like themselves so that teaching can be adapted to their needs. However, research shows that it has a significant negative impact on those placed in the lower levels (Hattie, 2009) and the evidence is mixed on the impact of tracking on high achievers, depending on the methodology and data used (Jakubowski, 2010). Data from OECD PISA confirm that countries with more differentiated instruction have greater inequality of performance between students, while there are no significant effects on overall performance (Hanushek and Wößmann, 2006). A study from Austria shows that students in the AHS in Austria do not benefit from the system of early selection as their achievement is below the students in academic schools in other countries (Schabmann et al., 2012).

The existence of lower level tracks and streams fuels a vicious cycle in the expectations of teachers and students. Teachers can have lower expectations for some students, especially disadvantaged and/or low performing ones, and assign them to slower-paced and more fragmented instruction; and students adjust their expectations and efforts, which results in even lower performance (Gamoran, 2011). Moreover, more experienced and capable teachers tend to be assigned to higher level tracks (Oakes, 2005). Students placed in lower performance groups experience a low quality learning experience, and may suffer stigmatisation and a decrease in self-esteem. Also, they do not benefit from the positive effects of being around more capable peers (Hanushek and Wößmann, 2006; Ammermueller, 2005).

To address these challenges, a number of policy options are open for consideration. Most importantly, Austria should consider completing the integration of NMS and AHS at the lower secondary level as was originally intended with the NMS reform. This would mean that all Austrian students are in the same type of school until age 14, which is the case in most OECD countries. The November 2015 reform proposal of the federal government envisages the creation of model regions of comprehensive education within individual provinces limited to 15% of students and to 15% of schools in this province, but does not go so far as to propose the lengthening of common schooling across the country (see Chapter 1, Annex 1.1). Although tracking in Poland already took place at a later age, the country provides an example for a successful structural reform that has had a significant success not only in terms of reducing inequities, but also in raising student performance overall. In 1999, Poland reduced the selectivity of its education system as part of a broader education reform that also covered the curriculum. The reform postponed tracking by one year until age 15 and thus extended the period of general education based on a common core curriculum and equal standards for all students. Since the reform, students complete six years of primary education and three years of common lower secondary education before moving to a three- or four-year upper secondary school that provides access to higher education or to a three-year basic vocational school. Furthermore, students' experience in schools has shifted towards common exposure to content and content difficulty. In OECD PISA 2003, 19% of 15-year-old lower-secondary students who took part in PISA attended schools whose principal reported that students were not placed in different groups for mathematics classes (either through groups within a particular class or between different classes in the same school). In the 2012 round of the assessment, the share of students not being placed in different ability groups had increased to 42% of 15-year-old lower-secondary students (OECD, 2013b; OECD, 2011).

However, if a move towards the full integration of the NMS and the AHS turns out not to be politically feasible, other options are available. One of these would be to reduce the distance between AHS and NMS schools, for example by bringing all lower secondary schools into one hand administratively so that educational planning for the whole age group is more coherent, and common oversight of the curricula, teaching and assessment is strengthened (see Chapter 2). One step further could be to twin AHS and NMS schools in the same regions, perhaps even bring them under joint management. This would facilitate transfer from school to the other and increase the likeliness that in terms of curricula the two types of schools grow closer together. Facilitating better transitions for students to move upstream from the NMS to the AHS and from one track to another at later moments in their education and providing adequate support to students that have changed tracks to cope with the new track could help reduce the impact of socio-economic background on student outcomes. The Austrian school system is more flexible than other models of early tracking and selection (e.g. in some German *Länder*) through its diversity of upper secondary vocational tracks which are open to students from the NMS as well. But NMS students face additional challenges to move across streams as they require specific grades for access to specific tracks and as implicit tracking through different grading schemes within the NMS has remained in place. NMS students may also face lower expectations concerning their educational career. It would, therefore, be important to provide better support to students to move up across different school types and to those struggling within a particular track to succeed (e.g. through differentiated teaching). Implementing a system of early diagnosis and remedial support for struggling students can be an effective policy tool in this regard. In Finland, for example, a special teacher who is specifically trained to work with struggling students is assigned to each school and works closely with teachers to identify students who need extra help. Multi-professional care groups, consisting of the school principal, special education teacher, the school nurse, the school psychologist, a social worker, teachers and parents, meet periodically to discuss individual students' learning progress (OECD, 2016). While the Dutch system of early tracking also faces increasing challenges (OECD, forthcoming), the Netherlands could provide some further inspiration for Austria. The Netherlands is a country with relatively early tracking, but with much more favourable outcomes in terms of the impact of socio-economic background on educational performance. Unlike in Austria, children in the Netherlands are tracked into different streams at age 12 after two years of kindergarten and six years of primary education, that is two years later than in Austria. Like in Austria, there are many transfer points throughout secondary education, but transfer possibilities also exist much earlier, including in the first year of lower secondary education.

Further promote all-day schooling

Although all-day schools are increasingly available in Austria, only a small fraction of these offer an integrated form of all-day schooling, which promises greater benefits for children from less advantaged socio-economic backgrounds. Currently the federal budgets available for all-day schooling are underused, suggesting that the provinces are not moving as quickly as the federal government would like them to.

If all-day schooling is introduced successfully in Austria, it may offer several positive outcomes. Until recently, the evidence for all-day schooling was rather thin, but an ambitious programme for all-day schooling combined with a large scale study in Germany shows evidence of several improvements. In Germany, the conversion and equipment of schools to the all-day format has been financially supported by the investment programme "Future of Education and Care" between 2003 and 2009. Federal states and governments have been investing in two areas: increasing the availability of all-day schooling for children and youths; and improving pedagogical work and teaching quality at those all-day schools. The number of all-day schools in Germany has risen greatly. In 2009, 47% of German schools were considered to be all-day schools. The criteria for classification as an all-day school are quite strict. All-day schools are "primary and secondary schools which, in addition to timetabled lessons in the morning, offer an all-day programme comprising at least seven hours per day on at least three days per week. Activities offered in the afternoon are to be organised under the supervision and responsibility of the head staff and to be carried out in co-operation with the head staff. The activities are to have a conceptual relationship with the lessons in the morning" (Secretariat of the Standing Conference of the Ministers of Education and Cultural Affairs of the *Länder* in the Federal Republic of Germany, 2008: 356). Different forms of all-day schools are distinguished based on student level of obligation. In schools with "open-all-day" programmes, participation is voluntary and students choose to participate individually. In "compulsory" all-day programmes, students are required to stay in school for extended hours at least three days a week. Consequently, even though more than 45% of schools offered all-day programmes in 2009, only about 25% of students participated.

The study attached to this major policy programme revealed a number of positive effects. First, the introduction and expansion of all-day schooling has led to an improvement in family-work balance for parents, particularly for parents from low socio-economic backgrounds who feel supported by all-day schools. Second, students have been very positive about the quality of extracurricular activities. Student ratings are based on student-staff relationship, student age, and other characteristics of students and their schools. Third, and perhaps most importantly, given sufficient quality of the extracurricular activities and duration and intensity of participation, all-day schools can enhance motivational and social development of students as well as their grades (Fischer and Klieme, 2013). The German study shows that quality matters, i.e. that the integrated form of all-day schooling is likely to have a greater effect on education outcomes. However, currently only a fraction of the schools in Austria offer this option. This is partly hampered by the fact that two-thirds of the parents and the teachers need to agree before schools can opt for the integrated forms of all-day schooling, which is understandable given that integrated all-day schooling affects all students. However, this procedure considerably slows down the further implementation of all-day schooling. If Austria is serious about introducing integrated all-day schooling, a campaign bringing parents on board will be essential.

Moreover, it needs to be better acknowledged that in order for any form of all-day schooling to be a success in urban areas there are serious infrastructure challenges that need to be addressed. The space requirements to keep children inside schools for longer periods, including cooking facilities and play areas need to be developed in line with the expansion of this type of schooling. All-day schooling is also likely to imply that teachers are present at schools to a larger degree and need workplaces, equipment and facilities to prepare teaching, collaborate and use their out-of-class time effectively.

Notes

1. For example, see *www.leerstandskonferenz.at* (accessed 6 April 2016).
2. For example, "*Oberösterreichischer Schulbaufonds*" [Upper Austrian Fund for the Construction of Schools], "*Niederösterreichischer Schul- und Kindergartenfonds*" [Lower Austrian Fund for Schools and Kindergartens], "*Wiener Schulsanierungspaket 2008-17*" [School maintenance package for Vienna].
3. Data from *BMBF, Abteilung IT/1 – Bildungsstatistik* [BMBF, Division IT/1 – Education statistics] *www.cisonline.at/fileadmin/kategorien/SPF-SchuelerInnen_2013-14_nach_besuchten_Klassen_-_Integration_20.3.2015.pdf.*
4. Data from *BMBF, Abteilung IT/1 – Bildungsstatistik* [BMBF, Division IT/1 – Education statistics] *www.cisonline.at/fileadmin/kategorien/SPF-SchuelerInnen_2013-14_nach_besuchten_Klassen_-_Integration_20.3.2015.pdf.*

References

Ammermüller, A. (2005), *Educational Opportunities and the Role of Institutions*, Research Memoranda 004, ROA, Research Centre for Education and the Labour Market, Maastricht.

Ares Abalde, M. (2014), "School Size Policies: A Literature Review", *OECD Education Working Papers*, No. 106, OECD Publishing, *http://dx.doi.org/10.1787/5jxt472ddkjl-en.*

Berry, C.R. and M.R. West (2010), "Growing pains: The school consolidation movement and student outcomes", *Journal of Law, Economics, & Organization* 26(1), pp. 1-29.

BMBF and BMWFW (2015), *Bildungsreformkommission Vortrag an den Ministerrat [Education Reform Commission Presentation to the Council of Ministers]*, Bundesministerium für Bildung und Frauen, Vienna, *www.bmbf.gv.at/ministerium/vp/2015/20151117.pdf?55kaz6.*

Borgonovi, F. and G. Montt (2012), "Parental Involvement in Selected PISA Countries and Economies", *OECD Education Working Papers*, No. 73, OECD Publishing, Paris, *http://dx.doi.org/10.1787/5k990rk0jsjj-en*.

Bruneforth, M. et al. (forthcoming), *OECD Review of Policies to Improve the Effectiveness of Resource use in Schools: Country Background Report for Austria*, Bundesministerium für Bildung und Frauen, Vienna.

Bruneforth, M. and L. Lassnigg (eds.) (2012), *Nationaler Bildungsbericht Österreich 2012 [National Education Monitoring Report for Austria 2012]*, Leykam, Graz, *www.bifie.at/buch/1914*.

Bruneforth, M., C. Weber and J. Bacher (2012), "Chancengleichheit und garantiertes Bildungsminimum in Österreich" [Equality of opportunities and guaranteed minimum education standards in Austria], in B. Herzog-Punzenberger (ed.), *Nationaler Bildungsbericht Österreich 2012, Band 2 [National Education Monitoring Report for Austria 2012. Volume 2: Focussed Analysis of Key Areas of Education Policy]*, Leykam, Graz, pp. 189-229.

Chmielewski, A.K. (2014), "An international comparison of achievement inequality in within- and between-school tracking systems", *American Journal of Education*, Vol. 120/3, pp. 293-324.

Duncombe, W.D. and J.M. Yinger (2010), "School district consolidation: The benefits and costs", *The School Administrator*, Vol. 67, No. 5, pp. 10-17.

Eder, F. et al. (eds.) (2015), *Evaluation der Neuen Mittelschule (NMS). Befunde aus den Anfangskohorten: Forschungsberich [Evaluation of the New Secondary School (NMS): Insights from the First Cohort. Research Report]*, Leykam, Graz.

Falch, T., M. Rønning and B. Strøm (2008), "A cost model of schools: School size, school structure and student composition", in N.C. Soguel and P. Jaccard (eds.), *Governance and Performance of Education Systems*, Springer, Dordrecht.

Field, S., M. Kuczera and B. Pont (2007), *No More Failures: Ten Steps to Equity in Education*, Education and Training Policy, OECD Publishing, Paris, *http://dx.doi.org/10.1787/9789264032606-en*.

Fischer, N. and E. Klieme (2013), "Quality and effectiveness of German all-day schools: Results of the study on the development of all-day schools", in J. Ecarius et al. (eds.), *Extended Education – an International Perspective*, Barbara Budrich, Opladen, pp. 27-52.

Gamoran, A. (2011), "Designing instruction and grouping students to enhance the learning of all: New hope or false promise?", in M. Hallinan (ed.), *Frontiers in Sociology and Social Research*, Vol. 1, Part 1, pp. 111-126.

Gibbs, C (2014), "Experimental evidence on early intervention: The impact of full-day kindergarten", *EdPolicyWork working papers*, University of Virginia, *http://curry.virginia.edu/uploads/resourceLibrary/34_Full_Day_KG_Impact.pdf*.

Hanushek, E. and L. Wößmann (2006), "Does educational tracking affect performance and inequality? Differences-in-differences evidence across countries", *Economic Journal*, Vol. 116, pp. 63–76.

Hattie, J. (2009), *Visible learning: A Synthesis of 800 Meta-Analyses Relating to Achievement*, Routledge, London.

Herzog-Punzenberger, B. and A. Unterwurzacher (2009), "Migration – Interkulturalität – Mehrsprachigkeit", in W. Specht (ed.), *Nationaler Bildungsbericht Österreich [National education monitoring report for Austria]*, Leykam, Graz, pp. 161-182.

Howley, C., J. Johnson and J. Petrie (2011), *Consolidation of Schools and Districts: What the Research Says and What It Means*, National Education Policy Centre, School of Education, University of Colorado, Boulder.

Humlum, M.K. and N. Smith (2015), "The impact of school size and school consolidations on quality and equity in education", *EENEE Analytical Report*, No. 24.

Im, Y. (2009), "Towards new directions for Korean rural education policy", in T. Lyons, J. Choi and G. McPhan (eds.), *Innovation for Equity in Rural Education. Symposium Proceedings*, University of New England, Armidale.

Jakubowski, M. (2010), "Institutional tracking and achievement growth: Exploring difference-in-differences approach to PIRLS, TIMSS, and PISA data", in J. Dronkers (ed.), *Quality and Inequality of Education. Cross-National Perspectives*, Springer, Dordrecht.

Killeen, K. and J. Sipple (2000), "School consolidation and transportation policy: An empirical and institutional analysis", *Working Paper for the Rural School and Community Trust Policy Program*, Cornell University, Ithaca.

Kolouris, P. and S. Sotiriou (2006), "Exploring teacher's innovative leadership roles in small rural schools", in *The Commonwealth Council for Educational Administration and Management (CCEAM) Conference 2006*, Nicosia, Cyprus, pp. 12-17.

Larsen, B.Ø., K. Houlberg and B.S. Rangvid (2013), *Metodenotat om udgiftsanalyser på folkeskoleområdet på skoleniveau [Methodological Note on the Cost Analysis of the Folkeskole by Level of Schooling]*, KORA.

Lyson, T.A. (2002), "What does a school mean to a community? Assessing the social and economic benefits of schools to rural villages in New York", *Journal of Research in Rural Education*, Vol. 17, No. 3, pp. 131-137.

Meyer, E.T. (2000), *Big or Small? A Policy Analysis of School Consolidation*, *http://users.ox.ac.uk/~inet0080/iuarchive/files/BigorSmall.PDF*.

Moulton, J. (2001), *Improving Education in Rural Areas: Guidance for Rural Development Specialists*, The World Bank, Washington, DC.

Nguyen, H., M. Schmidt and C. Murray (2007), "Does school size matter? A social capital perspective?", *Review of Educational Policy Literature, Faculty of Education and School of Communication*, Simon Fraser University.

Nitta, K., M. Holley and S. Wrobel (2010), "A phenomenological study of rural school consolidation", *Journal of Research in Rural Education*, Vol. 25, No. 2, pp. 1-19.

Oakes, J. (2005), *Keeping Track: How Schools Structure Inequality*, Yale University Press, New Haven.

OECD (forthcoming), *OECD Education Policy Review: The Netherlands*, OECD Publishing, Paris.

OECD (2016), *Low-Performing Students: Why They Fall Behind and How to Help Them Succeed*, PISA, OECD Publishing, Paris, *http://dx.doi.org/10.1787/9789264250246-en*.

OECD (2015), *Education at a Glance 2015: OECD Indicators*, OECD Publishing, Paris, *http://dx.doi.org/10.1787/eag-2015-en*.

OECD (2013a), *PISA 2012 Results: Excellence through Equity Giving Every Student the Chance to Succeed*, PISA, OECD Publishing, Paris, *http://dx.doi.org/10.1787/9789264201132-en*.

OECD (2013b), *PISA 2012 Results: What Makes Schools Successful? Resources, Policies and Practices*, PISA, OECD Publishing, Paris, *http://dx.doi.org/10.1787/9789264201156-en*.

OECD (2012), *Equity and Quality in Education: Supporting Disadvantaged Students and Schools*, OECD Publishing, Paris, *http://dx.doi.org/10.1787/9789264130852-en*.

OECD (2011), "The Impact of the 1999 Education Reform in Poland", *OECD Education Working Papers*, No. 49, OECD Publishing, Paris, *http://dx.doi.org/10.1787/5kmbjgkm1m9x-en*.

Pfeffer, F.T. (2008), "Persistent inequality in educational attainment and its institutional context", *European Sociological Review*, 24(5), pp. 543-565.

PSBA (2009), *Merger/Consolidation of School Districts: Does It Save Money and Improve Student Achievement?*, Education Research and Policy Centre, Pennsylvania School Boards Association.

Rechnungshof (2014), *Schulstandortkonzepte/–festlegung im Bereich der allgemein bildenden Pflichtschulen in den Ländern Oberösterreich und Steiermark, Rechnungshofbericht, Bund 2014/12 [Concept for the School Offer in the Area of General Compulsory Schooling in the Provinces of Upper Austria and Styria, Report of the Court of Audit, Band 2014/12]*, Austrian Court of Audit, Vienna.

Schabmann, A. et al. (2012), "Lesekompetenz, Leseunterricht und Leseförderung im österreichischen Schulsystem. Analysen zur pädagogischen Förderung der Lesekompetenz" [Reading competencies, reading teaching and support in the Austrian school system. Analysis of pedagogical support of reading competencies], in B. Herzog-Punzenberger (ed.), *Nationaler Bildungsbericht Österreich 2012 - Band 2. Fokussierte Analysen bildungspolitischer Schwerpunktthemen [National Education Monitoring Report for Austria 2012. Volume 2: Focussed Analysis of Key Areas of Education Policy]*, Leykam, Graz.

Schratz, M. and M. Hartmann (2009), *Studie zur Evaluation der Auswirkungen der Leadership Academy an Schulen [Study of the Evaluation of the Impact of the Leadership Academy on Schools]*, Universitat Innsbruck.

Sell, R.S. and F.L. Leistritz (1997), "Socioeconomic impacts of school consolidation on host and vacated communities", *Community Development Society*, Vol. 28, No. 2, pp. 186-205.

Shavit, Y. and W. Müller (2006), "Vocational secondary education, tracking, and social stratification", in M. Hallinan, *Handbook of the Sociology of Education*, pp. 437-452.

Sigbórsson, R. and B. Jónsdóttir (2005), "Small rural schools: An Icelandic perspective", in A. Sigsworth and K. J. Solstad (eds.), *Small Rural Schools: A Small Inquiry*, Interskola, Cornwall.

Sigsworth, A. (2005), "Summary and reflections", in A. Sigsworth and K.J. Solstad (eds.), *Small Rural Schools: A Small Inquiry*, Interskola, Cornwall.

Statistik Austria (no date), online database, *www.statistik.at/web_de/statistiken/menschen_und_gesellschaft/bildung_und_kultur/formales_bildungswesen/schulen_schulbesuch/index.html*.

Chapter 4

Management of the teaching workforce in Austria

This chapter analyses the management of the teaching workforce in Austria, from initial teacher education and professional development to the organisation of teachers' employment conditions and working time. It also analyses the availability and organisation of administrative and other pedagogical support staff and the local management of schools through school leadership. It considers recent reforms of initial teacher education and teachers' employment conditions – major milestones in the creation of a common teaching profession beyond school types. But it also highlights the difficulties the complex governance arrangements create for the effective organisation of human resources in schools from a broader perspective and across primary and lower secondary education as a whole as well as the need to develop a vision of teacher professionalism and the need to further develop the leadership of schools. The chapter concludes in suggesting a number of policy recommendations to address these issues.

The statistical data for Israel are supplied by and under the responsibility of the relevant Israeli authorities. The use of such data by the OECD is without prejudice to the status of the Golan Heights, East Jerusalem and Israeli settlements in the West Bank under the terms of international law.

Context and features

Initial teacher education

A comprehensive reform of initial teacher education (*PädagogInnenbildung NEU*) was passed in 2013 and has been implemented for new primary teachers since 2015/16. For new secondary teachers, it is planned to be implemented from 2016/17 onwards. Prior to the implementation of the new model, teachers of federal schools were required to complete a five-year programme at a university, culminating in a master's degree, as well as an additional year of post-graduate part-time professional practice (*Unterrichtspraktikum*). Teachers of provincial schools were required to attend one of nine public and five private university colleges of teacher education (*Pädagogische Hochschulen*, PH) to complete a three-year programme which was only recently given the status of a bachelor's degree.

The reform seeks to enhance the quality of teaching by improving future teachers' academic and practical training. Although the reform maintains the institutional division between university colleges of teacher education (PHs) and universities, the two types of institutions will be required to collaborate more closely, particularly to provide master's degree programmes. The teacher education reform introduces a common set of qualification requirements across school types. All new teachers will need to complete an eight-semester bachelor's degree, plus a master's degree of two to three semesters within the first five years of teaching. Part-time master's degrees will be made available before 2019/20. From 2029, however, new teachers will need to attain their master qualification before entering the profession.

The creation of a common teacher education scheme is also intended to reduce structural differences between the training of teachers for federal and provincial schools. Following the reform, the education of all future teachers will be geared towards age groups (primary or secondary level) rather than the different school types. This change seeks to raise the status of teachers of provincial schools relative to the currently more highly qualified federal school teachers and to increase teachers' mobility between different types of schools. In addition to these changes, the new system aims to make the teaching profession more attractive for side entrants from other professions through the development of supplementary study programmes and the recognition of previous experience and pedagogical competences. It also seeks to raise the profile of students and to provide guidance and orientation by extending compulsory admissions tests to universities. Previously, only students at university colleges had to participate in such admissions proceedings.

The new teacher education programmes will focus on legally defined competency areas and include instruction in subject-related theory, pedagogy and the basics of general education. The new programmes will provide students with practical teaching experience and the possibility to specialise (e.g. in special-needs pedagogy or multilingualism). Prospective primary school teachers will acquire the whole range of skills necessary for teaching all subjects while prospective secondary school teachers will be qualified in two subjects. Under the new model, inclusive pedagogy will be an integral part of the training for all new teachers. This reflects the fact that 30.3% of Austrian lower secondary school teachers reported a high level of need for further training in teaching special needs students for the OECD 2008 Teaching and Learning International Survey (TALIS) (although only 10.0% compared to the TALIS average of 13.9% reported a strong demand for training concerning the teaching in multicultural environments in the TALIS study) (OECD, 2009).

A quality assurance council (*Qualitätssicherungsrat für Pädagoginnen- und Pädagogenbildung*, QSR) comprising six external experts has been created to follow the reform. It monitors, analyses and gives advice on the implementation of the new model and issues an annual report on the reform's progress to the Austrian National Parliament (*Nationalrat*) (Bruneforth et al., forthcoming; Eurydice, 2015; QSR, 2015).

Workload and organisation of teachers' time

In Austria, teachers' workload is regulated in the federal teacher service code (*Bundeslehrer-Lehrverpflichtungsgesetz*, BLVG) for teachers of federal schools and the federal service code for provincial teachers (*Landeslehrer-Dienstrechtsgesetz*, LDG) for teachers of provincial schools. For federal teachers, legislation does not specify the working time, but the teaching time only; for provincial teachers, legislation specifies both the total working time and the teaching time. The actual hours of presence at school are not regulated for neither federal nor provincial teachers.

Teachers in federal schools have a basic teaching assignment of 20 teaching hours per week. However, there is a complex system to weight the total teaching hours per subject taught. Subjects that are considered more challenging to teach have a proportionally higher weighting (e.g. German-language teaching has a higher weighting than physical education). In addition, specific tasks such as administrative support to the school principal or other tasks in the schools such as the management of the school library can further reduce the basic teaching load of 20 hours if a certain school size is met. In the most common subjects, teachers have an actual teaching load of 17-21 hours.

The workload of teachers in provincial schools is regulated according to an annual working hours scheme. This scheme stipulates 1 736 hours of work per year for teachers aged 43 or older, and 1 776 hours of work per year for all younger teachers. The annual standard is divided into three activity areas: teaching duty including supervision; preparation, follow-up and correction; and hours for other activities such as substitute teaching, class co-ordination, administrative tasks and school-projects. Over one year, 720 to 792 hours, that is about 20 to 22 hours a week, have to be dedicated to direct teaching, 600 to 660 hours are foreseen for the planning and follow-up of lessons, and the remaining 324 to 456 hours of the annual standard are available for other activities. For all teachers, the task of student assessment is regulated and typically takes up a substantial amount of teaching time relative to direct teaching.

A new teacher service code (*Dienstrechts-Novelle 2013 – Pädagogischer Dienst*) will harmonise the working time arrangements for all new teachers across federal schools and provincial schools. With the new regulations, teachers will have an increased teaching load of 24 teaching units of 50 minutes per week. Twenty-two of these teaching hours have to be dedicated to direct instruction, two hours have to be spent on other tasks, such as student counselling and mentoring of new teachers. For teachers of subjects that require a large amount of preparation and follow-up in upper secondary education, only 20 hours of direct teaching are required. The new service code has been implemented from September 2015 onwards, but until September 2020 new teachers can choose between the old and the new system (Bruneforth et al., forthcoming; Eurypedia, 2015).

Teacher appraisal

Teacher appraisal in Austria is primarily the responsibility of the school principal and carried out through sporadic classroom visits and observations of teaching. In addition, for teachers on fixed-term contracts, there is a mandatory annual appraisal for contract renewal, and in federal schools, teachers on fixed-term contracts are also regularly appraised during their one-year probationary period (OECD, 2013c). In the case of complaints, the school inspectorate can initiate an evaluation of a teacher's work that involves a teacher appraisal commission at the level of the province usually composed of school inspectors and teaching staff representatives. Following a second formal statement that a teacher's performance does not meet expectations, a teacher can be dismissed. Besides appraisal, teachers are encouraged to evaluate themselves (e.g. through student feedback), but this is not a requirement (Bruneforth et al., forthcoming; Eurypedia, 2015).

Teacher professional development

All teachers are obliged by the respective service codes to ensure that their teaching reflects the latest subject-specific didactics and pedagogy. Specific requirements for participation in professional development, however, differ depending on the service code and the employment status. For teachers of general compulsory schools employed by the provinces it has been obligatory to undertake 15 hours of professional development per year. For teachers of academic secondary schools employed by the federal level, there has been no such requirement in place for those employed as civil servants, but those employed as contract agents have had to also complete 15 hours of professional development. The reform of the teacher service code harmonises the regulations for teachers' continuing professional development across different school types. Since September 2015, all newly employed teachers are employed under the contract agent scheme and are, therefore, required to take 15 hours of professional development per year.

Professional development courses are offered at university colleges of teacher education (PHs) which offer a broad range of courses that reflect current policy priorities. Teachers should usually undertake their professional development outside of their regular teaching hours, i.e. in the afternoon, evening, weekends or vacations. Only if this is deemed necessary by the school authorities and if a replacement is provided can teachers participate in professional development during teaching hours. Professional development does not need to be linked to a teacher's specific subjects (Bruneforth et al., forthcoming). There are few statistics on participation, but OECD TALIS 2008 indicated that almost all Austrian teachers participate in professional development, although the number of days per participant was comparatively low (11 days compared to the TALIS average of 15 over the 18 months preceding the survey) (OECD, 2009).

Administrative and other support staff

A number of different social and administrative support staff roles exist in the Austrian school system. Educational psychology and career guidance (*Schulpsychologie-Bildungsberatung*) is available through 77 school psychological service units throughout Austria. These units are run by the Federal Ministry for Education and Women's Affairs

(BMBF) and employ around 150 educational psychologists. School psychological service units offer psychological information, counselling, support and treatment with the focus of health promotion and personality development, and expert services according to legal provisions. Their work focuses on issues related to students' school career decisions, maturity for school, learning difficulties, behavioural problems, personal difficulties and crises and emergencies, for example. All students, parents and teachers can make use of this psychological guidance and counselling service free of charge. As a second area of work, school psychological service units support schools in prevention (such as violence prevention, social learning, student engagement and motivation, school absenteeism and early school leaving) and intervention (such as class intervention, mediation and conflict resolution), the promotion of a sense of community, the management of crises (such as in the case of violence and bullying), and in the development of school development plans. As a third area of work, school psychological service units offer training and professional development for teachers and school principals to develop their competencies in special focus topics, such as dyslexia, dyscalculia, behavioural problems, violence and maturity for school.

Social workers are only employed at schools if necessary. Where social workers are required, their role is to identify social problems as early as possible and to develop relevant solutions and strategies to solve them. As part of the 2014-20 European Social Fund Operational Programme, the Federal Ministry of Education and Women's Affairs (BMBF) published a call for project proposals to find innovative ways to organise social work at schools to prevent school dropout in socially disadvantaged contexts. Social pedagogues may also be available. Typically, social pedagogues work in school-based day care, youth welfare, school-based and non-school-based youth work and also therapeutic and special pedagogy. School medical services (*Schulärztlicher Dienst*) are provided at all schools in different ways (e.g. through a local physician or dedicated school doctors that provide advice on a range of issues).

Some further support staff related to vocational guidance, counselling and early school leaving is available in secondary education. In Years 7 and 8 of lower secondary education, students take one lesson of career guidance per week. In lower secondary education overall, students take 32 lessons of career guidance per year. These career guidance classes and activities are typically organised by career guidance co-ordinators on behalf of the school leadership. At New Secondary Schools (NMS) and academic secondary schools (AHS), specially trained student counsellors provide career guidance and personal counselling (e.g. on learning or behavioural difficulties) directly at the school. And in 2013, the Federal Ministry for Social Affairs (*Bundesministerium für Arbeit, Soziales und Konsumentenschutz*, BMASK) and the Federal Ministry for Education and Women's Affairs (BMBF) introduced the 'Youth Coaching' initiative to tackle early school leaving. As part of this initiative, youth coaches advise and accompany young people aged 15 to 19 at risk of dropping out from school or of being marginalised to look for the educational pathway that works for them. Youth coaches generally have a background in social work, therapeutic pedagogy, social pedagogy, social management or psychology.

Schools may also employ administrative staff, but administrative staff is generally not widely available. The recruitment of administrative support personnel is the responsibility of the provincial school board in the case of federal schools, and the responsibility of the provincial government authorities or school maintainers (*Schulerhalter*) in the case of provincial schools.

The federal government's November 2015 reform proposal foresees giving schools the possibility to convert up to 5% of their teaching staff positions into pedagogical support staff positions (BMBF and BMWFW, 2015, see Annex 1.1 in Chapter 1).

School leadership

Profile

The organisation of school leadership in Austria depends on the size of the school. In schools with at least ten teachers, a school principal needs to be appointed. In schools with less than ten teachers, there are no school principal positions, but teachers are entrusted with the leadership and management of the school and in return partly exempt from their obligation to teach. School leadership in Austria is still predominantly exercised by an individual school principal and middle leadership roles are rare except for some medium-sized and large schools, particularly in technical and vocational upper secondary education. A few large secondary schools have a permanent deputy principal position. In all other schools, school principals are assisted by a teacher that functions as an administrator and not by an officially appointed deputy.

In medium-sized and larger schools, there are some more middle management positions, such as heads of departments (*Abteilungsvorstehung*) and heads of subjects (*Fachvorstehung*). Teachers taking on such roles have a reduced teaching load (50-75% less) and receive a bonus of between EUR 300 and EUR 850 per month. In addition, teachers can take on leadership roles through functions such as class co-ordinators which includes administrative tasks related to one specific class as well as the pedagogical co-ordination of the different subject teachers in New Secondary Schools (NMS) and academic secondary schools (AHS) (Bruneforth et al., forthcoming; Eurypedia, 2015).

Employment

The employment of school principals is organised according to the same federal statutory regulations that regulate the recruitment and remuneration of teachers (Civil service code [*Beamten-Dienstrechtsgesetz*, BDG] for school principals of federal schools, and federal service code for provincial teachers [*Landeslehrer-Dienstrechtsgesetz,* LDG] for school principals of provincial schools).

Vacant school principal positions are filled following a public call for applications and through a regulated appointment process. All interested candidates with at least six years of professional experience as a teacher in a relevant school type must submit their applications to the responsible administration (*Dienstbehörde*). Following the introduction of an amendment to the teacher service code in 2013, candidates will also need to complete a training programme in school management (*Schulmanagement: Professionell führen*, currently 30 ECTS, 90 ECTS from 2030) at a University College of Teacher Education (PHs) before applying for a position. Completion of school management training was previously only required within the first four years of appointment. According to a central framework provided by the Ministry for Education and Women's Affairs (BMBF), the training programme in school management should develop educational leaders' pedagogical, functional, social and personal competencies. Participants should acquire knowledge and skills in the following areas: leadership and management; personnel and team development; quality management and development; school and lesson development; and community relations. All programmes should consider gender and diversity issues.

Selection and appointment procedures differ between federal schools and provincial schools. The appointment of school principals of federal schools is regulated through federal legislation only and the appointing authority is the Federal Ministry for Education and Women's Affairs (BMBF). The appointment of school principals of general compulsory schools is regulated according to the basic federal framework for the recruitment of school principals and the provinces are responsible for the development of implementation legislation that details the procedures for the appointment of school principals.[1]

With the amendment to the teacher service code in 2013, school principals of all schools will be initially appointed for a period of five years (previously four years). At the end of the initial appointment, the employer, i.e. the provincial authorities or the federal authorities, can reappoint the school principal without an open call for applications and a new appointment process for an unlimited period of time. School principals must be informed about decisions on their reappointment at least three months prior to the end of their initial appointment. School principal positions are linked to a specific school and school principals have a right to be employed at that school. School principals can, however, be transferred from one school to another under certain conditions set out in the teacher service codes.

The federal government's November 2015 proposal for education reform envisages some changes to the organisation of the school leadership employment framework, including the establishment of school leadership as a separate professional group, the introduction of a standardised job profile and recruitment process, and a five-year limit to all school principal appointments, including re-appointments (BMBF and BMWFW, 2015; see Annex 1.1 in Chapter 1).

School principals receive a service bonus in addition to their salary as teachers. The new teacher service code will increase the size of the bonus and abolish age-related aspects in its calculation to make school leadership more attractive for younger teachers. While the bonus ranges currently from EUR 218 to EUR 907 per month, it will increase to EUR 300 to EUR 1 650 per month and the amount of the bonus will vary by school size only. School leaders of small and very small schools will receive an additional allowance of up to EUR 463 per month. School principals who are responsible for two or several schools receive the bonus for each school they manage. In addition, school principals can receive a one-off bonus for outstanding performance or involvement in particularly successful projects (Bruneforth et al., forthcoming; Eurypedia, 2015). Table 4.1 provides an overview of basic statutory salaries of school principals in public schools by level of education and school size.

Tasks and responsibilities

School principals' duties and responsibilities are regulated through laws established by the federal legislator irrespective of the school type, including provincial schools. Accordingly, school principals are the direct supervisors of the teachers and other staff at their school. School principals have to advise teachers in their teaching and pedagogical work and to regularly monitor instruction and student performance. They may visit classrooms and observe instruction at any time. Concerning the recruitment and assignment of teachers to their school by the responsible authority (provincial school board or school department of the office of the provincial government), school principals must prepare a plan to project the future demand and development of human resources in their school and submit data (e.g. on the distribution of teaching subjects, absences, overtime)

Table 4.1. Annual gross salaries of full-time fully qualified school principals in public schools, 2014/15

	Basic statutory salary (EUR)	
	Minimum	Maximum
Primary (big)	41 320	67 120
Primary (small)	36 376	61 513
Lower secondary (> 4 classes, General schools)	41 320	67120
Lower secondary (small)	36 376	61 513
Upper secondary (> 12 classes, Academic secondary schools)	54 083	82 334
Upper secondary (small)	49 721	77 381

Note: Data on basic statutory salaries (basic statutory teacher salaries plus school leadership bonus) are from the Federal Remuneration Act.

Source: Eurydice (2015), *Teachers' and School Heads' Salaries and Allowances in Europe, 2014/2015*, Eurydice Facts and Figures, Brussels/Luxembourg.

Figure 4.1. Ratio of school leader and maximum teacher salaries to the minimum annual statutory salary for teachers, 2014/15

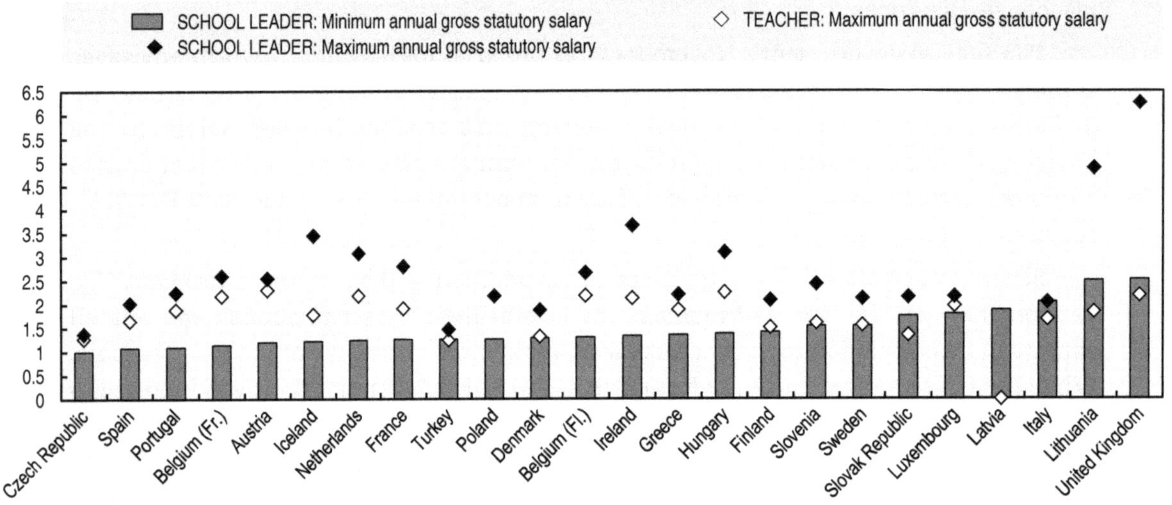

Note: Countries are presented in ascending order of ratio of minimum school leader salary to minimum teacher salary.
Minimum salaries are based on the lowest salary across primary and secondary education. Maximum salaries are based on the highest salary across primary and secondary education.

Source: Calculated from data in Eurydice (2015), *Teachers' and School Heads' Salaries and Allowances in Europe, 2014/2015*, Eurydice Facts and Figures, Brussels/Luxembourg.

to electronic data management systems (see Chapter 2). Further, they can give their opinion with regard to the suitability of teachers who have applied to be assigned to their school and, although principals have no formal decision making power with regard to the recruitment of teachers, they can have some informal influence. School principals are responsible for the running of the school and the liaison between the school, students and the parents. They are also responsible for implementing laws and other legal regulations as well as instructions and decrees (*Erlässe und Rundschreiben*) issued by the educational authorities. They prepare the meetings of the school partners and are responsible for executing the decisions adopted at these meetings. School principals allocate the annual budget granted to the school and prepare the school's annual financial statements (in the case of federal schools). While in the past school principals had to teach a certain number of hours depending on the size of their school in addition to their school leadership responsibilities, they have been exempt from this requirement since September 2014 if their school has at least ten full-time teachers. School leaders of small and very small schools can receive a 25-50% reduction of their teaching duties (Bruneforth et al., forthcoming; Eurypedia, 2015).

The federal government's November 2015 reform proposal envisages some changes to school principals' tasks and responsibilities as part of the plan to give schools greater pedagogical, organisational, staff and financial autonomy. This includes giving school principals the responsibility for the organisation of the work schedule, greater flexibility for the adaptation of school hours to meet the demands of parents' and guardians' work schedules, and autonomy for school principals to set aside time for quality development projects and annual planning with all staff outside of teaching hours. Concerning the management of schools' human resources, it is planned that school leaders are consulted in the selection of staff, that they hold a veto right against new appointments, and that they should be involved in employment decisions, such as contract renewal. School leaders should be responsible for staff development and evaluations and arranging and approving teachers' further training within the available resources. And school leaders are planned to receive the possibility to convert up to 5% of their teaching staff positions into support staff positions and to use external teaching staff for special areas of focus (BMBF and BMWFW, 2015, see Annex 1.1 in Chapter 1).

Strengths

There are a range of aspects that provide teachers in Austria with good working conditions and Austria has undertaken first steps to make teaching a more attractive career for young people

Job satisfaction and morale among Austrian teachers appears high, even though there are also some concerns (e.g. as suggested by high early retirement rates of teachers). According to data from OECD TALIS 2008 36.9% of lower secondary teachers were strongly satisfied with their jobs (TALIS average: 24.3%) (OECD, 2009, Table 4.19). This was one of the highest proportions among countries participating in the survey. And according to data from the OECD Programme for International Student Assessment (PISA) 2012, all 15-year-olds were in a school whose principal agreed or strongly agreed that the morale of teachers in their school was high and that teachers worked with enthusiasm (OECD, 2013b, Figure IV.5.8).

Neither TALIS 2008 nor PISA 2012 provide further data on teachers' perceptions of their working conditions and the underlying reasons for their job satisfaction and morale at work. However, some factors may positively influence teachers' job satisfaction and morale which are essential as they influence teachers' ability to do their job well and their willingness to remain in the profession. In particular, teachers in Austria benefit from relatively low teaching hours and small classes. For the OECD *Education at a Glance 2015* publication, Austria reported a total annual net teaching time of 779 hours for primary education, 607 hours for general lower secondary education and 589 hours for general upper secondary education, compared to an OECD average of 772, 694 and 643 hours respectively (OECD, 2015a). When looking at class size (more on this in Chapter 3), the average primary school class in Austria had 18 students, the average lower secondary school class (general programmes) had 21 students, both well below the OECD average (21 and 24 students per class respectively) (OECD, 2015a). Research from different countries suggests that small classes can have a positive effect on teachers' working conditions (Hattie, 2009; OECD, 2009). However, one needs to bear in mind that both low teaching loads and small classes imply considerable costs for the school system as these factors influence the number of teachers required.

With the introduction of a new teacher service code and a new teacher education system, Austria has undertaken first steps to make teaching more attractive for young people and side entrants through changes to qualification requirements and remuneration, even though more measures may be needed in the future. This is an urgent issue as Austria faces a considerable retirement wave in the near future – according to a parliamentary inquiry (*parlamentarische Anfrage* Nr. *8597/J-NR/2011*, BMUKK, 2011),[2] about half of all teachers in Austria are expected to retire by 2025. Concerning teachers' qualification requirements, the new teacher education system will raise the status of the teaching profession with the requirement for all future teachers to acquire a master's qualification, also for those in general compulsory education. For side entrants, the switch to the Bologna system and the creation of supplementary study programmes that award credits for subject-related and pedagogical competencies as part of the new teacher education scheme will make the teaching profession more easily accessible. With regards to teachers' remuneration, the new teacher service code will significantly change the salary progression (also see Chapter 2 for a discussion of teachers' salaries). Statutory salaries for beginning teachers will start at a higher level and the slope of the salary scale will be compressed while roughly maintaining lifetime earnings (at present, the slope of salary increases in Austria is much steeper than in many other countries). Under the new service code, teachers will benefit from seven salary steps in the first 15 years of their career instead of the current system of a biannual salary increase. This change implies a considerable financial risk during the transition period until all teachers under the old salary scheme have retired considering the high salaries for ageing teachers, but it has the potential of making the profession more attractive than was the case previously. Nevertheless, whether the reverted salary will help to attract highly qualified candidates in the future will have to be seen. It is also important to bear in mind that qualification requirements for new teachers in provincial schools have been raised – new teachers of provincial schools will have to acquire a master's degree and complete 11-12 semesters of study compared to a three-year programme before – and that the teaching load will slightly increase, particularly for teachers of federal schools. For professionals from outside education, the recognition of up to 12 years of professional experience and the new salary progression that come with the new teacher service code will offer more attractive salaries when switching careers.

The new initial teacher education system (PädagogInnenbildung NEU) has a number of positive elements

The new teacher education scheme aims to harmonise qualification requirements and programmes for provincial and federal schools. While the distinction between university colleges of teacher education (PHs) and universities will be maintained, only primary school teachers will be predominantly educated at university colleges. For all other levels of schooling both kinds of institutions will have to collaborate, at least at the master's level. The development of a common initial teacher education appears as an important milestone to break down barriers between different school types and to create a common teaching profession. A common initial teacher education for all teachers should help teachers feel part of a larger community of teachers that goes beyond school types and focuses on the common goal of raising achievement for all students in the education system as a whole. It is likely to create the basis for greater mobility and flexibility to teach at different school types and, therefore, reduce some rigidity in the teacher labour market. This is particularly relevant for lower secondary education where teacher education, like the teacher service codes, used to differ between teachers of federal and provincial schools at the same level of education. Together with the new teacher service code (more on this below), the new teacher education model, therefore, also constitutes a further step towards the creation of a common school form for all children up to age 14, and for raising the quality and profile of the NMS relative to the AHS.

The new teacher education scheme could also help raise the quality of initial teacher education in Austria more generally thanks to a number of positive changes. First, collaboration between university colleges of teacher education (PHs) and universities has the potential of bringing together the strengths of both types of institutions and to strengthen both training in subject-related theory on the one hand and pedagogical training on the other hand for all new teachers across the education system. Second, all new teachers will have to complete a master's degree, including those wanting to teach at provincial schools. This sends a strong signal that teaching should be a highly-qualified profession and provides new teachers with the opportunity to gain additional competencies provided that the additional time studying is used well. Third, the introduction of a compulsory orientation and admissions procedure for prospective students in teacher education programmes at universities – previously, such admissions procedures were only required at university colleges of teacher education (PHs) – has the potential of raising the quality of prospective teachers and of providing guidance and orientation for prospective teachers if teaching is the right career choice for them. Finally, the creation of an independent quality assurance council (QSR) provides support for the development of new teacher education programmes as well as continuous advice for the further development of initial teacher education in Austria.

The new teacher service code (Dienstrechts-Novelle 2013 – Pädagogischer Dienst) has some beneficial aspects

There are a range of positive aspects in the new teacher service code that are likely to strengthen the teaching profession in Austria. First, while the review team notes that additional measures could be undertaken in the long run to develop further opportunities for teachers to take on different roles and responsibilities (see further below), the new teacher service code has created some specialist functions (*Fachkarrieren*) in addition to school principal and administrator roles (in federal schools only). Functions include mentoring roles for new teachers, learning and career counsellors (*Bildungs- und Berufsberater*), learning designers (*Lerndesigner*) (for more details, see Box 4.1), special needs and remedial pedagogues (*Heil- und Sonderpädagogen*), and mentors of teacher students (*Mentoren für Praxisschulunterricht*). Teachers who take on such roles will receive additional allowances of up to EUR 156 per month for their tasks and the new teacher education model should provide training in related competencies (Bruneforth et al., forthcoming).

Second, the new teacher service code will harmonise the working conditions and remuneration of future teachers of different school types (Bruneforth et al., forthcoming). Therefore, the new teacher service code together with the new teacher education model (see above) provides the basis for the long-term development of a common professional identity among all teachers irrespective of the school they are teaching at. It provides the basis for greater flexibility and mobility for teachers to work in different school types, and it provides the same remuneration for teachers that have completed an equivalent teacher education programme. Like the changes to the teacher education system, this is particularly relevant for lower secondary education. Prior to the introduction of the new

Box 4.1. **The creation of teacher leadership roles in Austria as part of the New Secondary School reform**

In Austria, the New Secondary School reform (NMS) to transform lower secondary education also involved the creation of a new role of learning designers (*Lerndesigners*) with specific expertise in areas of curriculum and instructional development related to the reform goals of equity and excellence. As part of this initiative, each school designates a teacher to be the learning designer who acts as change agent in a shared leadership dynamic with school principals and other teacher leaders, such as subject co-ordinators and school development teams. As legislation and teacher statutes do not yet foresee an official function of teacher leaders, learning designers create their own role in the context of their school. The effectiveness of learning designers as change agents therefore depends to a significant degree on the culture and leadership in their schools.

Learning designers are trained and qualified for their role and attend national and regional workshops and local networking events. A two-year national qualification programme enables learning designers to acquire theoretical and practical insights in areas of expertise related to instructional quality, to develop the knowledge and skills to be effective teacher leaders and to network with one another. This programme also contributes significantly to their profile and professional identity. It comprises six development areas: mindfulness of learning, diversity, competence orientation, backwards design curriculum development, differentiated instruction and assessment. Learning designers earn a certificate worth 12 ECTS relevant for further study towards a master's degree. The programme consists of national and regional symposia for networking and qualification purposes as well as a self-study component which is co-ordinated on line and includes practice based tasks for exploration in school based professional learning communities. A virtual networking and learning space is also available to connect learning designers across generations, to promote exchange, learning and development, and to foster a professional identity. To foster school networks and communities of practice and to support learning designers, federal education authorities established a National Centre for Learning Schools.

Learning designers are not alone, but as part of the educational reform several other teacher leadership roles have emerged. These include contact persons or co-ordinators with specific agendas required by the Ministry (e-learning, gender issues, culture and arts programming, standards and school quality), and school development team members and co-ordinators created at the school level.

Source: OECD (2013d), "Approaches to learning leadership development in different school systems", in OECD, *Leadership for 21st Century Learning, http://dx.doi.org/10.1787/9789264205406-7-en*; OECD (2015d), *Schooling Redesigned: Towards Innovative Learning Systems, http://dx.doi.org/10.1787/9789264245914-en*.

teacher service code, teachers in the NMS and in the AHS were employed and remunerated according to two different service codes (*Bundeslehrer-Lehrverpflichtungsgesetz*, BLVG and *Landeslehrer-Dienstrechtsgesetz, LDG*). However, considering prior differences in service codes and related working conditions, the new teacher service code may affect the attractiveness of teaching in provincial and federal schools differently. While new teachers in provincial schools seem to have opted for the new service code since its introduction, new teachers in federal schools seem to have been less likely to do so. Also, the new teacher service code only applies to future teachers and within the first five years, i.e. until September 2020, new teachers can choose between the old and the new system. It will, therefore, take about 40 years for the new service code to apply to all teachers. Until then, teachers will be employed on the basis of three different service codes. As some teachers remarked during the review visit, this may create problems for the school climate and between younger and older teachers.

Third, the introduction of the new teacher service code will also provide stronger in-service development requirements for all teachers. While a one-year induction phase (*Unterrichtspraktikum*) was previously only required for teachers of academic secondary schools, the new teacher service code will provide new teachers of all school types and levels of education with an employment contract from their first year onwards and support new teachers with experienced mentors throughout a one-year professional entry phase. The traditional induction phase for teachers of general secondary schools will be offered for the last time in the school year 2018/19 (Bruneforth et al., forthcoming). As the OECD review of teacher policies and OECD TALIS have pointed out, new teachers often face additional challenges, particularly in disadvantaged schools (e.g. in terms of classroom management and student behaviour and discipline) (OECD, 2005; OECD, 2009). If not addressed, these challenges can reduce teachers' confidence and influence teachers' decision to change careers. A difficult start to the career can, then, imply high costs for individual teachers as well as schools and students. Effective induction and mentoring arrangements can increase the effectiveness and job satisfaction of new teachers, and increase the likelihood that teachers grow into mentoring roles themselves and participate in professional development later on in their career. Experienced teachers can also benefit from their mentoring role as it provides a source of new ideas about curriculum and teaching and an opportunity to reflect about experiences and beliefs with regard to teaching and learning (OECD, 2005; Jensen et al., 2012; OECD, 2015e). However, the impact of the new induction and mentoring phase in Austria will also depend on the training and time that mentors receive for their role. In that respect, it is positive that the new teacher service code also includes two hours per week, which, among others, can be used for mentoring activities. In addition, all new teachers will be required to undertake 15 hours of professional development per year.

The introduction of systematic team teaching in New Secondary Schools (NMS) has the potential to improve teaching and learning

The NMS reform involved the introduction of teacher collaboration as one of its central elements. The reform provides additional teaching resources for the NMS to build teacher teams that work together in one classroom. While team-teaching was initially concentrated on specific subjects (German, mathematics and English), this restriction has recently been lifted and the NMS have more flexibility to decide about the use of the additional teaching resources, i.e. it is now possible to double-staff a third of posts for subjects other than German, mathematics and English with the overall number of hours remaining the same. The additional resources amount to six additional teaching units per NMS class. This systematic team teaching initiative provides an opportunity for teachers to learn from each other and to work together, but also to provide more individualised instruction and additional support for low-achieving students. The additional teaching resources should be provided by teachers from academic secondary schools so that a team is made up of one academic secondary school teacher and one New Secondary School teacher. Considering differences in the traditional model of teacher education between teachers of general compulsory schools and teachers of academic secondary schools – the former are educated at university colleges of teacher education (PHs) in more practical programmes, the latter at Universities in more theoretical programmes – this provides an interesting opportunity for teachers with different backgrounds to learn from each other. It also provides an opportunity for cultural change towards a common teaching profession and acceptance of more time in a common school. Furthermore, the NMS reform has introduced networking opportunities for teachers and school principals across New Secondary Schools with the creation of a Centre for Learning Schools (*Bundeszentrum für Lernende Schulen*) (Bruneforth et al., forthcoming).

However, it may be necessary to provide further support for the implementation of the team-teaching concept and collaboration between the AHS and the NMS, and to encourage school principals and teacher leaders to take greater responsibility for the management of team teaching. As interviews with teachers and students suggest, teachers may not be prepared to effectively work together to provide additional opportunities for learning. Teachers may simply use the support provided by each other to reduce their workload and the time required for preparation, and assessment and marking, for example. Concerning the collaboration of teachers from different school types and the use of AHS teachers in the NMS, there are no incentives for AHS teachers to participate in this initiative and collaboration depends on the willingness of individual teachers and school principals of different schools. Not all teacher teams are, therefore, made up of AHS and NMS teachers. In 2012/13, AHS teachers accounted for only slightly more than half of the total additional teaching time in the NMS, even though this differed greatly across provinces (Bruneforth et al., forthcoming). Teaching in another school also has costs for individual teachers in terms of time, e.g. for participation in teacher conferences at two schools. As mentioned in Chapter 2, the split in regulatory competencies between the federal and provincial governments for AHS and NMS teachers makes it difficult to monitor and manage the secondment of AHS teachers. The secondment of AHS teachers would, therefore, benefit from an ending of the formal divide between federal and provincial schools as well as between federal and provincial teachers.

The Austrian education system provides additional teaching resources for students with particular learning needs

In primary education, students at risk of falling behind can benefit from one remedial teaching hour (*Förderunterricht*) per week – either separately as an additional lesson or integrated within the regular schedule (also see Chapter 3). Students with particular language needs can also receive additional teaching resources. Students with difficulties to follow the language of instruction when starting school can receive special support for up to two years as "non-regular students" (*außerordentliche Schüler*). Classification of "non-regular students" typically takes place when children enter school, but is also possible if students migrate to Austria at a later age. Schools receive up to 11 lessons per week depending on the number of non-regular students, and lessons can be integrated or parallel to regular instruction. If provided in integrated form, the additional weekly instruction time for a student must not exceed five hours. The federal government also provides funding for specialised staff within the general staff allocation so schools can offer additional language courses (German as a second language) for students who are not classified as "non-regular students". Besides additional teaching resources for remedial teaching, "non-regular students" and German as a second language, the provincial school boards have some discretion to allocate additional teaching resources if such needs are identified, often through the school inspection (Bruneforth et al., forthcoming).

While these additional teaching resources exemplify that Austria pays attention to providing additional teaching resources to particular learning needs, there is also scope for improvement. As Nusche, Shewbridge and Lamhauge Rasmussen (2010) pointed out multilingualism in Austria is sometimes still seen as a problem rather than a resource and the allocation of additional resources focuses on children's deficits. This might lead to a labelling and stigmatisation of students and lower expectations by teachers. Also, additional instruction focuses on students' progression in language learning rather than on the standard subject content. It provides resources only at the beginning of a student's schooling even though it is important to support the continuous language learning of students also in the higher grades. And it leaves the organisation of additional instruction entirely to schools, which might lead to an inconsistent provision of additional resources and to the additional resources not being used in the best way. Furthermore, while the resources are provided by the federal level, the way they are used in schools is not controlled or monitored, and since classification of students as "non-regular" is only possible when students enter the education system and is not based on a standardised process, there can be an incentive for school principals to label students pre-emptively to receive the additional teaching resources (Bruneforth et al., forthcoming).

Schools have a fair degree of pedagogical autonomy and Austria has taken steps to build school leadership

As highlighted in Chapter 2, the review team gained the impression that Austrian schools (as well as individual teachers) have a relatively high degree of autonomy in some pedagogical matters, i.e. in choosing preferred teaching methods and in developing new subjects. Curricula are developed by the federal ministry, but schools have some autonomy in how to implement them. Within the pre-set framework curricula, schools can develop their own specific profile and set priorities by modifying the number of instruction hours for subjects, introduce additional compulsory or non-compulsory subjects and offer tutoring (*Förderunterricht*). Pedagogical autonomy for schools to develop a school profile is greatest in lower secondary and upper secondary education. In addition, teachers have full autonomy in choosing the methods they deem appropriate to implement the curricula and achieve set learning objectives (Bruneforth et al., forthcoming; Eurypedia, 2015).

All schools visited as part of the review visit offered additional subjects or had created a specific profile (e.g. with a focus on specific pedagogies). One primary school, for example, had developed a focus on Montessori teaching methods as well as a transversal focus on ecology and nature that was implemented across all subjects. One NMS had developed a technical profile; another NMS had decided to offer bilingual and mother-tongue instruction in Bosnian, Serbo-Croatian and Turkish. One AHS had introduced optional subjects in health and sports, management and leadership, and chess; another AHS had introduced a focus on Croatian-language instruction as a minority language, sports, music, and autonomous learning.

Comparative data from *Education at a Glance 2012* and OECD PISA 2012 also suggest that schools have a relatively high level of pedagogical autonomy. According to *Education at a Glance 2012*, lower secondary schools make 88.9% of decisions related to the organisation of instruction, compared to 75.4% on average across OECD countries (OECD, 2012).[3] For PISA 2012, Austrian principals also reported having a say on a number of curricular issues, but more principals than in other countries reported that higher authorities are also involved in the decision-making process (see Table 4.2). This most likely reflects that specific curricula

Table 4.2. **School autonomy over curricula and assessments, PISA 2012**

Percentage of students in schools whose principals reported that only "principals and/or teachers", only "regional and/or national education authority", or both "principals and/or teachers" and "regional and/or national education authority", or "school governing board" has/have considerable responsibility for the following tasks:

	Austria			OECD average		
	Principals and/or teachers	Both principals and/or teachers and regional and/or national education authority or school governing board	Only regional and/or national education authority	Principals and/or teachers	Both principals and/or teachers and regional and/or national education authority or school governing board	Only regional and/or national education authority
Establishing student assessment policies	38.4	38.4	23.2	46.6	40.5	12.9
Choosing which textbooks are used	60.1	39.7	0.1	64.9	27.1	8.0
Determining course content	34.7	39.4	25.9	39.7	35.8	24.5
Deciding which courses are offered	10.2	71.8	18.0	35.6	46.1	18.2

Source: OECD (2013b), *PISA 2012 Results: What Makes Schools Successful (Volume IV): Resources, Policies and Practices, http://dx.doi.org/10.1787/9789264201156-en*, Table IV.4.3. and Figure IV.4.3.

as implemented by schools are developed within national framework curricula and need to be presented to the school forum and be reported to the school inspection (Bruneforth et al., forthcoming). Principals and teachers have relatively high levels of autonomy (similar to the OECD average) with respect to choosing textbooks, deciding on the course offer and determining the school content. Fewer students were in a school whose principal reported to be involved in the establishment of student assessment policies, which reflects that assessment criteria are set out in federal legislation (OECD, 2013b).[4] However, one needs to bear in mind that most 15-year-olds in Austria already go to upper secondary schools. This complicates comparisons of structural aspects with other countries where 15-year-olds typically still attend lower secondary education (Bruneforth et al., forthcoming).

Schools often seemed to draw on teachers' interests and competencies beyond their qualification for a specific subject when developing optional subjects. The creation of individual school profiles also seemed to help schools respond to students' background and interests and attract students to their school. However, various schools also mentioned that resource constraints, i.e. the lack of teachers and teaching hours, can make it difficult to use this pedagogical freedom. This may be particularly challenging for small schools. One school, for example, was interested in offering nutrition, but did not have the teaching hours to do so, and the principal of one larger school commented that only the large number of students made it possible to maintain the wide range of optional subjects currently available at that school. In addition, several principals mentioned that the number of autonomous hours had been reduced in recent years. As far as teaching methods are concerned, various interview partners also mentioned that the introduction of educational standards and standardised assessments may lead to some reduction of pedagogical autonomy.

As part of its work programme for 2014-18 and as part of its six-point programme for education, the Austrian federal government plans to extend current school autonomy, including the autonomy to manage pedagogical matters. Planned measures include the introduction of alternative assessment and grading up to Year 3, more flexible time structures (e.g. combination of classes, more project-based work and more flexible breaks), more scope for the development of school profiles, additional quotas of hours and cross-location pools of hours to meet support needs in the form of "project pots" (subject to budgetary limits), especially in primary education, and more freedom to co-operate with other institutions and associations within the region and municipality (e.g. kindergarten, sports clubs and music schools, arts and cultural institutions) (BMBF, 2014; Austrian Federal Chancellery, 2013). The November 2015 reform package proposed by the federal government also intends to give schools greater autonomy, including further responsibilities for pedagogical matters. As is planned, schools should have more flexibility to devise learning groups according to pedagogical targets and more opportunities for the flexible formation of classes and groups, and they should have greater autonomy to determine their focus and curriculum timetables where this will enhance the quality of learning (BMBF and BMWFW, 2015; see Annex 1.1 in Chapter 1).

The review team also notes that Austria has implemented some measures to strengthen the leadership capacity of schools over the last 15 years, even if more still needs to be done in this area (see further below). Since 1997, school principals have been required to undertake compulsory training within the first four years of their first appointment and initial preparation has now been strengthened with the introduction of the new teacher service code in 2013 that will require school principals to undertake preparation before taking up a position. This is in line with recommendations from an international research project on Improving School Leadership in Central Europe which suggested reconsidering the induction requirement for recruitment and to introduce preparatory training prior to appointment instead (Schratz et al., 2010).[5] In 2004, Austria undertook a further step towards the professionalisation of school leadership with the creation of a Leadership Academy. While professional development for school principals was previously organised through short-term training at university colleges of teacher education (PHs), the development of a Leadership Academy has established more systematic opportunities for ongoing professional learning. The Leadership Academy seeks to develop leadership at all levels of the education system, from principals to managers in the school administration, the inspection and teacher education (Schratz, 2009; NLQ Hildesheim, 2011). In addition, the new teacher service code provides more time for school principals to focus on their leadership tasks by eliminating school principals' teaching obligation if their school has at least ten teachers, and by reducing school leaders' teaching duties if they manage a small or very small school. This reflects a growing realisation that it may be necessary to reduce school leaders' teaching role to fulfil their increasingly complex role (NLQ Hildesheim, 2011).

Challenges

There are a number of rigidities in the organisation of the teacher labour market

The OECD review team formed the impression that there were a number of rigidities in teacher recruitment and allocation that formed obstacles to a more efficient organisation of the teacher labour market. First, the complex distribution of responsibilities for the employment of human resources between federal and provincial levels makes it difficult to organise the teaching workforce efficiently and to steer and monitor the use of teachers in schools across Austria (more on this in Chapter 2). The distinction between provincial and federal schools and teachers in lower secondary education also makes it difficult for teachers to work in different schools at this level, although the team teaching arrangements in the NMS have created first opportunities for teachers from the AHS to work in both school types.

Second, despite some initiatives to give schools more input into the selection of teachers and informal opportunities to influence selection decisions and plans to extend schools' human resource management autonomy as part of the November 2015 reform proposal, schools are still limited in their autonomy to manage their human resources (also see Chapter 2 and Figure 4.2). The selection of staff is largely the responsibility of the provincial school boards and the school departments of the provincial governments. This may not always ensure that the allocation of teachers matches schools' needs, although input of the school inspections – which have, however, limited capacity – may facilitate some steering. An important criterion for the allocation of teachers seemed to be new teachers' age and the age profiles of schools rather than the schools' profile and needs. It was also not clear in how far the allocation of teachers reflected equity concerns and in how far the best teachers were allocated to the most disadvantaged schools. In addition, teachers interviewed by the OECD review team voiced concerns that they had little influence on where they would be allocated and contract teachers might face particular challenges of only being informed at short notice of where they would have to teach.

Figure 4.2. **School leader reports on school responsibility for resource management, PISA 2012**

Percentage of students in schools whose leader reports only he/she and/or teachers are responsible for:

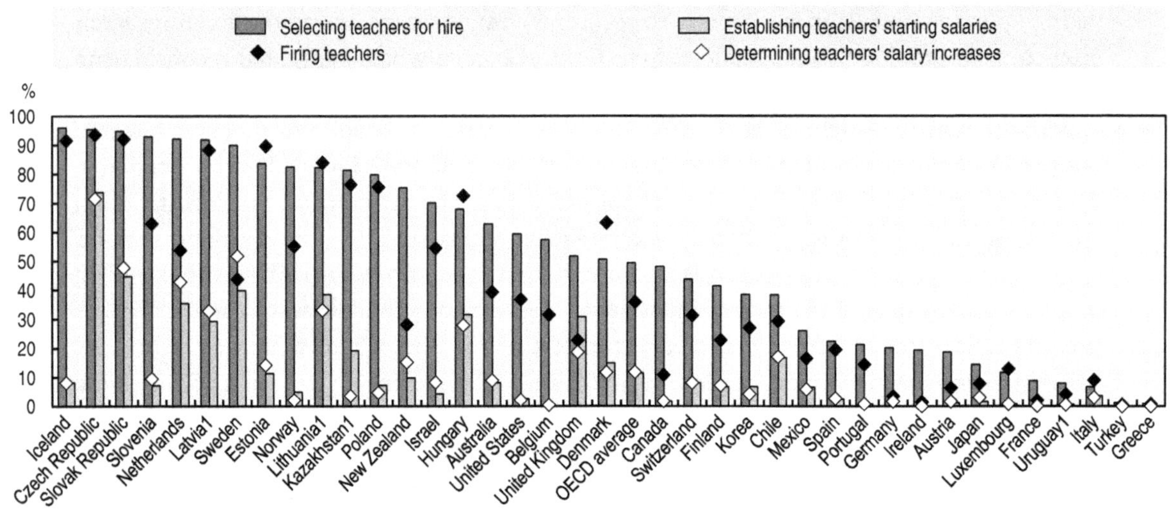

Note: Countries are ranked in descending order of schools principals' and/or teachers' responsibility for selecting teachers for hire.
1. Not an OECD member country.
Source: OECD (2013b), *PISA 2012 Results: What Makes Schools Successful (Volume IV): Resources, Policies and Practices, http://dx.doi.org/10.1787/9789264201156-en.*

Third, the current definition of teachers' remuneration does not set incentives to organise the teaching workforce more effectively. According to the old and the new teacher service codes, teachers with a given set of qualifications and seniority receive the same pay irrespective of other factors that could steer the supply of teachers to areas most in need, such as specific school contexts (e.g. rural schools, disadvantaged schools) and subjects with a shortage of qualified teachers. More generally, teacher mobility seems low and it can be difficult for teachers to move to another school, as interviews during the review visit suggest. Low teacher mobility can be an obstacle to the sharing of practices and spread of knowledge across the education system (OECD, 2005).

Finally, teachers at general compulsory schools interviewed by the OECD review team noted that their employment by the provincial level makes it difficult for them teachers to move to another province. The statutory rights which teachers acquire through seniority, such as the progression in the salary scale and pension entitlements, may not always be recognised in a different province. This essentially reduces teachers' mobility and creates regional labour markets with different balances of demand and supply.

The complex governance structure complicates the monitoring of the teacher labour market and the effective steering of the supply of teachers

While detailed data are not available, there does not seem to be a shortage of teachers across the Austrian education system overall. According to OECD PISA 2012, school principals believed that teacher shortages hindered instruction less than in many other countries (OECD, 2013b, Figure IV.3.5).[6] However, as various stakeholders reported to the OECD review team, the situation differs greatly between different provinces and regions. In Vorarlberg and Vienna, for example, it has apparently become more difficult to fill vacant teaching positions. Vorarlberg seems to compete for teachers with neighbouring Switzerland and the working conditions offered there. In Vienna, authorities already had to employ AHS teachers prior to completing their post-graduate part-time professional practice as well as non-qualified staff on special contracts to compensate for a shortage of graduates in certain teaching subjects. These regional differences are also related to demographic developments and an increase or reduction of the school age population in different parts of the country (see Chapter 3). Vienna, for instance, is projected to grow in population and concentrates a considerable share of international migrants to Austria. The need for new teachers is, therefore, likely to increase in the future, whereas rural areas of Austria such as parts of Carinthia and Styria are projected to lose population (*parlamentarische Anfrage Nr. 8597/J-NR/2011*).

As reported by some of the OECD review team's interview partners, it has become more difficult to find sufficient teachers for specific subjects, such as mathematics and the natural sciences. In these subjects, stakeholders raised concerns that a number of teachers teach in subjects for which they are not qualified. This seems to be a particular problem in the NMS and small schools. A further hidden form of teacher shortage is the significant use of overtime. For the school year 2010/11, the Austrian Court of Audit reported that, on average, federal teachers in lower and upper secondary education taught 2.7 hours a week more than their stipulated teaching time. This amounts to 3.74 million hours of overtime for all 36 500 federal teachers in lower and upper secondary education (Bruneforth et al., forthcoming). However, the use of overtime also seems to create a certain level of flexibility for the management of the teaching workforce. Compensation for overtime is cheaper than the recruitment of additional teachers and overtime can be reduced or increased more easily according to changing student numbers than teacher positions.

To get a complete picture of the teacher labour market and to steer the supply of teachers effectively, processes to analyse demand and supply and a possible shortage or oversupply of teachers across the country need to be in place. Considering the large number of teachers who are expected to retire in the near future, sound forward planning and monitoring will be essential to identify existing and emerging teacher shortages. Austria disposes of measures for forward planning and labour market monitoring (European Commission/EACEA/Eurydice, 2015). However, the distribution of responsibilities for the employment, monitoring and data management of human resources between federal and provincial authorities for different school types (also see Chapter 2) seems to make projections and forecasting overly challenging. Forecasting and planning seem to require a substantial amount of co-ordination between the different responsible authorities (the Ministry for Education and Women's Affairs, the provincial school boards and the school departments of the provincial governments). For example, to gather data on the share of teachers who teach a subject they are not qualified for, it would be necessary to analyse all individual teachers' working contracts filed at the level of the nine provincial school boards or provincial school departments. None of the authorities seemed to assume the overall responsibility for planning and monitoring the supply and demand for future teachers across the education system as a whole and for taking steps to mitigate potential bottlenecks in the supply of new teachers. For the Ministry for Education and Women's Affairs (BMBF), which holds responsibility for teacher education at university colleges of teacher education (PHs), it is difficult to take on such a system-wide planning and monitoring role considering the lack of easy access to data on provincial teachers. For example, there are no national data on the number of counsellors (*Beratungslehrer*) employed at special needs centres (*Sonderpädagogische Zentren*) as these are provincial teachers (Schmich, 2010).

There are challenges related to the implementation of the new initial teacher education scheme

The introduction of the new initial teacher education system entails a number of promising features that have the potential to raise the quality of the future teaching workforce. However, the impact of the reform will necessarily take time and depend on how it is implemented. The success of the reform rests to a large extent on the ability of university colleges of teacher education (PHs) and universities to develop new curricula and to raise the quality of teaching. As a monitoring report of the quality assurance council pointed out, each of the two types of institutions faces their own challenges considering their particular traditions and strengths and weaknesses (QSR, 2015). At university colleges, this concerns the institutions' limited capacity to undertake research and their relatively low managerial and organisational autonomy – university colleges are directly dependent on the Ministry for Education and Women's Affairs (BMBF). At universities, this concerns in particular the institutions' more limited tradition in offering students more practice-oriented professional education. There are limited links between universities and schools, and universities are not involved in the further professional development of teachers which could ensure links between initial education and actual practice.

The quality assurance council's report further identified the lack of sufficient qualified staff and personnel and adequate organisational and managerial structures at both institutions as a major challenge for effecting real change in the quality of teacher education (QSR, 2015). Besides long-term strategies such as the development of doctoral schools for teacher education, this will require adequate collaboration between institutions, the development of profiles and areas of expertise in different institutions, and the development of joint organisational and administrative units. The implementation of the reform through collaboration of institutions in four regions should help in this regard. Considering that university colleges and universities are under two different ministries (the Ministry for Education and Women's Affairs and the Ministry of Science, Research and Economy respectively), the effective steering of the new teacher education also requires productive collaboration between the two ministries. According to a judgement of the quality assurance council, however, collaboration between both has been good so far and platforms that have been built should be maintained. More generally, all institutions involved in teacher education should take shared responsibility for developing and offering a high quality education (QSR, 2015).

Stakeholders interviewed during the OECD review visit pointed to further concerns, in particular how the new teacher education scheme and the increasing length of programmes will affect the attractiveness of the profession. While this constitutes a valid concern, the longer duration may also influence and raise the profile of future students.

The number and quality of enrolments will, therefore, be an important area to monitor. A further concern relates to the feasibility of new teachers completing the required master's degree programme while working in schools.

A stronger professional approach to conceive teaching might be needed

The quality of teaching is key for effective learning and considered the single most important factor within schools that impacts student learning. Austria has taken some important steps to increase the quality of teaching, such as the introduction of a new initial teacher education system (see above) and the development of quality assurance, school development and self-evaluation practices through the SQA and QIBB initiatives (see Chapter 2). However, the review team noted that there seems to be a need for further reflection in Austria about the nature of teachers' professional work today in a context of changing conceptions of teaching and learning. The OECD review team formed the impression that the main lever of the Austrian education system to raise student performance was seen to be the provision of additional teaching hours rather than the implementation of steps to improve teaching practice in schools, which also requires the development of greater capacity for the school-level management of teachers and the learning environment (more on this below). The main political debates about education focus on governance and the distribution of responsibilities for the employment of teachers, but less on the nature of teachers' work in schools and classrooms.

Recent research on organisational learning has stressed the importance of new ways of working in schools that focus on collaboration in teams and larger professional learning communities. This requires teachers to adapt to collaborative work cultures based on shared goals, continuous professional development, reflective practice, peer observation and feedback on a daily basis (OECD, 2013a; OECD, 2013c). In Austria, both policy and practice do not yet fully reflect such reconceptualisations of the teaching profession. As elaborated further below, the new teacher service code, for example, failed to create a real change in the conception of the teaching profession, teachers' working time and teachers' roles and responsibilities. During its school visits, the review team gained the impression that teachers mostly identify with their own school rather than a larger profession. Teachers seemed to be rather isolated in their classrooms and schools did not seem to manage teaching and learning collectively. OECD TALIS 2008 and PISA 2012 substantiate these impressions. Data from OECD TALIS 2008, for example, suggest that teachers in Austria are more likely to favour simpler exchanges and co-ordination over more in-depth forms of professional collaboration than teachers in other countries. In the PISA 2012 index of teacher participation in school management, Austria ranked comparatively low. For instance, 11.2% of students were in a school whose principal reported that they never engage teachers to help build a culture of continuous improvement in the school or at most 1-2 times a year (OECD average: 7.7%). Only 15.2% of students were in a school whose principal reported that they do so more than once a week (OECD average: 23.3%) (OECD, 2013b, Table IV.4.8).

There are limited opportunities for horizontal and vertical differentiation of the teaching career

Even though the new teacher service code constitutes a step into the right direction, teachers in Austria do still not benefit from distinct and flexible pathways that would help schools meet their needs and give teachers more development opportunities and recognition, including for those teachers who wish to remain focused on classroom teaching.

The new teacher service code provides limited opportunities for specialist functions (*Fachkarrieren*), the NMS reform has created some additional teacher leadership roles such as teacher leaders with specific expertise in instructional development (*Lerndesigners*) and co-ordinators of specific areas, such as e-learning, gender issues, culture and the arts, and the introduction of the SQA process has created the role of SQA co-ordinators. There is also a school pilot on middle management that provides opportunities for teachers to take on roles for prevention and integration, school development, assessment and evaluation, community relations, etc.).

But there could still be more systematic opportunities for horizontal differentiation of the teaching career across the entire education system as part of a defined teacher career structure (e.g. co-ordinators of in-service training, school project co-ordination). This would better reflect that teachers need to take on a greater range of tasks and responsibilities and that teachers can also exercise leadership in different roles. According to the new teacher service code, salary progression is still defined in terms of qualifications and seniority and there are no opportunities for formal promotion within teaching (only out of teaching into school principal positions). This traditional approach does not convey the important message that the guiding principle for career advancement should be merit and it does not provide possibilities to reward teachers who choose to remain in the classroom. The lack of opportunities for promotion may reduce the attractiveness of the profession, possibly contributing to both attrition among young teachers and burn-out among older teachers (OECD, 2005; OECD, 2013c).

The conception of teachers' working time does not promote greater teacher professionalism and teachers and school principals spend considerable time on administrative tasks

Employment is conceived of mostly in terms of teaching hours (as opposed to working hours)

While the employment of provincial teachers is based on overall working hours and an annual standard that allocates working time to three different task categories (teaching; preparation, follow-up and correction; and other activities), the employment of federal teachers in Austria is limited to teaching hours only. The new teacher service code that will apply to all new teachers from 2019/20 onwards similarly conceptualises teachers' working time in terms of teaching hours only, even if two hours are allocated to other tasks, such as mentoring, for example.

Such a regulation of teacher employment does not reflect current conceptions of teacher professionalism and effective teaching that entails a range of further activities within the school beyond classroom instruction. It constitutes an implicit assumption that teachers work further hours to complete tasks like the preparation of lessons and the assessment of students' work, but fails to explicitly recognise these tasks and responsibilities. It also limits teachers' engagement in whole-school responsibilities, such as collaboration and peer feedback among teachers, school self-evaluation and improvement planning, which are important for raising the overall quality of teaching and learning at schools (OECD, 2005; OECD, 2013c).

For general compulsory schools, the change from the old teacher service code that defined annual working hours to the new teacher service code may also reduce schools' scope and autonomy to strategically organise teachers' working time. Furthermore, the current and future conceptions of teachers' working time in Austria do not differentiate between teachers with different work experience. As Jensen et al. (2012) argued, it is likely to be inefficient to have teachers of different levels of effectiveness and levels of experience having the same teaching responsibilities. Giving more experienced teachers more teaching hours or more students or classes to teach and reducing new teachers' teaching hours so they can focus on developing their teaching skills at the beginning of their careers could improve teaching and learning.

Teachers and school principals have to fulfil various administrative tasks

As already mentioned in Chapter 2, the review team noted that many schools lack administrative support staff. While both provincial and federal schools may employ secretaries and administrators, and while higher authorities may take on some administrative responsibilities, logistical and secretarial tasks tend to be taken over by school leaders and teachers in return for a reduced teaching load. This means that not all teachers and school leaders are able to fully focus on their core pedagogical responsibilities and tasks, including preparation and follow-up of classes. Some teachers pointed out that the distribution of administrative tasks among teachers in a school may come at the expense of beginning teachers who are asked to take on tasks that no one else wants to take care of, thus placing an additional burden on new teachers. And as the Court of Audit has highlighted, it is also very costly to have teachers take over administrative tasks that could be fulfilled by less expensive administrative staff (Bruneforth et al., forthcoming).[7] In this context, it is also important to bear in mind that the lack of sufficient career differentiation for teachers means that administrative tasks, such as the co-ordination of IT, provides one of the few possibilities for teachers to take on more managerial tasks.

The lack of administrative support is also an issue that came across in OECD TALIS 2008. According to lower secondary principals' reports, there was one administrative or managerial staff available for about 23 teachers, compared to a TALIS average ratio of 1 to 8, by far the worst ratio among participating countries (OECD, 2009, Table 2.4). When looking at the ratio of administrative staff to students, the picture is similar. In Austria, there was one administrative or managerial staff for 221 students. Only schools in Turkey had less administrative support in relation to students among the countries participating in the survey (Schmich, 2010). Not surprisingly then, more than three out of four lower secondary teachers were in a school whose principal reported that instruction was hindered to some extent or a lot by a lack of other support personnel (77.5%, compared to a TALIS average of 45.9%) (OECD, 2009, Table 2.5).

In the general compulsory school sector, the municipalities as school maintainers (*Schulerhalter*) are responsible for the employment of administrative personnel, while the provinces are responsible for the employment of teachers. The local organisation of administrative staff has advantages as it allows, in theory, to organise staff needs so they meet local needs. But the split in responsibilities also means that the provinces cannot influence the employment of administrative staff to ease the administrative burden on their teachers while municipalities may have little financial means to employ such staff or simply be unwilling to do so as the provincial and federal levels compensate by increasing the number of teachers' working hours. Municipalities may, furthermore, lack pressure from their school leaders to employ secretarial staff as they are content to accept these tasks themselves or to delegate them to their teachers (see below). In addition, in the absence of a mechanism that would equalise funding levels across municipalities (see Chapter 2) some municipalities may have less means to hire administrative staff than others. This can create inequities between schools in the education system. In the case of federal schools, the federal government has taken some steps to address the lack of administrative staff. It has pledged to provide up to 2 000 additional administrative staff for schools (e.g. through the redeployment of civil servants who have become redundant in other public services) and started to organise administrative staff more innovatively (e.g. by providing IT support to groups of schools within a region). Nevertheless, funding constraints (for federal schools and provincial schools) and governance arrangements (for provincial schools) pose barriers for employing and organising sufficient administrative personnel in all sub-systems. The current governance arrangements prevent a systematic reflection of the effective use of human resources in schools. Also, there are no roles for particular tasks in Austria, such as the management of the school library and lab facilities, a further issue mentioned during school visits.

There are challenges for the school-level management of the teaching workforce

School principals are not equipped to manage the teaching workforce effectively at the school level

Despite some efforts to foster school leadership, particularly with the establishment of the Leadership Academy in 2004 and the strengthening of the preparation requirement for new school principals with the introduction of the new teacher service code, school principals in Austria do often not yet focus on their pedagogical leadership (and tasks such as strategic goal-setting and monitoring, human resource management, and the development of strong relations with the community) which research indicates has the potential to have a great impact on teaching and learning (Leithwood et al., 2004; Day et al., 2009; Louis et al., 2010), As OECD TALIS 2008 indicated, school principals in Austria are less likely than in most other participating countries to favour instructional school leadership (OECD, 2009). More recent data from OECD PISA 2012 paint a similar even if slightly more mixed picture, which may also be related with the constructs that are measured (OECD, 2013b, Tables IV.12, IV.13, IV.14 and IV.15). Principals in Austria practice slightly more instructional leadership than principals in other countries and economies, but they are less involved in framing and communicating the school's goals and less active in promoting instructional improvements and professional development. Principals in Austria are also less likely to involve teachers in the management of the school. This was also the impression the review team gained through its interviews with school principals and teachers. School principals did not perceive their role as a pedagogical one, but rather as administrative and managerial in nature. In fact, school principals seemed quite content with this role. This is also true for the level of school autonomy. With the exception of teacher recruitment for which school principals wanted to have a greater say, school principals did not seem to want greater overall autonomy. School principals were, in particular, wary of more managerial autonomy that could place a further burden on them. The review team also had concerns about the employment conditions of school principals. These do not necessarily ensure that school leadership is attractive and that the most qualified candidates are selected. Interviews with teachers and school principals provide anecdotal evidence that the school leadership profession is not very attractive and that compensation may not reflect the higher level of responsibility. Data collected by Eurydice (2015) indicate that both minimum and maximum gross statutory salaries do not differ greatly between school principals and teachers (see Figure 4.1). Nevertheless, the new teacher service code may lead to some improvement, especially for younger teachers, by removing age-related aspects in the determination of school principal allowances. Both federal and provincial schools, and particularly small rural schools, struggle to find a large number of candidates (Bruneforth et al., forthcoming). These issues may become more pressing considering that the current school leadership profession is ageing. There are no detailed statistical data on the age distribution of school principals, but according to the latest national education report (*Nationaler Bildungsbericht 2012,* NBB) 2 out of 3 school principals are between 50 and 59 years-old (Vogtenhuber et al., 2012).

Concerning the recruitment of school principals, even though aptitude tests and assessment centres have become more prominent in recent years, the selection process is often considered as being driven by political networks rather than by an objective assessment of the candidates' skills and competencies (Schratz, 2009; Bruneforth et al., forthcoming). This was also mentioned in the review team's interviews. The risk for "political" appointments stems from the political nature of the federal and provincial bodies responsible for the selection process. In particular, the members of the collegiate boards of the provincial school boards are nominated by the political parties relative to their number of seats in the provincial parliaments (Chapter 2). In addition, there are no professional standards for school leadership that could provide a clear and transparent reference of necessary competencies for the selection and recruitment process. The November 2015 reform package may lead to some changes, however, with the introduction of a standardised job profile and recruitment process (BMBF and BMWFW, 2015, see Annex 1.1 in Chapter 1).

Similarly, the review team considers it necessary to improve the working conditions of school principals so as to facilitate greater pedagogical leadership. First, schools lack administrative support personnel and, therefore, school principals often have to deal with many secretarial tasks. This was also the result of a study by Huber, Wolfgramm and Kilic (2013). Schools typically do not have any deputy principals or secretarial staff, even though the situation may be slightly better in academic secondary schools where administrators typically provide some support to school principals. Second, the concept of distributed leadership has not yet gained ground in schools in Austria and school principals are often still "lonely fighters" as Schratz (2009) put it. This can be a hindrance for school principals to concentrate on pedagogical leadership and also lead to burn-out problems for engaged school principals. Third, schools' limited autonomy for resource management, in particular for the management of human resources (e.g. the selection of teachers), can be a barrier to pedagogical leadership. And fourth, the small size of many schools in Austria does not give all school principals the leeway to exercise pedagogical leadership (more on this in Chapter 3).

There are almost no possibilities for school leaders to incentivise high performance or to respond to underperformance

Schools' and school principals' responsibility for human resource management decisions in Austria is very limited (see Figure 4.2). This restricts school principals' scope for encouraging improvement among their teachers and for responding to concerns about a teacher's performance through human resource management decisions (e.g. through influence on teachers' salary progression). Besides school principals' limited autonomy, the lack of sufficient horizontal and vertical differentiation of the teacher career in Austria also weakens school principals' possibilities for setting incentives and for rewarding teachers for their work (e.g. through promotions to middle leadership positions).

It is, therefore, no surprise that teachers in lower secondary schools reported for OECD TALIS 2008 that a teacher's performance would not lead to positive or negative consequences. Teachers in Austria were less likely to believe that they would be rewarded for high performance than teachers in other countries and teachers in Austria were less likely to believe that consistent underperformance would be picked up or addressed than teachers in other countries (see Figure 4.3) (OECD, 2009).

Figure 4.3. **Teacher rewards and incentives, TALIS 2008**

Percentage of teachers of lower secondary education who agree or strongly agree with the following statements about aspects of appraisal and/or feedback in their school:

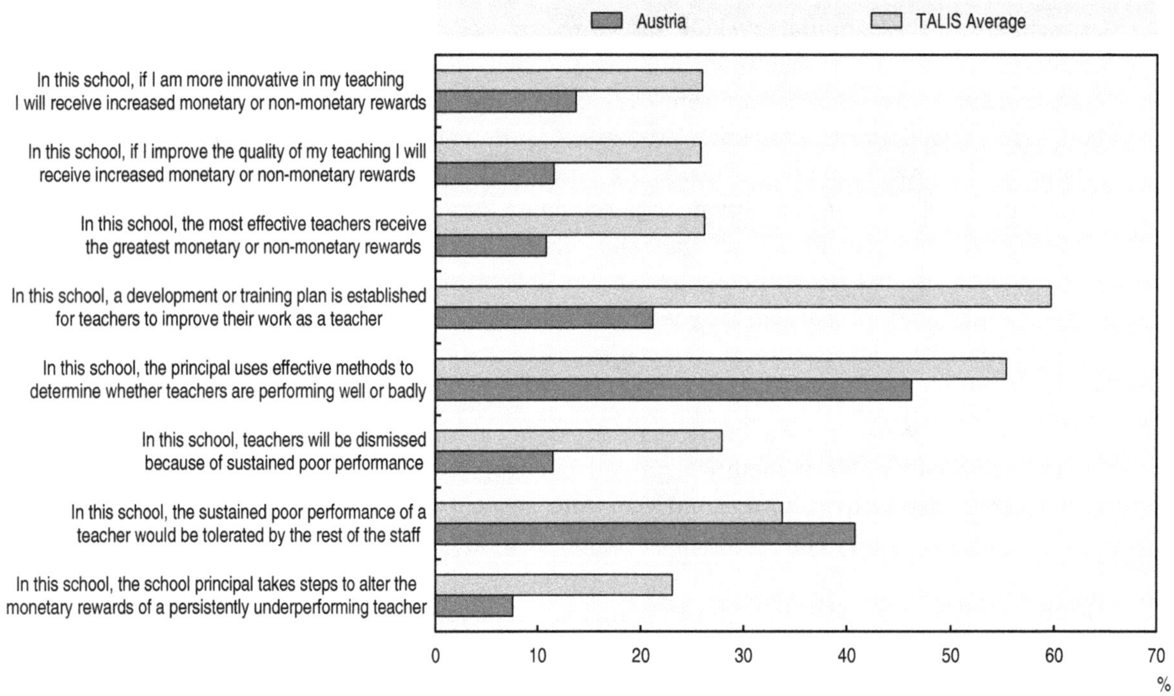

Source: OECD (2009), *Creating Effective Teaching and Learning Environments: First Results from TALIS, http://dx.doi.org/10.1787/9789264068780-en*, Table 5.9.

Teachers have few opportunities to receive feedback and professional development is not used strategically

While school principals are, in theory, responsible for appraising their teachers, both school principals and teachers interviewed by the OECD review team repeatedly indicated that, given the heavy workload of school principals, such formal appraisal was not always systematically implemented for all teachers. Appraisal seems too often to be concentrated on the least experienced teachers and to be less common for more experienced teachers. For OECD TALIS 2008, 18% of Austrian lower secondary teachers reported that they had never received any appraisal/feedback from their school principal (against a TALIS average of 22%) and 29% reported that they had received such appraisal/feedback only once every 2 years or less (against a TALIS average of 13.7%) (OECD, 2009). As already stated above, the review team also gained the impression that there seems to be little tradition of peer feedback, classroom observation and collaborative professional learning among teachers in Austria. Few teachers seemed to work as "critical friends" or peer mentors for one another in developing their practice. In small schools, the sheer size of the school limits teachers' opportunities for feedback from one another (also see Chapter 3). Furthermore, teachers in Austria have limited sources of external feedback and there is no external teacher appraisal process in place. For OECD TALIS 2008, 42.5% of teachers reported that they had never received any appraisal or feedback from an external source (against a TALIS average of 50.7%) and 39.8% had received such external feedback only once in two years or less (against a TALIS average of 24.4%) (OECD, 2009). In Austria, external appraisal typically only takes place in case of serious or frequent complaints of parents about a teacher. In such cases, the school inspectorate may initiate a special appraisal of the particular teacher (OECD, 2013c).

If teachers are appraised by their school principal, the process seems to have only a weak formative function and a limited impact on teachers' professional development. Only 41.4% of Austrian teachers indicated that appraisal or feedback that they had received contained suggestions for improving certain aspects of their work (against a TALIS average of 58%) (OECD, 2009). School principals have full autonomy in deciding how to appraise their teachers and, as a result, teacher appraisal is likely to vary across schools in terms of the methods used, the criteria applied and the use of the results. There are no teacher standards which could inform appraisal and provide a reference against which teachers could be appraised (OECD, 2013c). Nevertheless, according to OECD TALIS 2008, teachers in Austria tend to be more likely to agree that their appraisal and feedback was a fair assessment of their work (OECD, 2009), and the introduction of national standardised assessments has introduced some element of external feedback to work with teachers to improve the quality of their practice.

With regards to the planning of professional development, strategic approaches to teachers' professional development in schools seemed to be rather rare and professional development seemed to be mostly the choice of individual teachers. Teacher appraisal in Austria does not systematically feed into a professional development plan, even if it may lead to a professional development plan or mandatory training for teachers in case of underperformance (OECD, 2013c). For the OECD TALIS 2008, only 21.2% of teachers surveyed in Austria agreed or strongly agreed that a development or training plan would be established for teachers in their school to improve their work. This was the lowest proportion among all TALIS countries, against a TALIS average of 59.7% (OECD, 2009). There is clearly further room in Austria for establishing teacher appraisal as a formative process and for better linking teacher appraisal to individual professional development. This is crucial given that teacher development is one of the main functions of teacher appraisal (OECD, 2013c). Concerning the quality of professional development, as some teachers and school principals pointed out during the review visit, the current offer of courses and programmes may benefit from more stimulation and input from external trainers and providers. Teacher trainers at university colleges of teacher education (PHs) that are in charge of professional development may fail to provide a new perspective on teaching and learning as well as new subject knowledge.

Schools may require greater support from pedagogical support staff, such as social workers and school psychologists

The OECD review team's interviews with school principals, teachers and parents raised concerns on whether sufficient pedagogical support staff was available to provide support for solving social, intercultural and behavioural problems. Social workers and social pedagogues, for example, are not typically available in schools. OECD TALIS 2008 substantiates these claims. According to school principals' reports, in 2008 there was one pedagogical support worker for 24 teachers, compared to a ratio of 1 to 13 on average across countries participating in the survey. This was the worst ratio of any country in the survey and was not related to class size (OECD, 2009, Table 2.4). From a student perspective, the situation is slightly better, also bearing low student-teacher ratios in Austria in mind. There was one pedagogical support staff for 263 students in Austria. This was, however, still much less than in various other countries like Denmark, Hungary, Norway and Poland. In Norway, the country with the lowest ratio, there was one pedagogical support worker for 78 students (Schmich, 2010). A relatively high proportion of lower secondary teachers in Austria were in a school whose principal reported that instruction was hindered to some extent or a lot by a lack of instructional support personnel (68.7%, compared to a TALIS average of 47.5%) (OECD, 2009). However, TALIS data do not give any information about the kind of pedagogical support personnel that is available and which kind of staff may hinder instruction the most.

There also appear to be some differences between the AHS and the HS (which have been replaced by the NMS). According to an analysis by Schmich (2010), there was less pedagogical support personnel available at the AHS than at the HS, which may also reflect the more disadvantaged student intake in the HS. But the use of pedagogical support staff seemed to be better targeted in the AHS. In AHS with a higher proportion of students with a non-German mother tongue, more pedagogical support staff was available than at schools with lower proportions of students with this background. Besides concerns about the number of pedagogical support staff, the review team's schools visits also suggested that there were concerns regarding the organisation of support services in schools and that pedagogical support may be more difficult to access compared to other countries like Finland which follow a more child-centred and open approach. School psychologists, for example, were only available through a number of school psychological service units which may not facilitate a close collaboration between teachers and school psychologists.

The lack of sufficient pedagogical support staff and an inefficient organisation of the staff that is available can have a number of negative consequences. For teachers, it can take time and focus away from their core task of teaching, as they are required to spend time on tasks for which they are not sufficiently qualified. And it means teachers may lack the support they need to provide differentiated teaching in classrooms. For students, it can mean that psychological and individual support is not available if needed. The lack of pedagogical support staff is also of concern considering the apparent problem of bullying in schools. According to data from the World Health Organization's (WHO) Health Behaviour in School-aged Children survey for 2009/10, 40% of children aged 11, 13 and 15 reported having been bullied at school at least once in the past couple of months (UNICEF Office of Research, 2013).[8]

Like the lack of administrative support personnel, the lack of pedagogical support staff is linked to the distribution of responsibilities for human resources in the Austrian education system which does not enable decision-making about staff recruitment based on a more general view of the staffing needs in schools and which gives schools a limited say in such decisions (also see Chapter 2).

Policy recommendations

Austria has undertaken important steps to improve the management of its teaching profession with the implementation of a new initial teacher education scheme and a new teacher service code. Both initiatives provide an important basis for the creation of a single teaching profession beyond school types, and, in fact, a common school until the end of lower secondary education (see also Chapter 3). They also have the potential to improve the quality of future teachers, as they aim to offer a more attractive career and improved initial education, induction and professional development. However, fundamental challenges remain to raise the quality of teaching and to make the most of the human resources that are available. This should be a key objective in the Austrian education system.

Two issues stand out. First, as discussed in detail in Chapter 2, the complex system of governance hinders the effective use of human resources across the education system as a whole. This concerns the split of responsibilities for funding, distributing and managing human resources between federal, provincial and municipal levels in the general compulsory school sector, the distinction between provincial and federal sub-systems, and the lack of school autonomy for human resource management. These features of the Austrian education system prevent a holistic vision and approach to the use of human resources in Austria's schools and set incentives for the allocation of human resources that does not necessarily best meet the needs of schools. The unnecessary complexity involved in the monitoring of the teacher labour market is a case in point, as is the lack of administrative staff, particularly in provincial schools, the general lack of pedagogical support staff, and the limited targeting of such staff to school needs in provincial schools.

Second, it is essential to develop a stronger professional approach to teaching in Austria that reflects the need for schools to become innovative learning-centred organisations that build on a better understanding of local processes and mechanisms to improve teaching and learning in partnership with parents and the community. Teachers' employment framework and conditions, that is the teacher career structure and working time arrangements, should reflect that teachers should be able to take on a broader range of roles that form an integral part of the teaching profession and collaborate to raise the quality of education at their school. This also requires a better local management of human resources in schools facilitated through greater school autonomy in this regard and greater capacity for pedagogical school leadership.

Teacher labour market and initial teacher education

Create greater transparency about the human resource needs of the system and steer the supply of teachers more effectively

While there appears to be no overall shortage of teachers in Austria at the moment, it is essential to ensure an adequate supply of qualified teachers. There already seem to be hidden shortages in certain geographical areas and specific subjects and Austria faces a considerable retirement wave of teachers in the next decade. This represents a loss of experienced teachers, but also an opportunity to renew the teaching workforce and to provide the system with new ideas and perspectives of greater teacher professionalism (more on this below). To steer the supply of new teachers more effectively and to address potential shortages and/or oversupply in specific geographical areas or subjects it is important to create greater transparency about the future demand for teachers which is linked to an overall concept of schools sizes and pedagogical concepts, like team teaching. Better information about the needs of the system could be useful both for teacher education institutions to define their offer and for graduates from secondary schools interested in teaching to gain a better picture of future opportunities to work in education. This requires a more systematic analysis of the teacher labour market overall, and the need for new teachers in different parts of the country and specific subjects. More systematic data on other aspects of the teacher labour market, such as teacher attrition and retention of old and young teachers should also be more readily available for analysis of the teacher labour market.

While there are some forecasting and planning processes in place, the current governance arrangements make these processes overly complicated. In particular, data on provincial teachers seem to be fragmented across provinces and not easily available for system-wide monitoring. Steering responsibilities are not clearly defined. Placing the responsibility for the employment of all teachers into one hand (see Chapter 2), would facilitate greater availability of data on the need and supply of teachers that could be used for systematic analysis and steering through one responsible institution. Considering the responsibility of the Ministry for Education and Women's Affairs (BMBF) for parts of initial teacher education, and its potentially central role for the funding of teachers (see Chapter 2), the ministry could take on such a role. Alternatively, another central institution such as the central statistical office (*Statistik Austria*), which already works with data on teachers, could take responsibility for the analysis of the teacher labour market if it is provided with a comprehensive reference framework to fulfil this role.

Improved availability and accessibility of information could also be used by the responsible authorities to steer the supply of teachers and to implement possible measures to further increase the attractiveness of the career (e.g. through greater teacher professionalism and a new teacher career, see below). Possible measures include, for example, scholarship, grant or loan programmes for subjects for which it is difficult to attract teachers; financial bonuses for specific geographical regions; and recruitment campaigns to attract teachers in areas of needs. Furthermore, the effective steering of the teacher labour market would benefit from eliminating current rigidities and barriers to teacher mobility. Teachers should be able to carry their statutory rights with them when moving to another province, but the streamlining of responsibilities for the employment and funding of teachers would also help. Austria should also consider the introduction of regulations or incentives to encourage greater teacher mobility between schools.

Give school leaders a greater say in the recruitment of teachers

As elaborated in Chapter 2, schools in Austria should gradually receive greater autonomy to select their personnel and teachers while maintaining the equity benefits of a more central teacher recruitment system and while possibly putting further mechanisms into place that work towards equity in teacher allocation. The introduction of salary allowances for schools in disadvantages areas, for example, could be one option. Such policies have been found to have clear positive effects on teacher recruitment (Falch, 2010). Greater school autonomy for human resource management could help promote pedagogical leadership. Despite long-standing efforts, it has been difficult to foster a cultural change towards greater pedagogical leadership and to change school leaders' practices in Austria. This is related to a number of challenges such as the lack of middle leadership structures and administrative support, but greater school autonomy for human resource management would help communicate that the school-level management of teachers, from selection to appraisal and development, is one of the key responsibilities of school principals. As Halász (2009) argued, school leaders also require a certain degree of autonomy to become pedagogical leaders. Also, giving schools more influence in selecting their teachers according to particular criteria (e.g. teaching methods, extracurricular activities, etc.) would allow schools to more effectively shape their profiles and meet the needs of their students.

Ensure the careful implementation and follow-up of the new initial teacher education scheme

The new initial teacher education model has great potential if all involved stakeholders work together with the ultimate goal of improving teacher education in Austria. As far as the government is concerned, the responsible ministries should continue to collaborate through the channels of communication that have been established and follow up on the suggestions of the independent quality assurance council to ensure the success of the reform. As highlighted by the QSR (2015), teacher education institutions require better personnel and organisational structures, i.e. an adequate supply of qualified staff and management structures with the capacity to manage quality development and create the desired changes in teacher education. Both ministries should support teacher education institutions to develop this capacity. This could imply the creation of doctoral schools that ensure a greater supply of research and teaching staff in the future. More funding opportunities for basic educational research could also strengthen the research capacity of institutions.

In addition, institutions could be supported and encouraged to collaborate further through the creation of common organisational structures and specific profiles of expertise. Both university colleges of teacher education (PHs) and universities also have their particular challenges in raising the quality of education. university colleges of teacher education would benefit from greater autonomy to manage their human resources; universities would benefit from stronger links with schools and the current teaching profession. Although this might be difficult to realise as universities are under the responsibility of the Ministry of Science, Research and Economy, universities could be involved in the new induction process for all teachers and further professional development for teachers. Universities' involvement in teachers' ongoing professional development would also address some concerns about the current quality of professional development and a lack of external input and expertise.

A number of further points merit further attention. It is essential that the teacher education reform helps to create a common teaching profession and raises the quality of education for all levels of education and school types. To this end, it would be important to incentivise universities to become sufficiently engaged in the preparation of primary teachers as well, traditionally the remit of university colleges of teacher education (PHs). Concerning the design of new curricula and programmes, these should foster greater teacher professionalism (more on this below) and foster a new conception of the teaching profession. This would help make teaching more attractive among young people and support other reforms, such as the effective implementation of new pedagogical approaches and team teaching in the NMS. It will also be important to monitor the ways in which the new teacher education model affects the supply of new teachers and students' progression through teacher education. Study regulations between different institutions should be harmonised and adequate guidance and counselling should be available for students. The feasibility for students to complete the required master's degree will also need to be evaluated and new teachers be supported to fulfil this requirement and to reconcile work, life and study.

Teacher professionalism

Develop a vision for teacher professionalism

While it is important to distribute responsibilities for the employment of teachers more effectively and to align funding and spending for human resources to ensure a better use of human resources in the Austrian education system (see Chapter 2), it is equally important to build a new conception of the teaching profession. A vision that promotes schools as professional learning communities that work together to improve teaching and learning for all students would help improve the quality of education. It would also help make teaching a more attractive career and create a more positive discourse around teaching. As the OECD (2015d) argued, "innovating learning environments offer a far more promising route for enhancing the attractiveness of teaching than backward-looking definitions of professionalism seen as the right of the individual teacher to be left undisturbed in his or her own classroom." The argument for greater teacher professionalism is further substantiated through an OECD report on teacher professionalism. Analysis of data from OECD TALIS 2013 suggests that teacher professionalism, and the development of teacher knowledge and collaboration/peer networks in particular, are positively associated with job satisfaction, confidence in the ability to teach and perceptions of the status of the teaching profession (OECD, 2016).

The OECD Innovative Learning Environment project formulated a number of principles that bring teachers' work in line with innovative ways of organising learning:

- Teachers should share a clear priority about the centrality of learning, for their students and themselves, and be fully engaged in meeting that priority; teachers as well as students should understand themselves as learners.
- Teaching should not be regarded as an individual matter and should often be done collaboratively.
- Teachers should work formatively – with their learners and with organisational strategies of design and development using rich evaluative information.
- Teachers should be strongly connected - across activities and subjects, in- and out-of-school, and with other partners and other schools and organisations.
- Schools should recognise diverse teacher motivations and understand that their professional performance is intricately linked to emotions (satisfaction, self-efficacy, avoidance of helplessness and anxiety, etc.).
- Schools should be sensitive to individual differences in the capacities and experiences of each teacher and build on those in personalised ways as well as through shared professional development (OECD, 2013a).

To support the development of a new vision of teacher professionalism, the OECD review team recommends developing a national teacher profile or standards of practice for the Austrian teaching profession. Such a national teacher profile would establish a foundation for teachers to explore their practice and for school to develop initiatives to improve. It would also provide orientation for the overall teacher development framework, including initial teacher education, professional development and appraisal. Tools and processes like school development planning and self-evaluation through the School Quality in General Education (SQA) process, more systematic work in schools with educational standards and assessments, and new opportunities for schools to collaborate could be used to help promote the new vision.

At present, there appears to be little organised engagement of teachers in professional matters and there is no professional organisation of teachers or a teaching council. The views and experience of effective teachers and school leaders should, however, be central for the development of their profession. Teachers themselves should be given greater responsibility for the self-regulation of their profession (e.g. in the development of professional standards, the design of teacher education programmes and the definition of entrance criteria) and the teacher union should recognise its responsibility for the development of the profession beyond the representation of teachers' political interests in terms of employment rights and working conditions. In other countries, teacher professional organisations have a lead role in determining processes for the development of teachers, such as the development of professional standards and teacher appraisal. In Australia, teaching colleges/institutes as independent statutory bodies provide teachers with professional autonomy and self-regulation and the right to have a say in the further development of their profession. The country has also established an Australian Institute for Teaching and School Leadership (AITSL),[9] with the ambition to establish a nationally shared understanding of what counts as accomplished teaching and school leadership. This institute has developed the Australian Professional Standards for Teachers to provide a national measure for teaching practice, in close collaboration with the profession, employers and teacher educators. In New Zealand, the New Zealand Teaching Council (NZTC) acted as the professional body of teachers holding the leading role in defining standards for the profession, with the extensive involvement of the teaching profession, employers and teacher unions (OECD, 2013c). In 2015, New Zealand introduced a new professional organisation for teachers of all education levels with a wider mandate to lead the teaching profession, promote good practice and raise its status, The Education Council of Aotearoa New Zealand.[10] The Council seeks to strengthen accountability and to bring consistently high standards across the education system. It is independent and sets its own agenda, commissions its own research, leads public discussions about teaching issues, and takes a position on education matters.

Similar professional bodies have also been established in some European countries, such as Ireland and Northern Ireland and Scotland in the United Kingdom. In Ireland, The Teaching Council takes core responsibility for the self-regulation of the profession, for promoting professional standards in teaching, and for supporting the quality of teaching and learning more generally.[11] As part of its recent programme of work, the Council has achieved establishing standards for all stages of teachers' careers, a new pilot model of induction and probation, the drafting of new registration regulations, the review and accreditation of all programmes of initial teacher education, preparation for *Fitness to Teach* and the commencement of consultation on a National Framework for continuing professional development (CPD) (OECD, 2015b). Northern Ireland (United Kingdom) provides a further example with the introduction of its General Teaching Council for Northern Ireland in 2002.[12] Similar to the other countries, the Council acts as a professional and regulatory body for teachers. It provides a research-informed voice on behalf of the profession on all matters relating to teaching and is in charge of establishing and promoting professional standards for teachers, developing and applying a code of professional practice for teachers, professional registration of teachers, accrediting education courses for teachers and pre-service teachers, and working closely with government and employers to promote continuous professional learning by teachers (Shewbridge et al., 2014). In Scotland, the General Teaching Council for Scotland is the independent professional body which sets teachers' professional standards and accredits initial teacher education. It also oversees a number of key programmes in induction, professional learning, and student placement (OECD, 2015c).[13]

Reconceptualise teacher employment on the basis of a workload system

Working towards a new concept of teacher employment could further facilitate the development of a new vision of teacher professionalism. While this may not be a present priority considering that a new teacher service code is currently being introduced, it should be an objective in the medium term to further develop the conception of employment and working time (possibly together with harmonising working conditions and education requirements for the early childhood education and care sector as part of a new service code in the future). Austria should consider moving to employment under a workload system, whereby teachers work a specified number of hours per week (e.g. 40 hours). This would involve stipulating the required number of working hours (and possibly hours required to stay at the school), but not necessarily the number of teaching hours. This conception of teacher employment recognises that teachers need time for engaging in a range of other tasks, including the adequate preparation of lessons. It is also likely to improve the opportunities for teachers to formally engage in activities other than teaching at the school level. In particular, school management would be in a better position to foster teacher collaboration, promote whole-school planning and develop professional learning communities. This would also favour the promotion of peer feedback and joint work among teachers. Of course, it is also important that school buildings and facilities provide the conditions for teachers for doing so. A number of countries require teachers to engage in non-teaching tasks during their statutory working time (see Box 4.2 for information on non-teaching tasks as part of teachers' working time from *OECD Education at a Glance*).

Box 4.2. **Non-teaching tasks are a part of teachers' workload and working conditions in a number of countries**

According to information collected for *OECD Education at a Glance 2014*, individual planning or preparing lessons, teamwork and dialogue with colleagues and communicating and co-operating with parents are the most common non-teaching tasks required of lower secondary teachers during their statutory working time at school or statutory total working time. These tasks are required in at least 20 of the 34 countries with available data for 2012. Marking/correcting student work, general administrative communication and paperwork and professional development activities are also required in around half of the countries with available data. Lower secondary teachers are required to supervise students during breaks, provide counselling and guidance to students, and/or participate in school management in around one-third of the countries. Eight countries require that lower secondary teachers engage in extracurricular activities after school. In most countries that record the non-teaching tasks required of teachers, the specific number of hours allocated for each task is, however, not specified. In Brazil, the Czech Republic, Hungary, Korea, the Netherlands, New Zealand and Slovenia, any of these non-teaching tasks may be required of teachers, but the decision is taken at the school level.

Source: OECD (2014), *Education at a Glance 2014: OECD Indicators, http://dx.doi.org/10.1787/eag-2014-en.*

Create further opportunities for teachers to take on other tasks and responsibilities as part of a dedicated career structure

The new teacher service code provides some further opportunities for teachers to take on additional roles in schools. However, the new service code has not yet created a dedicated career structure that provides teachers with opportunities to develop professionally and to take on a variety of roles and responsibilities. The lack of a real career structure fails to reflect the different needs that teachers may have at different stages of their career. And it fails to provide school leaders with the possibility to tailor teachers' roles to the needs of the school and to distribute leadership more formally. In the medium term, Austria should therefore consider the development of a differentiated career structure that allows for vertical and horizontal progression (see Box 4.3 for an example of a teacher career structure). A career structure would contribute to promoting a new conception of the teaching profession and increase the attractiveness of the teaching career. The development of a career structure would also provide an opportunity to rethink the administratively complex system of salary allowances for school-level staff which furthermore lacks transparency. The career structure could build on the promising roles that have been established as part of the new teacher service code and the NMS reform

Box 4.3. **The development of a teacher career structure in Estonia**

The teaching profession in Estonia has typically been differentiated vertically through a multi-step career structure. This was originally implemented through an attestation career system, but in 2013, a new system of teacher professional qualifications was been introduced in association with a new career structure. Unique features of the career structure are that it has no formal links to salary levels and access to its higher levels is voluntary. Its main aim is to serve as a reference for teachers' competency development. There are four career grades, which reflect different levels of professional competencies and experience:

- **Teacher (level 6):** applies only to pre-primary teachers upon entrance in the teaching profession, following the completion of an initial teacher education programme (at bachelor's degree level) or following the recognition of professional qualifications for this level by the teacher professional body. This career stage is awarded indefinitely.
- **Teacher (level 7.1):** is awarded upon entrance in the teaching profession, following the completion of an initial teacher education programme (at master's degree level) or following the recognition of professional qualifications for this level by the teacher professional body. This career stage is awarded indefinitely.
- **Senior teacher (level 7.2):** is awarded to a teacher who, in addition to conducting teaching activities, supports the development of the school and of other teachers and is involved in methodological work at the school level. This career stage is awarded for five years, period after which the teacher needs to submit a new application.
- **Master teacher (level 8):** is awarded to a teacher who, in addition to conducting teaching activities, participates in development and creative activities in and outside his or her school and closely co-operates with a higher education institution. This career stage is awarded for five years, period after which the teacher needs to submit a new application.

The career structure is associated with a set of teacher professional standards, which define the competencies associated with each career stage. The development of the teacher professional standards is the responsibility of the Estonian Qualifications Authority while the certification processes to reach the different career stages are the responsibility of a teacher professional organisation (the Estonian Association of Teachers). Teachers can apply for certification at any of the levels twice a year (April and November). The certification procedure involves two stages: i) an evaluation of a set of documents submitted by the candidate; and ii) an interview. The certification procedure is undertaken by a three member committee. A separate career structure, based on a distinct set of professional standards, exists for teachers in vocational education who teach vocational subjects.

Source: Santiago, P. et al. (2016a), *OECD Reviews of School Resources: Estonia 2016*, *http://dx.doi.org/10.1787/9789264251731-en*.

(e.g. Lerndesigners) and create further roles for school development. The experience of school pilots on middle management could also be institutionalised through the new career structure. Progression in the career structure should be voluntary and be associated with a formal process of evaluation to promote the principle of merit.

Management of the teaching workforce

Develop pedagogical leadership in schools

Research has highlighted the importance of school leadership for teaching and learning, which provides a strong rationale for implementing policies that ensure the effective management and development of the school leadership profession (Pont, Nusche and Moorman, 2008, Day et al., 2009, Louis et al., 2010). Furthermore, as school leaders constitute a relatively small, but central, group of actors in any education system, policies that target school leadership constitute highly cost-effective measures for improving education (Louis et al., 2010). It is against this background that various education systems, such as Australia (Victoria), Canada (Ontario), Chile and New Zealand, have implemented coherent school leadership development strategies (OECD, 2013c). In the Austrian context, the further development of the school leadership profession is also key considering the current calls for greater school autonomy. As pointed out in Chapter 2, greater school autonomy will need to go hand in hand with greater capacity and accountability of school leaders.

Austria has already undertaken steps to foster effective school leadership, but the past initiatives have failed to create a cultural change towards pedagogical leadership. The current age profile and the retirement of many school principals provide a window of opportunity for recruiting a new generation and profile of school leaders. However, to ensure that promising candidates are selected, the recruitment process will need to be further professionalised to reduce the risk for political appointments, as is already envisaged in the federal government's November 2015 reform proposal (BMBF and BMWFW, 2015). Necessarily, the employer of school principals should take responsibility for the management of school principals, including the recruitment, but the responsibility for recruitment should not be in the hands of a highly politicised body such as the collegiate boards of the provincial school boards. Irrespective of the institution that will take over the employment of school leaders following the governance reform (e.g. the proposed education directorates), the recruitment process should be managed by an administrative body that has the capacity to conduct a high quality recruitment process. To increase objectivity and to match the selection better to the needs of the school, further actors, such as the school inspectorate and the school forum, should have greater prominence in the selection process. Involvement of the school inspectorate would bring in additional expertise and involvement of the school forum would strengthen horizontal accountability. In some countries, school boards take on a very prominent role for the employment of school principals. School boards can even take complete responsibility for the school leader selection process and propose a ranking of candidates from which employers are then required to choose, or draw up a profile of a desired candidate that then serves as a reference for a central recruitment process. In some countries, school boards can also propose the dismissal of a school principal or initiate an evaluation process in the case of concerns.

The development of professional school leadership standards would also help introduce greater objectivity in the selection process by providing a clear reference what kind of skills and competencies school principals should have. More generally, such standards would help promote a vision of pedagogical leadership. In the development of professional school leadership standards, involvement of the school leadership profession should be central. Austria has taken part in other international projects on school leadership that it could build on in the development of professional standards (e.g. Halász, 2009; Schratz, 2009; Schratz et al., 2010; Schratz et al., 2013). Considering the apparently low number of applicants, it would be important to further analyse the attractiveness of the school leadership profession, including the competitiveness of current school leader remuneration compared to teachers and other professions and the possibility to create career development opportunities for school leaders (e.g. system leadership roles, such as learning consultants in Denmark or national and local leaders of education in England (United Kingdom), see Nusche et al., forthcoming).

To improve pedagogical leadership in schools, the employer of school principals – the federal, provincial or new hybrid administration as proposed in Chapter 2 and as part of the November 2015 education reform proposal – should take more responsibility for the ongoing management of individual school leaders. This could involve the development of personnel management processes such as the mandatory individual appraisal of school leaders. Individual appraisal constitutes a tool to set clear expectations, to provide school leaders with formative feedback, and to hold principals accountable for their performance (Radinger, 2014; OECD, 2013c). The School Quality in General Education (SQA) process also provides a tool for providing school leaders with feedback on their work as part of conversations around targets and performance agreements for the school.

Creating more opportunities for schools to collaborate and facilitating school leadership networks can be a further strategy to foster greater pedagogical leadership and to improve the quality of education across the education system more widely. For example, New Zealand has initiated "Learning and Change Networks" to establish a web of knowledge-sharing networks among schools, families, teachers, leaders, communities, professional providers and the Ministry of Education. Network participants work collaboratively to accelerate student achievement in Years 1 to 8 and address equity issues (OECD, 2015d). Chile has established local networks of small rural smalls (*microcentros*) that offer opportunities for regular development and exchange. Schools meet on a monthly basis for two-hour workshops to analyse the situation of learning in schools, reflect on the pedagogical work of teachers to decide on the necessary innovations to improve student learning, exchange educational experiences, develop teaching strategies that suit the local contexts, agree on criteria for the formulation of improvement plans according to the needs of the students, and receive the support of the advice of the Ministry of Education or technical assistance institutions where appropriate (Ministerio de Educación de Chile, forthcoming; Santiago et al., forthcoming). And in England (United Kingdom), The London Challenge and City Challenge initiatives to improve education in London, Greater Manchester and the Black Country were built around a belief that school-to-school collaboration has a central role to play in school improvement. Some of the best schools and best principals were, therefore, encouraged to lead improvement networks with other schools and other school leaders. The lead schools were designated as teaching schools as hubs for professional development and their principals as national and local leaders of education (NLEs and LLEs) with an outreach responsibility for the improvement of other schools (Baars et al., 2014). In Austria, the new initiative of Centre for Learning Schools (*Bundeszentrum für Lernende Schulen*) could be expanded to the whole system beyond New Secondary Schools, if successful. This could also facilitate collaboration between school types.

Also, school leaders in Austria will need to benefit from greater support structures in the form of administrative support staff (see further below) and middle leaders (see further above on the development of a teacher career structure). Some countries, such as Chile, the Czech Republic and the Slovak Republic, have established subject committees and teacher councils in schools that provide a structure to facilitate exchange and collaboration, for example (Santiago et al., 2016b; Santiago et al., forthcoming; Shewbridge et al., forthcoming).

Ensure that all teachers have opportunities for regular professional feedback and relevant professional learning

As highlighted above, teachers do not have sufficient opportunities for regular professional feedback, especially as they progress in their career. School principals should appraise their teachers, but owing to a heavy workload, appraisal often only focuses on beginning teachers. To strengthen school-based teacher appraisal and feedback it is important to enhance pedagogical leadership in schools as just described. This would imply improving school leader's skills for effective observation, feedback and coaching.

In this context, it is also important to promote more distributed leadership and involvement of senior peers in regular teacher evaluation, classroom observation, and planning of professional development in line with a new conception of the teaching profession. Incentives could be provided for teachers to engage in informal observations of each other's practices with the objective of fostering mutual learning among teachers. Younger teachers may also be able to support their senior peers, e.g. in using new technologies and media. These practices can clearly benefit from a new concept of teacher employment based on working hours (rather than teaching hours, see above) whereby the formal recognition of activities other than teaching at the school would promote collaborative work among teachers.

For teacher appraisal to have an impact on learning outcomes in the school, it needs to be closely connected to professional development. This link is not well established in Austrian schools. At the school level, teachers' individual choices of professional development should be more strongly influenced by i) their own appraisal results and identification of areas for improvement, and ii) priorities of the school development plan and self-evaluation results from the SQA process. Effective teacher appraisal should give teachers a choice from a range of professional learning activities that meet their individual needs in relation to the priorities of the school's overall development plan. The appraisal results of individual teachers should also be aggregated to inform school development plans. In order to guarantee the systematic and coherent application of school-based teacher appraisal across Austrian schools, it would be important to ensure external validation of the respective school processes (e.g. through the introduction of an individual school leader appraisal process).

Administrative and pedagogical support staff in schools

Find ways to increase the availability of both administrative and pedagogical support staff

In Austria, there are serious concerns about the lack of sufficient administrative and pedagogical support staff. As a result, school principals and teachers have to take over many of the related tasks. This takes away time and focus for teaching and learning, which teachers generally value very highly. As research suggests, teachers in general are typically motivated by the intrinsic benefits of teaching – working with children and young people, helping them to develop, and making a contribution to society – and structures need to ensure that teachers are able to focus on these tasks (OECD, 2005). Specialised pedagogical support, such as school psychologists, are not always easily available for students if needed. Considering the current need to integrate a large number of young refugees and asylum seekers into the education system, the need to provide more pedagogical support staff in schools might become more pressing in the near future. Also, the lack of administrative support staff will make it difficult to give schools greater autonomy as this implies more tasks and responsibilities for school leaders.

As suggested in Chapter 2, and also in the November 2015 reform proposal (schools are planned to be able to convert 5% of their teaching staff into pedagogical support staff), Austria should, therefore, find ways to increase the availability of both administrative and pedagogical support staff. This should not necessarily involve an increase in overall staff numbers, but involve a reflection of how human resources can be shifted to better meet schools' and students' needs. Most importantly, a reform of education governance which places the responsibility for human resources (and teachers and other pedagogical support staff, in particular) in one hand and gives schools a greater say for human resource decisions could help the responsible agencies develop a more strategic approach to the distribution of human resources that meets schools' needs. Under the current system, provinces have an incentive to hire teachers at the expense of other pedagogical support staff as the number of required teachers is part of the negotiations of staff plans with the federal level. And although more pedagogical support personnel seem to be available in provincial schools despite this disincentive to hire such staff, provinces do not seem to target the recruitment of such staff at the schools with the greatest needs.

With regards to administrative staff, the lack of such staff seems greatest in provincial schools, even though there are concerns about an adequate supply at federal schools as well. For provincial schools, the current model of municipalities holding responsibility for financing and managing operational costs as school maintainers reflects that related expenditures depend on many diverse factors and local prices of inputs (e.g. the price of energy expenditure and communal services). It avoids trade-offs between investments in infrastructure (such as modern heating) and maintenance staff and it theoretically ensures proximity to the community for the local recruitment of administrative and maintenance staff, such as cleaners and janitors. However, like provinces in the case of pedagogical support staff, municipalities have little incentives to hire sufficient administrative support staff such as secretaries as costs for teachers that take over administrative tasks in the absence of such staff are covered by the provincial/federal levels. Also, different municipalities may have different means to finance and hire administrative support, thus possibly creating inequities between schools. If the policy options suggested in Chapter 2 are implemented, the employment of other pedagogical support staff could become part of the responsibilities of the new authority responsible for the employment of teachers, while schools could assume responsibility for the recruitment of administrative and maintenance staff, for example. But to limit the administrative burden on schools, the responsibility for the recruitment of administrative staff could also be delegated to the same level as the recruitment for teachers and other pedagogical staff.

If the streamlining of overall human resource responsibilities does not prove feasible, the federal authorities could take advantage of their power to set central policies and regulations. Federal authorities could consider the introduction of central standards or guidelines on minimum staff-teacher or staff-student ratios for pedagogical support staff and a minimum number of administrative staff for schools of a certain size. For pedagogical support staff, other contextual factors, such as the proportion of disadvantaged students, could also be taken into account to ensure that schools with the greatest needs have the support they require. Minimum regulations or guidelines could help ensure a baseline level of support in schools and work towards an equitable distribution of pedagogical and administrative support staff irrespective of school type and maintainer. Of course, in the case of administrative staff, under the current model of governance, potential inequities between municipalities and funding constraints by individual municipalities would have to be taken into account and be addressed in the case of provincial schools (e.g. through an equalisation mechanism, see Chapter 2). A further alternative lies in including decisions about the recruitment of pedagogical support staff in the negotiation of staff plans between the federal and the provincial authorities.

In addition, Austria could further test out innovative and cost-effective ways of organising schools and administrative and pedagogical support. If municipalities maintain their role as school maintainers, this could involve the collaboration of different municipalities, particularly in rural areas (e.g. through *Schulgemeindeverbände*). And schools could be encouraged to collaborate more with other social services and non-formal education initiatives to provide support for children and young people in a more open format.

Besides the implementation of steps to make more administrative and pedagogical support available in schools, there seems to be a need to clarify teachers' roles and responsibilities as part of the new conception of teacher professionalism and the development of a teacher career structure. Teachers often seem to understand tasks related to student assessment, school self-evaluation and subject co-ordination as administrative tasks, even though such tasks should be seen as part of their involvement in school development. A new teacher career could also provide an opportunity for creating additional roles in the Austrian education system, such as school librarians and lab assistants, which could support teachers and students.

Notes

1. For federal schools, the collegiate board (*Kollegien*) of the provincial school board (*Landesschulrat* and *Stadtschulrat* in the case of Vienna) selects a shortlist of three candidates from all applications. The school community committee or the school forum (*Schulforum*) as well as the teaching staff representative body have the right to comment on the applications received and, while not binding for the collegiate board, these comments still form an important basis for the board's decision-making process. Ultimately, the education minister selects one candidate from the three-candidate shortlist and proposes that candidate to the federal president for appointment. For provincial schools, the provincial government is responsible for selection and appointment through the office of the provincial government (*Amt der Landesregierung*) and the respective school department (*Schulabteilung*) of that office. According to the service code for provincial teachers, the regional boards of education (municipal board of education in Vienna) have the right to submit a shortlist of three candidates. School forums have the right to provide their opinion on the suitability of the candidates within three weeks, which is not binding, but needs to be considered by the board. In some provinces, the selection and appointment process may also involve the provincial school board. The province of Vienna, for example, has transferred its competencies for the appointment of its school principals to the provincial school board.
2. See *www.parlament.gv.at/PAKT/VHG/XXIV/AB/AB_08500/fname_226576.pdf*.
3. The domain "organisation of instruction" includes the following areas: student admissions; student careers; instruction time; choice of textbooks; choice of software/learningware; grouping of students; additional support for students; teaching methods; day-to-day student assessment.

4. Almost all 15-year-olds were in a school whose principal reported that "only school principals and/or teachers" or that "both school principals and/or teachers, and regional and/or national education authorities or the school governing board" chooses which textbooks are used (OECD average: 92.0%). Eighty-two percent of students were in a school whose principal reported that "only school principals and/or teachers" or that "both school principals and/or teachers, and regional and/or national education authorities or the school governing board" decided which courses are offered (OECD average: 81.8%), and 74.1% of students were in a school whose principal reported that "only school principals and/or teachers" or that "both school principals and/or teachers, and regional and/or national education authorities or the school governing board" determine the school's course content (OECD average: 75.5%). 76.8% of students were in a school whose principal reported that "only school principals and/or teachers" or that "both school principals and/or teachers, and regional and/or national education authorities or the school governing board" establish student assessment policies (OECD average: 87.1%).
5. Austria participated in a three-stage project on school leadership realised within the framework of collaboration between five countries (Austria, the Czech Republic, Hungary, Slovakia and Slovenia) in form of the Central European Co-operation for Education (CECE), under co-ordination of the Tempus Public Foundation, and with support of the Hungarian Ministry of Education and the European Commission.
6. According to OECD PISA 2012, 14% of 15-year-olds were in a school whose principal reported that a lack of qualified mathematics teachers hindered student learning "to some extent" or "a lot" (OECD average: 17%); 16% of 15-year-olds were in a school whose principal reported that a lack of qualified science teachers hindered student learning "to some extent" or "a lot" (OECD average: 17%); 14% of 15-year-olds were in a school whose principal reported that a lack of qualified language-of-instruction teachers hindered student learning "to some extent" or "a lot" (OECD average: 9%); and 21% of 15-year-olds were in a school whose principal reported that a lack of qualified teachers of other subjects hindered student learning "to some extent" or "a lot"(OECD average: 21%).
7. The Court of Audit stated in a recent report that at federal level out of a total of 36 500 federal teachers (full-time equivalents) around 2 500 fulltime equivalents (i.e. about 6.8%) were withdrawn from teaching to execute functions of school leadership, administration and IT maintenance in 2011/12 (Rechnungshof 2013/5). The Court of Audit estimated cost savings of EUR 13 million per year if support functions at federal schools were executed by administrative staff instead of (more expensive) teaching staff.
8. The 2009/10 Health Behaviour in School-aged Children survey asked young people aged 11, 13 and 15 how often they had been bullying others and how often they had been bullied by others at school in the past couple of weeks. The children who took part in the survey were given the following definition of bullying: "We say a student is being bullied when another student, or a group of students, say or do nasty and unpleasant things to him or her. It is also bullying when a student is teased repeatedly in a way he or she does not like or when he or she is deliberately left out of things. But it is not bullying when two students of about the same strength or power argue or fight. It is also not bullying when a student is teased in a friendly and playful way."
9. For further information, see *www.aitsl.edu.au/* (accessed 25 March 2016).
10. For further information, see *http://educationcouncil.org.nz/* (accessed 25 March 2016).
11. For further information, see *www.teachingcouncil.ie/en/* (accessed 25 March 2016).
12. For further information, see *www.gtcni.org.uk/* (accessed 25 March 2016).
13. For further information, see *www.gtcs.org.uk/* (accessed 25 March 2016).

References

Austrian Federal Chancellery (2013), *Work programme of the Austrian Federal Government 2013-2018 Austria, A Story of Success*, Austrian Federal Chancellery, Federal Press Service, Vienna.

Baars, S. et al. (2014), *Lessons from London Schools: Investigating the Success*, CfBT Education Trust, Centre for London, LKMco. Ltd., Reading, London, Cambridge, *http://centreforlondon.org/publication/lessons-london-schools*.

BMBF and BMWFW (2015), *Bildungsreformkommission Vortrag an den Ministerrat [Education Reform Commission Presentation to the Council of Ministers]*, Bundesministerium für Bildung und Frauen, Vienna, *www.bmbf.gv.at/ministerium/vp/2015/20151117.pdf?55kaz6*.

BMUKK (2011), *Anfragebeantwortung auf parlamentarische Anfrage Nr. 8597/J-NR/2011 [Response to the Parliamentary Enquiry No. 8597/J-NR/2011]*, *www.parlament.gv.at/PAKT/VHG/XXIV/AB/AB_08500/fname_226576.pdf*.

BMBF (2014), *Der Weg zur besten Bildung:6-Punkte-Programm [The Way Towards the Best Education: 6 Step Programme]*, Bundesministerium für Bildung und Frauen, *www.bmbf.gv.at/ministerium/vp/2014/20140927.pdf?4k5kks*.

Bruneforth, M. et al. (forthcoming), *OECD Review of Policies to Improve the Effectiveness of Resource Use in Schools, Country Background Report for Austria*, Bundesministerium für Bildung und Frauen, Vienna.

Bruneforth, M. and L. Lassnigg (eds.) (2012), *Nationaler Bildungsbericht Österreich 2012, Band 1 Das Schulsystem im Spiegel von Daten und Indikatoren [National Education Monitoring Report for Austria 2012. Volume 1: The School System in Light of Data and Indicators]*, Leykam, Graz.

Day, C. et al. (2009), *The Impact of School Leadership on Pupil Outcomes: Final Report*, University of Nottingham, *http://dera.ioe.ac.uk/11329/1/DCSF-RR108.pdf*.

European Commission/EACEA/Eurydice (2015), *The Teaching Profession in Europe: Practices, Perceptions, and Policies*, Publications Office of the European Union, Luxembourg.

Eurydice (2015), *Teachers' and School Heads' Salaries and Allowances in Europe, 2014/2015*, Eurydice Facts and Figures, Brussels/Luxembourg.

Eurypedia (2015), European Encyclopedia on National Education Systems: Austria, *https://webgate.ec.europa.eu/fpfis/mwikis/eurydice/index.php/Austria:Overview*.

Falch, T. (2010), "The elasticity of labour supply at the establishment level", *Journal of Labor Economics*, Vol. 28, pp. 237-266.

Halász, G. (2009), "School leadership and leadership development in five Central European countries – synthesis report", in M. Schratz et al. (eds.), *The Role of School Leadership in the Improvement of Learning, Country Reports and Case Studies of a Central-European Project*, Tempus Public Foundation, Budapest, pp. 185-267, *www.schoolleadership.eu/sites/default/files/the_role_of_school_leadership_in_the_improvement_of_learning_-_tpf_2009_9.pdf*.

Hattie, J. (2009), *Visible Learning: A Synthesis of Over 800 Meta-analyses Relating to Achievement*, Routledge, London.

Huber, S.G., C. Wolfgramm and S. Kilic (2013), "Vorlieben und Belastungen im Tätigkeitsspektrum: Was tun Schulleiterinnen und Schulleiter gern und was belastet sie?" [Preferences and burden in the domain of responsibilities: What do school leaders like to do and what do they see as a burden?], *b:sl Beruf Schulleitung*, Vol. 7, pp. 10-11.

Jensen, B. et al. (2012), *The Experience of New Teachers: Results from TALIS 2008*, TALIS, OECD Publishing, Paris, *http://dx.doi.org/10.1787/9789264120952-en*.

Leithwood, K. et al. (2004), *How Leadership Influences Student Learning*, University of Minnesota, University of Toronto, a report commissioned by the Wallace Foundation, *www.wallacefoundation.org/knowledge-center/school-leadership/key-research/Pages/How-Leadership-Influences-Student-Learning.aspx*.

Louis, K.S. et al. (2010), *Investigating the Links to Improved Student Learning – Final Report of Research Findings*, University of Minnesota, University of Toronto, a report commissioned by the Wallace Foundation, *www.wallacefoundation.org/knowledge-center/school-leadership/key-research/Pages/Investigating-the-Links-to-Improved-Student-Learning.aspx*.

Ministerio de Educación de Chile (forthcoming), *Reporte nacional de Chile: Revisión de políticas para mejorar la efectividad del uso de recursos en las escuelas [Country Background Report for Chile: Review of Policies to Improve the Effectiveness of Resource Use in Schools]*, Ministerio de Educación de Chile, Santiago.

NLQ (2011), *The Making of: Leadership in Education A European Qualification Network for Effective School Leadership, Framework of Reference*, Niedersächsisches Landesinstitut für schulische Qualitätsentwicklung, Hildesheim, *www.leadership-in-education.eu/fileadmin/reports/European_Synopsis.pdf*.

Nusche, D., C. Shewbridge and C. Lamhauge Rasmussen (2010), *OECD Reviews of Migrant Education: Austria 2010*, OECD Reviews of Migrant Education, OECD Publishing, Paris, *http://dx.doi.org/10.1787/9789264086180-en*.

Nusche, D. et al. (forthcoming), *OECD Reviews of School Resources: Denmark*, OECD Publishing, Paris.

OECD (2016), *Supporting Teacher Professionalism: Insights from TALIS 2013*, TALIS, OECD Publishing, Paris, *http://dx.doi.org/10.1787/9789264248601-en*.

OECD (2015a), *Education at a Glance 2015: OECD Indicators*, OECD Publishing, Paris, *http://dx.doi.org/10.1787/eag-2015-en*.

OECD (2015b), *Education Policy Outlook 2015: Making Reforms Happen*, OECD Publishing, Paris, *http://dx.doi.org/10.1787/9789264225442-en*.

OECD (2015c), *Improving Schools in Scotland: An OECD Perspective*, OECD Publishing, Paris, *www.oecd.org/education/school/Improving-Schools-in-Scotland-An-OECD-Perspective.pdf*.

OECD (2015d), *Schooling Redesigned: Towards Innovative Learning Systems*, Educational Research and Innovation, OECD Publishing, Paris, *http://dx.doi.org/10.1787/9789264245914-en*.

OECD (2015e), "Supporting New Teachers", *Teaching in Focus*, No. 11, OECD Publishing, Paris, *http://dx.doi.org/10.1787/5js1p1r88lg5-en*.

OECD (2014), *Education at a Glance 2014: OECD Indicators*, OECD Publishing, Paris, *http://dx.doi.org/10.1787/eag-2014-en*.

OECD (2013a), *Innovative Learning Environments*, Educational Research and Innovation, OECD Publishing, Paris, *http://dx.doi.org/10.1787/9789264203488-en*.

OECD (2013b), *PISA 2012 Results: What Makes Schools Successful (Volume IV): Resources, Policies and Practices*, PISA, OECD Publishing, Paris, *http://dx.doi.org/10.1787/9789264201156-en*.

OECD (2013c), *Synergies for Better Learning: An International Perspective on Evaluation and Assessment*, OECD Reviews of Evaluation and Assessment in Education, OECD Publishing, Paris, *http://dx.doi.org/10.1787/9789264190658-en*.

OECD (2013d), "Approaches to learning leadership development in different school systems", in OECD, *Leadership for 21st Century Learning*, OECD Publishing, Paris, *http://dx.doi.org/10.1787/9789264205406-7-en*.

OECD (2012), *Education at a Glance 2012: OECD Indicators*, OECD Publishing, Paris, *http://dx.doi.org/10.1787/eag-2012-en*.

OECD (2009), *Creating Effective Teaching and Learning Environments: First Results from TALIS*, TALIS, OECD Publishing, Paris, *http://dx.doi.org/10.1787/9789264068780-en*.

OECD (2005), *Teachers Matter: Attracting, Developing and Retaining Effective Teachers*, Education and Training Policy, OECD Publishing, Paris, *http://dx.doi.org/10.1787/9789264018044-en*.

Pont, B., D. Nusche and H. Moorman (2008), *Improving School Leadership, Volume 1: Policy and Practice*, OECD Publishing, Paris, *http://dx.doi.org/10.1787/9789264044715-en*.

QSR (2015), *Bericht des Qualitätssicherungsrates für Pädagoginnen- und Pädagogenbildung an den Nationalrat [Report of the Quality Assurance Council to the National Council]*, *www.qsr.or.at/?content/der-qsr/beschluesse/bericht-an-den-nationalrat-2014/index*.

Radinger, T. (2014), "School Leader Appraisal – A Tool to Strengthen School Leaders' Pedagogical Leadership and Skills for Teacher Management?", *European Journal of Education*, Vol. 49, No. 3, pp. 378-394, *http://onlinelibrary.wiley.com/doi/10.1111/ejed.12085/abstract*.

Santiago, P. et al. (forthcoming), *OECD Reviews of School Resources: Chile*, OECD Publishing, Paris.

Santiago, P. et al. (2016a), *OECD Reviews of School Resources: Estonia 2016*, OECD Reviews of School Resources, OECD Publishing, Paris, *http://dx.doi.org/10.1787/9789264251731-en*.

Santiago, P. et al. (2016b), *OECD Reviews of School Resources: Slovak Republic 2015*, OECD Reviews of School Resources, OECD Publishing, Paris, *http://dx.doi.org/10.1787/9789264247567-en*.

Schmich, J. (2010), "Ressourcen an Schulen und Unterrichtsbeeinträchtigungen – wunder Punkt in Österreich?" [Resources at Schools and drawbacks for teaching and learning – a weak point in Austria?], in J. Schmich and C. Schreiner (eds.), *TALIS 2008: Schule als Lernumfeld und Arbeitsplatz. Vertiefende Analysen aus österreichischer Perspektive [TALIS 2008: Schools as Learning Environment and Working Place: In-depth Analysis from an Austrian Point of View]*, Leykam, Graz, pp. 127-142, *www.bifie.at/buch/1053*.

Schratz, M. et al. (2013), *The art and science of leading a school – Central5: A Central European view on competencies for school leaders*, Tempus Public Foundation, Budapest, *www.leadershipacademy.at/downloads/20140422_Central5.pdf*.

Schratz, M. et al. (2010), *Improving School Leadership in Central Europe: final report of the project School Leadership for Effective Learning involving the countries of Austria, the Czech Republic, Hungary, Slovakia and Slovenia*, Tempus Public Foundation, Budapest.

Schratz, M. (2009), "Country report and case studies – Austria", in M. Schratz et al. (eds.), *The Role of School Leadership in the Improvement of Learning - Country Reports and Case Studies of a Central-European Project*, Tempus Public Foundation, Budapest, pp. 7-38, *www.schoolleadership.eu/sites/default/files/the_role_of_school_leadership_in_the_improvement_of_learning_-_tpf_2009_9.pdf*.

Shewbridge, C. et al. (2014), *OECD Reviews of Evaluation and Assessment in Education: Northern Ireland, United Kingdom*, OECD Reviews of Evaluation and Assessment in Education, OECD Publishing, *http://dx.doi.org/10.1787/9789264207707-en*.

Shewbridge, C. et al. (forthcoming), *OECD Reviews of School Resources: Czech Republic*, OECD Publishing, Paris.

Specht, W. and F. Sobanski (2012), *OECD Review on Evaluation and Assessment Frameworks for Improving School Outcomes: Country Background Report for Austria*, Bundesministerium für Unterricht, Kunst und Kultur (BMUKK), Vienna, *www.oecd.org/edu/evaluationpolicy*.

Statistik Austria (2015), *Bildung in Zahlen 2013/14 Schlüsselindikatoren und Analysen [Education in Figures 2013/14, Key Indicators and Analyses]*, Statistik Austria, Wien.

UNICEF Office of Research (2013), *Child Well-being in Rich Countries: A Comparative Overview*, Innocenti Report Card 11, UNICEF Office of Research, Florence, *www.unicef-irc.org/publications/683*.

Vogtenhuber, S. et al. (2012), "B: Inputs – Personelle und finanzielle Ressourcen" [B: Inputs – Personnel and financial resources], in M. Bruneforth and L. Lassnigg (eds.) (2012), *Nationaler Bildungsbericht Österreich 2012, Band 1 Das Schulsystem im Spiegel von Daten und Indikatoren [National Education Monitoring Report for Austria 2012. Volume 1: The School System in Light of Data and Indicators]*, Leykam, Graz, pp. 31-60.

ANNEX A

The OECD Review of Policies to Improve the Effectiveness of Resource Use in School

The ***OECD Review of Policies to Improve the Effectiveness of Resource Use in Schools*** (also referred to as the *School Resources Review*) is designed to respond to the strong interest in the effective use of school resources evident at national and international levels. It provides analysis and policy advice on how to distribute, utilise and manage resources so that they contribute to achieving effectiveness and efficiency objectives in education. School resources are understood in a broad way, including financial resources (e.g. expenditures on education, school budget), physical resources (e.g. school buildings, computers), human resources (e.g. teachers, school leaders) and other resources (e.g. learning time).

Fifteen education systems are actively engaged in the review. These cover a wide range of economic and social contexts, and among them they illustrate quite different approaches to the use of resources in school systems. This will allow a comparative perspective on key policy issues. Participating countries prepare a detailed background report, following a standard set of guidelines. Some of the participating countries have also opted for a detailed review, undertaken by a team consisting of members of the OECD Secretariat and external experts. Insofar, the participating countries are (in bold those that have opted for an individual review): **Austria, Belgium (Flemish Community)**, Belgium (French Community), **Chile**, the **Czech Republic**, **Denmark**, **Estonia**, Iceland, **Kazakhstan**, **Lithuania**, Luxembourg, the **Slovak Republic**, Spain, Sweden and **Uruguay**. A final comparative report from the OECD Review, bringing together lessons from all countries, is planned to be completed in 2016.

The project is overseen by the Group of National Experts on School Resources, which was established as a subsidiary body of the OECD Education Policy Committee in order to guide the methods, timing and principles of the review. More details are available from the website dedicated to the review: *www.oecd.org/education/schoolresourcesreview*.

ANNEX B

Composition of the OECD Review Team

Marius R. Busemeyer is a Full Professor of Political Science at the University of Konstanz. His research focuses on comparative political economy and welfare state research, education and social policy, public spending, theories of institutional change and public opinion on the welfare state. Marius studied political science, economics, public administration and public law at the University of Heidelberg and the Harvard Kennedy School of Government. He holds a doctorate in political science from the University of Heidelberg. He worked as a senior researcher at the Max Planck Institute for the Study of Societies in Cologne and was a post-doctoral visiting fellow at the Center for European Studies at Harvard. His publications include a forthcoming book on Skills and Inequality, an edited volume (with C. Trampusch) on The Political Economy of Collective Skill Formation and numerous articles in international peer-reviewed journals.

Deborah Nusche is a Policy Analyst in the OECD Directorate for Education and Skills, where she has been since 2007. She currently leads the country-specific work for Austria, Belgium and Denmark in the OECD School Resources Review. Prior to this, she conducted policy analysis for three major cross-country studies at the OECD: a review of school leadership policy and practice leading to the two-volume publication *Improving School Leadership* (2008); a review of migrant education leading to the OECD publication *Closing the Gap for Immigrant Students* (2010); and a review of evaluation and assessment in education, leading to the OECD publication *Synergies for Better Learning* (2013). As part of these, she conducted education policy reviews in 15 countries producing tailored analysis and policy advice.

Thomas Radinger is a Junior Policy Analyst with the OECD Directorate for Education and Skills, currently working for the OECD School Resources Review. He joined the organisation in September 2011 to contribute to the *OECD Review on Evaluation and Assessment Frameworks* for Improving School Outcomes. Thomas is a co-author of the project's final synthesis report *Synergies for Better Learning* (2013) and took the lead in the analysis of school leader appraisal. Between October 2012 and January 2015, he was involved in the development of the OECD Education GPS, an online platform to disseminate OECD data and research on education to a broader audience.

Henno Theisens is a Professor of Public Management at The Hague University for Applied Sciences. His work focusses on the effective governance of today's complex public systems, like education, health or public safety. He has extensive experience in the area of education on issues related to governance and long term strategy. Previously he was an Analyst at the OECD Centre for Educational Research and Innovation and a Senior

Research Associate at the Centre for Higher Education Policy Studies. Henno holds a Ph.D. in Comparative Higher Education Policy Research from the University of Twente (Center for Higher Education Policy Studies, CHEPS), an M.Sc. in European Politics and Policy from the London School of Economics and Political Science (LSE) and an M.A. in Public Policy and Public Administration from the University of Twente.

ANNEX C

Visit programme

Wednesday, 24 June 2015, Vienna	
09:30-10:00	Meeting with project co-ordinator
10:00-11:00	Budget and infrastructure of federal schools (planning, maintenance, budget)
11:00-11:45	Statistics and monitoring
11:45-12:50	Federal Ministry for Finance
12:50-13:50	Working Lunch: Vienna School Authorities
14:00-15:00	Federal budget for education, management and monitoring of teaching resources
15:00-16:00	Representatives of institutions providing initial and continuing teacher training • University College of Teacher Education, Lower Austria • Rectors Conference of University Colleges of Teacher Education • Teacher Training Centre, University of Vienna
16:00-16:45	Parents Representation • Parents Association of General Compulsory Schools (APS) • Parents Association of Academic Secondary Schools (AHS) and Colleges for Higher Vocational Education (BHS)
16:45-17:30	Teacher Unions • Teacher Union General Compulsory Education (APS) • Teacher Union Academic Secondary Schools (AHS)
17:30	Pupils and youth representation • Federal Student Representation • Federal Youth Representation (Bundesjugendvertretung)

Thursday, 25 June 2015, Vienna	
09:00-10:00	Association of Municipalities (Gemeindebund)
10:00-11:00	Social Partners • Federal Chamber of Labour (AK) • Federal Chamber of Economy (WKÖ)
11:15-12:00	Minister of Education Gabriele Heinisch-Hosek
12:00-12:50	School strategy development, school quality, educational research (BMBF and BIFIE)
13:10-13:55	Federal Court of Audit
14:30-17:00	**School visit 1: AHS Wien Bernoullistraße 3, 1220 Wien** • 14:30-15:15: School principal + administrator • 15:15-16:00: Teachers • 16:00-16:20: Students • 16:20-16:40: Parents

Friday, 26 June 2015, Salzburg, Oberalm	
09:00-09:50	School Authorities, Land Salzburg • General compulsory schools, provincial school board of Salzburg LSR • Schools Department, Province Government of Salzburg
10:30-13:00	**School visit 2: VS Oberalm** • 10:30–11:20: School principal + administrator • 11:20-12:10: Teachers • 12:10-12:30: Students • 12:30-13:00: Parents
14:00-17:00	**School visit 3: NMS Salzburg Maxglan I** • 14:00-14:50: School principal + administrator • 14:50-15:40: Teachers • 15:40-16:00: Students • 16:00-16:20: Parents
Monday, 29 June 2015, Sieggraben, Eisenstadt	
09:00-10:00	School Authorities Burgenland • Department for General Compulsory Schools (APS) • Department for Academic Secondary Schools (AHS) • School Department, Province Government of Burgenland
10:30-13:00	**School visit 4: VS Sieggraben** • 10:30-11:20: School principal • 11:20-12:10: Teachers • 12:10-12:30: Students • 12:30-12:50: Parents
13:00-14:00	Working Lunch: Municipality Council Sieggraben • Mayor • Member of municipality council, responsible for education • Head of municipality office
14:30-17:00	**School visit 5: AHS Eisenstadt** • 14:30-15:15: School principal + administrator • 15:15-16:00: Teachers • 16:00-16:20: Students • 16:20-16:40: Parents
Tuesday, 30 June 2015, Vienna	
09:00-11:30	**School visit 6: NMS Wien Selzergasse** • 09:00-09:50: School principal + administrator • 09:50-10:40: Teachers • 10:40-11:00: Students • 11:00-11:30: Parents
12:00-12:45	Federation of Austrian Industries (IV)
14:00-14:40	Expert Commission on School Administration Reform
15:00-16:45	Researchers' Seminar • Lorenz Lassnigg, Institute for Advanced Studien (IHS) • Kurt Schmid, Institut für Bildungsforschung der Wirtschaft (IBW) • Michael Bruneforth, Dept. Educational Standards and International Assessments, BIFIE • Ferdinand Eder, Univ. of Salzburg
16:45	Preliminary Impressions by OECD Review Team

ORGANISATION FOR ECONOMIC CO-OPERATION AND DEVELOPMENT

The OECD is a unique forum where governments work together to address the economic, social and environmental challenges of globalisation. The OECD is also at the forefront of efforts to understand and to help governments respond to new developments and concerns, such as corporate governance, the information economy and the challenges of an ageing population. The Organisation provides a setting where governments can compare policy experiences, seek answers to common problems, identify good practice and work to co-ordinate domestic and international policies.

The OECD member countries are: Australia, Austria, Belgium, Canada, Chile, the Czech Republic, Denmark, Estonia, Finland, France, Germany, Greece, Hungary, Iceland, Ireland, Israel, Italy, Japan, Korea, Luxembourg, Mexico, the Netherlands, New Zealand, Norway, Poland, Portugal, the Slovak Republic, Slovenia, Spain, Sweden, Switzerland, Turkey, the United Kingdom and the United States. The European Union takes part in the work of the OECD.

OECD Publishing disseminates widely the results of the Organisation's statistics gathering and research on economic, social and environmental issues, as well as the conventions, guidelines and standards agreed by its members.

OECD PUBLISHING, 2, rue André-Pascal, 75775 PARIS CEDEX 16
(91 2016 06 1 P1) ISBN 978-92-64-25670-5 – 2016

www.ingramcontent.com/pod-product-compliance
Lightning Source LLC
Chambersburg PA
CBHW061211240926
51846CB00006B/1187